W9-BTR-901

THE BOAT MAINTENANCE AND REPAIR BOOK

Also by Tony Meisel

The Rule of St. Benedict
American Wine
A Manual of Singlehanded Sailing
Under Sail
Nautical Emergencies
Singlehanding: A Sailor's Guide
Yachting: A Turn-of-the-Century Treasury

THE BOAT MAINTENANCE AND REPAIR BOOK

Tony Meisel

Macmillan Publishing Company
New York
Collier Macmillan Publishers
London

Macmillan Publishing Company
866 Third Avenue, New York, NY 10022
Collier Macmillan Canada, Inc.

Library of Congress Cataloging-in-Publication Data
Meisel, Tony.
The boat maintenance and repair book / Tony Meisel
p. cm.
Includes Index
ISBN: 0-02-583910-1
1. Boats and boating–Maintenance and repair. 2. pc07 03-10-88; pc02 to br00 03-11-88; br07 to SCD 03-15-88; fd03 03-16-88; fn24 03-22-88. I. Title.
VM322.M45 1988
623.8'223'0288–dc19 88-9635
CIP

Macmillan books are available at special discounts for bulk purchases for sales promotions, premiums, fund-raising or educational use.
For details, contact:
Special Sales Director
Macmillan Publishing Company
866 Third Avenue
New York, NY 10022

This book has been designed and typeset by the author on a Macintosh Plus computer and an Apple LaserWriter Plus printer using MicroSoft Word software.

Illustrations by Clive Spong and Tony Gibbons, Linden Artists, Ltd., London.

10 9 8 7 6 5 4 3 2

Printed in the United States of America.

Contents

Every effort has been made by the author and the publisher to assure the accuracy of the information contained herein. However, neither assumes responsibility for accidents, mishaps or injuries which may occur repairing or maintaining a boat. Standard safety procedures should be followed at all times, and care should be taken when working with toxic compounds and power tools.

Introduction

Owning a boat is a major investment in time, labor and money. Keeping the boat seaworthy and cosmetically pristine demands extraordinary effort, no matter how old, what she is built from or how much she cost to start with. This volume attempts to guide the boat owner in all aspects of maintenance and repair that can be undertaken by the owner himself, as well as outlining the more complex jobs usually left to a professional. After all, even if the yard does the work, it is imperative that the owner understands the nature of what is being done, if only to protect himself from excessive charges or slipshod repairs.

This book is not divided into maintenance and repair sections. Rather, each area of concern is dealt with separately–hulls, propulsion, electrics, etc.–for both repair and maintenance. The reason for this is quite simple: during routine maintenance is the time when you find items needing repair. Too often things go wrong at exactly the worst possible moment: as you start your holiday cruise, or while entering a harbor at night. Fixing things before a malfunction puts you in a dangerous or difficult position is only seamanlike. After all, boats are like children: they need constant looking after.

The goal of any boat owner should be to keep systems running as smoothly as possible. To do this most effectively, maintenance and repairs should be treated as a system. An outline of all possible areas of concern for regular maintenance should be made: items for commissioning, for midseason overhaul, and for haulout and winterizing. Such lists should be kept to with the regularity of a heartbeat. Otherwise, you will surely start to overlook and ignore potential problems. Even if you installed new winches this season, they must be included in the list of things to do–clean, lubricate, inspect pawls and springs, check mountings, tighten bolts and so on. We all forget, so write it down!

In writing this book, I have made no attempt to cover every possible area of repair and maintenance. To do so with any comprehensiveness would be to court disaster, as well as to spend the next ten years at it filling several volumes in the process. My intention is to cover broad areas of concern to the average yachtsman in construction, hardware, rigging, propulsion systems and electrics and the rest. I have attempted to trace general outlines of what to look for, with the captions to the illustrations going into greater detail where necessary. More than anything, my goal has to be to get you to think about a particular problem constructively.

Every boat is different, as is every system and installation. To do justice to one would inevitably slight all. Therefore, the approach is meant to be thought-provoking rather than highly specific. There are dozens of fine books available on specific aspects of boat repair. I make no attempt to show you how to replank a hull or weld. These are generally jobs for the professional. I am well aware that a growing number of amateur builders are undertaking major repair and rebuilding projects. This book may help them, but it is not intended for them.

If this volume can help some of you keep your boat looking better, safer and more useful, then I have accomplished my task. I hope this book will make your spring and winter chores around the yard simpler and swifter and give you more time on the water.

–Tony Meisel
New Suffolk, New York

1
TOOLS AND TECHNIQUES

Any repairs you undertake will be made much easier if you provide yourself with good tools, properly cared for. Too often, we buy our tools cut-rate, then wonder why we are unable to do a professional-looking job, why we curse and why we eventually abandon a task to yard personnel. Any professional craftsman knows that a large part of any repair job–whether it be piping, woodwork or wiring, glasswork or welding–is manipulating tools. If those tools are designed for the job and kept up to snuff, chances are the work will be accomplished faster, neater and with longer lasting results.

Assuming you are starting from scratch, there are certain items which belong in every tool kit, no matter what type of repairs, fitting out or maintenance is undertaken.

GENERAL TOOLS

Claw hammer
Hacksaw with extra blades
Tape measure, plastic or GRP (glass-reinforced plastic)
Combination square with adjustable bevel
Assorted screwdrivers, slotted and Phillips
Hand drill, with bits
Files, flat and round
Crosscut wood saw
Slip-joint pliers
Adjustable wrench
Socket set, with plug socket and rachet handle
Utility knife
Chisels
Sharpening stone
Clamp base vise
Vise-grips
3/8-inch or larger electric drill (used *only* when laid-up ashore)

The above should be kept in a well-secured, noncorrosive box, preferably of wood, belowdecks and firmly chocked off. Well-secured because tools are expensive, and if the cover cannot be clamped down in heavy weather, the chances are that someone will get hurt by a flying wrench. Most plastic tool boxes are flimsy affairs. If you cannot purchase a good wood box (heavily varnished and with brass or bronze hardware), it is easy enough to build one without much time or skill necessary for a utilitarian effort. For the sake of convenience, the box should have a lift-out tray for small tools and oft-used items and the bottom can be divided lengthwise to keep things from getting too tangled up. Keep the kit belowdecks to ward off temptation by casual thieves and for protection from weather. Keep it chocked down to avoid serious structural damage in storm conditions. Fifty pounds or so of steel can breach the hull or cabin trunk in a knockdown.

Obviously, the size of this container depends on the size of your boat, but good for most cruising yachts would be something about 18 inches long by 10 inches high by 10 inches deep (outside dimensions). This will allow for a 2-inch-deep tray and still leave plenty of room for larger tools and especially a small saw. Also, it will hold all the general tools and leave room for additions to the kit you will make as time goes on.

Despite the temptation to save money, tool buying is one time when you should get the best quality commensurate with your budget. If you want to go all out, by all means buy copper-nickel alloy, nonsparking wrenches. For most of us, good-quality, medium-range tools will suffice. After all, they will last a lifetime and can travel from boat to boat with you. Hammers with GRP handles can save you oily palms and will absorb shock better than metal ones. Chrome-plated wrenches and pliers will stand up better to salt air. Any wood parts should be kept varnished or painted. Some steels are more resistant to corrosion than others, but the sad fact is that though chrome vanadium stainless steel makes for good knives, working hand tools made of this alloy can be brittle.

Since all, or almost all, tools are made from steel they will rust in a marine environment at a prodigious rate. The best preventative measure is to coat all tools with a light film of machine oil, such as WD-40, trying to keep the grips dry, if possible. Saws especially are prone to excessive rusting and scaling, and these should be wrapped in an oiled cloth to keep them in shape.

WORKING WITH HAND TOOLS

Quality craftsmanship in any medium is much like cooking. It's a collection of simple steps strung together in rational order. Unfortunately, very few of us do mechanical tasks rationally. We've lost the natural rhythm of working with our hands, unlike our forefathers–or some of them–who could take a balk of wood and fashion a chair or a house or a boat from it. We've also lost our respect for materials; we think we can do anything to one and transfer the same procedures and techniques to another. One sure fact of life is that wood, plastic, and metal are all very different in their structures, properties and working qualities. Once that is accepted, and you don't try to force them into unnatural uses or work them against the grain, so to speak, you will find much greater pleasure in working with your hands.

By far, the largest number of yachts in the water today are built of GRP with wooden boats the runner-up. GRP is not really one material. Depending on layup composition, it can contain any number of combinations and permutations of glass, exotics and resins. Likewise, a wooden boat can be built from many different woods using hundreds of different techniques. Choosing and using tools depends, to a great degree, on what has to be done to what.

The key to working with either of these materials, in fact with any material, is to use any particular tool economically and with a rhythm equal to its capabilities and yours. Now this may sound a bit philosophical, so let's illustrate this with an example. Suppose you have to cut a round hole, 2 inches in diameter, in 3/4-inch plywood. You could first drill a starting hole with a brace and bit, then cut out a hole slightly smaller than the final diameter with a keyhole saw, and finally use a 1/2-round rasp to enlarge the hole to its final dimensions, always allowing for a final sanding. Much simpler would be to use a 2-inch hole saw with an electric drill and a sanding drum for the final finish. One procedure would take about an hour. The electrified version could be finished in about five minutes. The final result will be much the same, but the effort expended will be greatly reduced and you will be far less tired by using the electric drill and the appropriate tools.

The best way to learn to use a tool effectively is to watch a professional at work. Too often, I have seen someone take a hammer in hand, grip it near the head and proceed to pound away with abandon and end up with bent nails, dented wood and crushed fingers. If you watch a good carpenter at work, he will hold the hammer by the bottom part of the handle and swing with a regular rhythm so as to hit the nail square on the head, this after an initial tap to set the nail in the stock. If he is doing rough framing, a dent won't matter, but if this is finish work, he will use a nail set for the final blow, keeping the hammer head clear of the board.

The same applies to working with most other hand tools. Think first what the tool is supposed to do and use it with circumspection. Brutality has no place in the workshop! Anything that can be accomplished with force can usually be accomplished better with forethough and a gentle touch. It may take longer, but the results will not cause you to cry yourself to sleep. In the old days of wooden boatbuilding, a good craftsman was one who could work precisely *and* quickly at repetitive tasks. This takes a lot of practice to do, and since the chance of any of us becoming boatbuilders is slight, work precisely. Speed is not that important, especially as you're not being paid for your work.

Boat carpentry demands precision, much greater precision, in fact, than house carpentry. Tolerances are in the neighborhood of 1/32 of an inch, and this can only be achieved by practice. Obviously, considering the time you have and the cost of materials, especially wood, these days certain jobs should probably best be left to professionals. Available equipment can also make that decision for you. Casting a lead keel is not something you should even consider if you live in an apartment. At the same time, a lead casting of 400 pounds is an entirely different matter than one of 4,000 pounds. One is within the capabilities of one or two men, the other becomes a major industrial operation. Yes, it can be done, but please think more than twice about it first.

Using specific hand tools is usually a matter of applied logic. If you plan to cut a mortise with a chisel, the tool is sharp and true and the wood is square and seasoned, you mark out the cut–width, height and depth–and cut bit by bit. Attempting to take a large chunk out at once will gouge, split, crack or ruin the stock. Use both hands, the right to hold the chisel and apply pressure and weight, the left to guide the blade. A slipped chisel may damage you as well as the work.

Likewise, drilling deep holes without a jig or bench press is to court disaster, as the chances of the boring running true are slight indeed. In other words, before tackling any job, make sure you have the proper tool to accomplish the task. Do not try to get by with a makeshift substitute. Trying to smooth a long bevel with a spokeshave is just as idiotic as attempting to drive a Phillips screw with a blunt knife point!

POWER TOOLS

Too often amateurs use power tools as fast substitutes for hand tools. They are not! Power tools have a specific place in the workshop, but they must be used with different techniques as they work at much higher speeds and with much greater force. They take greater practice than hand tools to use effectively and must always be taken in hand with care and circumspection.

Since power tools work at far greater speeds than you can by hand, any mistakes you make will be catastrophic compared to the measured–and ofttimes repairable–pace of hand operations. You should get the best you can afford. Since power tools are rated as homeowners, mechanics and professional quality, the choice is made somewhat easier. Homeowners-rated tools will last a certain number of hours and then give up. The motor, more than likely, will burn out and there's nothing for it but to chuck the tool in the dustbin. For most repair work a midrange power tool will suffice. These are rated for several hundred hours of work and, unless you are going into boat repair as a profession, will suffice for all but the largest jobs.

Do not be misled by the materials of the casing of a particular tool. Modern plastics are more resilient to wear and banging about than the old metal castings which used to be used to encase the works of a tool. The key to quality is in machining and the motor capacity. The higher the amperage rating–as a rule–the more powerful the tool.

2
HULLS

A boat's hull is the major structure upon which all else is built. If the hull is not sound, no matter of care or expense will save the ship from possible disaster. As recently as 1960, most yachts were constructed of wood–backbone, frames, planking and all the thousands of other bits and pieces which together made a strong, unified vessel. Then came the fiberglass revolution which put most oldtime boat builders out of business and changed the way we think of boats. Of course there were other materials used before this–and still used–steel, aluminum, cold molding and ferrocement. But the majority of boats built in the Western world today are varying combinations of glass-fiber cloth and polyester resins, molded together into a strong monocoque form.

GRP CONSTRUCTION

It should be fairly obvious that all hulls are not created equal. Unfortunately, most boat buyers buy on looks, not layup schedules. As a result, many of the problems associated with hull maintenance and repair are inevitable. How a hull is constructed, and from what materials, is far more important than its color or decorative qualities. The principle of GRP construction is simple: layers of glass cloths, mats and rovings are sandwiched together with heat-setting resins. When the whole cures, it assumes the shape of the mold in which the layering took place. But temperature, humidity, glass-to-resin ratio, evenness of resin saturation, and dozens of other factors play a part in the quality and strength of the finished product.

Assuming you have a hull to start with, and are not buying a new boat, the only way you can be sure of knowing what you have is to take or have taken a core sample of the laminate at keel, turn of the bilges and sheer. This is a tricky business, since you are left with three holes to fill. Try first to get a copy of

GRP building materials: A. mat provides bulk and fast layup B. woven roving provides strength and bulk C. cloth provides strength and smoothness D. chopped strands are used for filler and for layup with spray equipment.

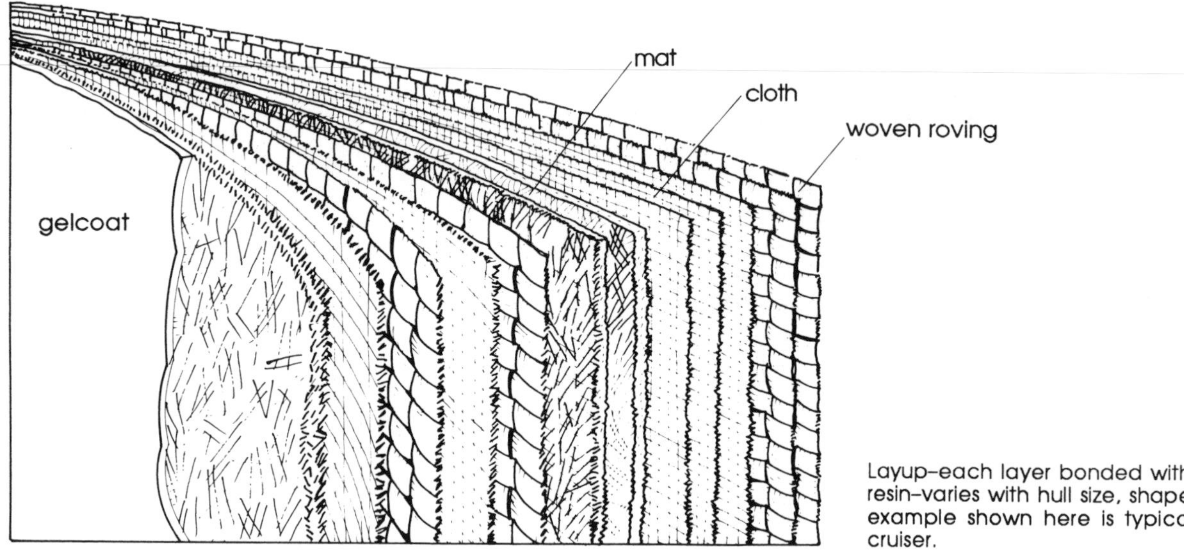

Layup–each layer bonded with polyester or epoxy resin–varies with hull size, shape and purpose. The example shown here is typical of a medium-size cruiser.

chopped strand

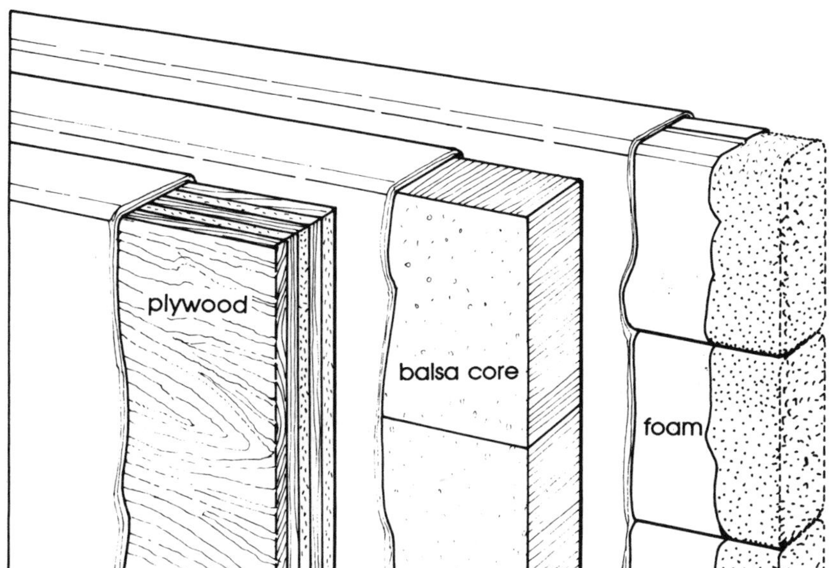

Core construction is used to gain strength (plywood), lightness (balsa) and insulation (foam). Within each type are many variants, but all are used to some degree in modern boat building to save weight and add insulating properties.

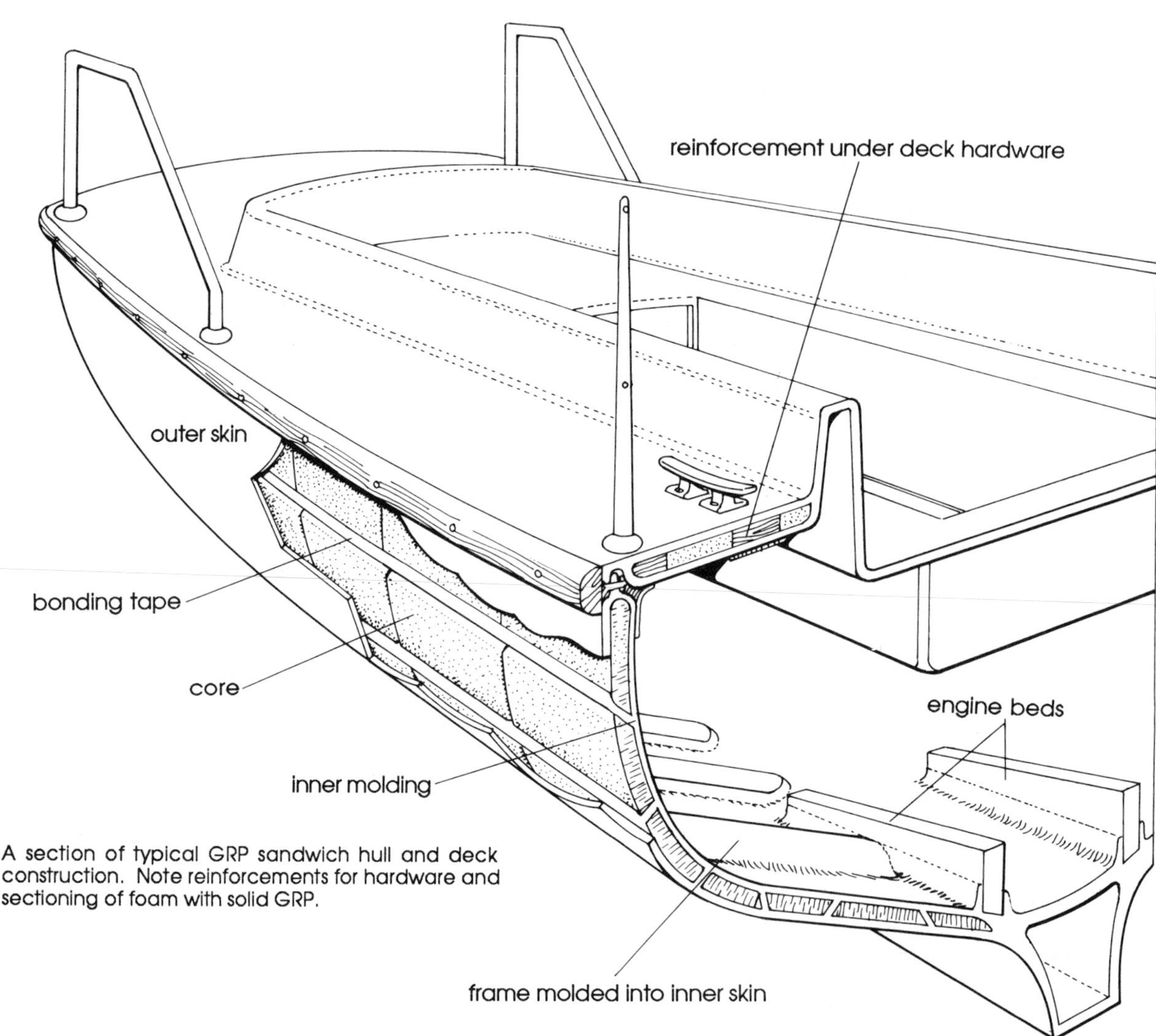

A section of typical GRP sandwich hull and deck construction. Note reinforcements for hardware and sectioning of foam with solid GRP.

the laminate specifications from the builder. If this is impossible, have a GRP specialist at your yard take a look at things. Chances are, the hull will be to a reasonable standard. However, there are many boats in the marketplace which are built to marginal safety standards. This is all a prologue, really, to the notion of increasing the hull strength of your boat through additional *internal* layups. Be forewarned, it is a lot of hard work! If you plan to venture into heavy-weather areas, however, it may well be worth the time and trouble (not to mention the expense).

But first, let's see what can be done with a minimum amount of expense and effort. Assuming the hull has not been breached in any area, and is one uninterrupted skin, the first task is to see if it flexes in a particular spot. This can be done in the water, by crossing powerboat wakes with a person stationed below. It can be done on land by pressing your torso against broad panel areas both inside and out and *feeling* any deflection. Despite all the technical advances, nothing quite makes up for what your fingertips can tell you.

Strengthening the Hull

Should you find that there are areas–particularly broad and flat expanses of glass–that have any appreciable degree of deflection, there are ways to stiffen them at reasonable expense. You will probably have to remove a certain amount of interior joinery to do this and, should the hull have a glass liner, you may have to cut away part of this. In modern auxiliaries, both furniture and/or liners are usually bonded to the hull with fiberglass tabs or adhesive foam in the case of liners. The best way to cut these out is to use a scrolling, reciprocating saw with a blade sized short enough so as not to puncture the hull. This has to be done slowly and carefully. Since flexing panels tend to be at the bows, you may have to deal with glassed-in bulkheads as well. Since these are stiffeners in themselves, they need not be removed. However, any stringers you install

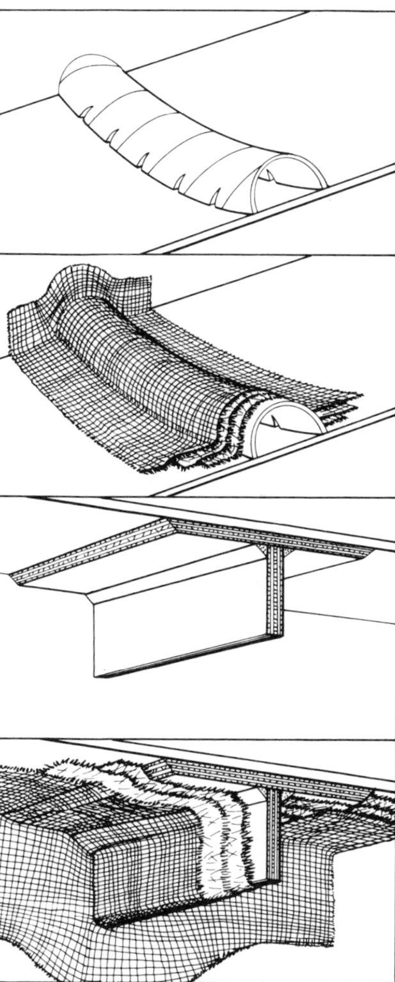

Bracing a hull or deck can be done in several ways. The easiest is to use a form–cardboard, foam, wood–totally encapsulated in layers of mat and cloth, each successive layer overlapping the preceding one. When using wood forms, make sure all edges are beveled and smooth to avoid any sharp breaks in the layup.

Other possible coring materials for reinforcement.

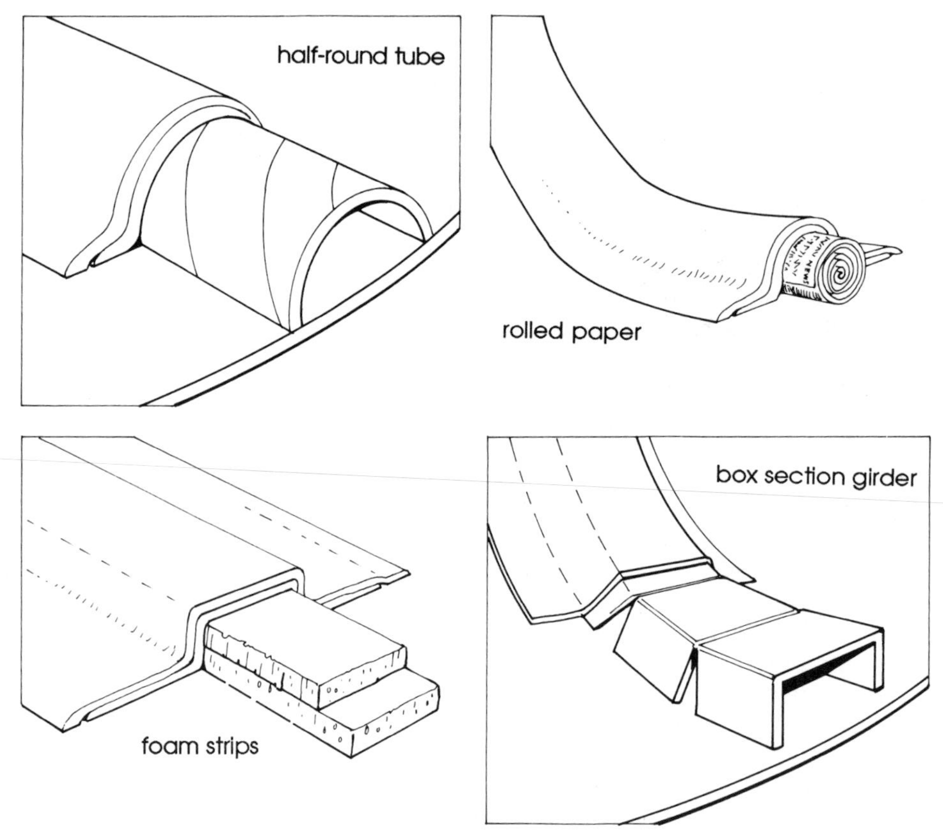

should run flush to either side of the bulkhead and be glassed to both the hull sides and the bulkhead as well.

Stringers–a normal part of wood construction rarely found in U.S.-made GRP hulls, though more common in European structures–supply fore-and-aft rigidity. Construction can be of varied materials: rigid foam, lightweight wood such as spruce, cardboard, Nomex, etc. Whatever the material used, its purpose is to act mainly as a form for the glass and resin mixture covering it. The lighter in weight, the better, providing it conforms *evenly* to hull shape, and creates a geometric structure with the required rigidity both in cross-section and fore-and-aft. Under ideal circumstances, a stringer should run the entire length of the hull, from just abaft the stem to just afore the transom. In some of the better boats, there will be three or four to each side of the hull.

In a fully fitted hull, however, this is not likely to be possible without major surgery. Partial stringers can be fitted where necessary. The ends cannot be abrupt, though. In other words, the core material must be shaped at either end to feather into the hull surface, much like one part of a scarf joint. If this is not done, hard spots are likely and fracture or distortion is possible in the topsides.

While all of this is being done, the hull must be supported strongly and evenly. Any sagging or pinching will be accentuated by the installation of a stringer. Likewise, the glassing in of the form must be done without hard spots, and by overlapping the glass layers to create a graduated base joint.

REPAIRING HOLES

If you have the misfortune to be holed or otherwise have a breach in the hull, rebuilding the glass structure is the only option. This is not as appalling as it might at first seem, for one of the advantages of GRP construction is that the structural members of the hull–the glass fibers–are held together by chemical reaction. However, since impact will invariably dam-

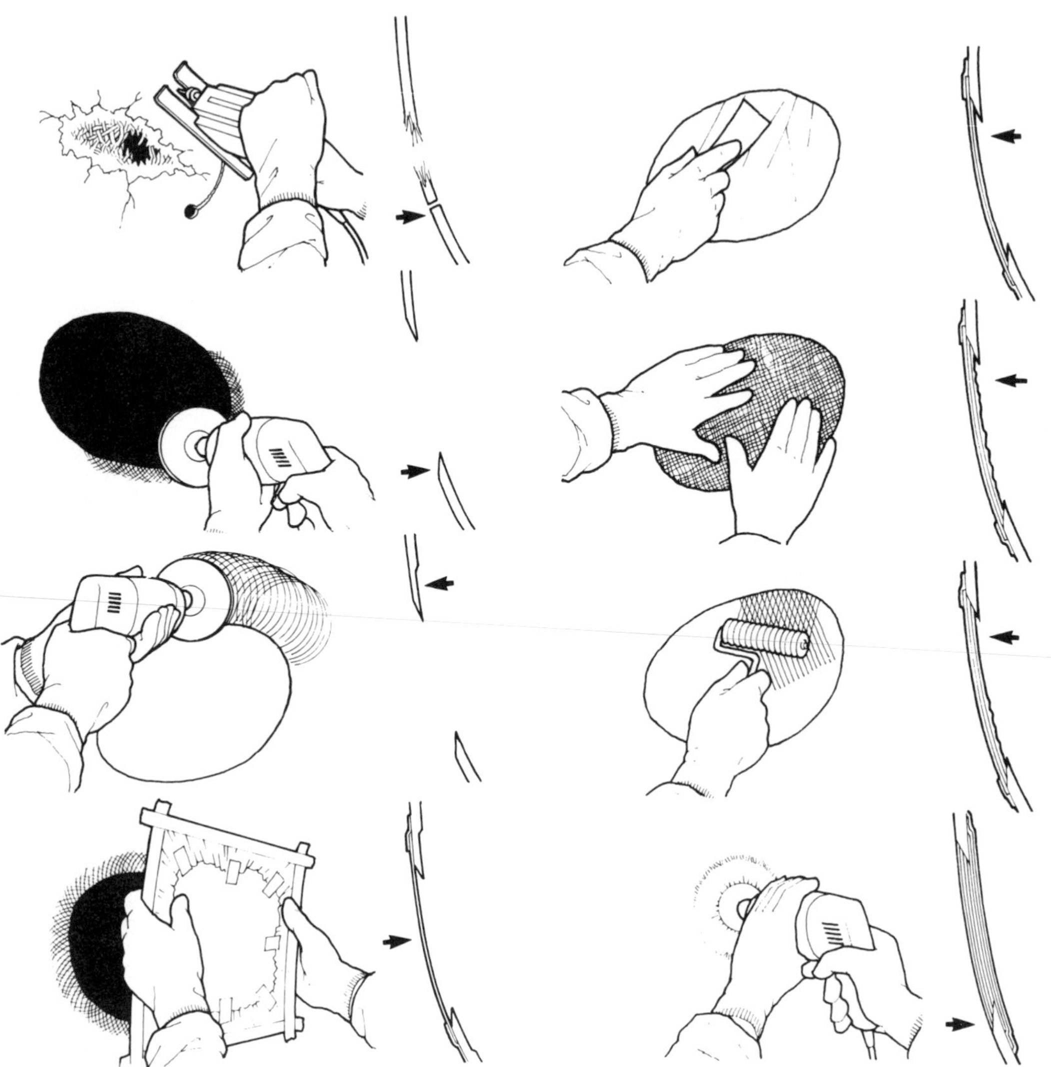

A fracture or hole in GRP can be repaired fairly easily with the proper tools and materials. First cut the damaged section back to sound GRP on all sides, then bevel the outside edges with a grinding wheel or abrasive disc and rabbet the inside as shown. Make a form from cardboard, masonite, etc. to fit the interior. Tape it in place; then build up layers of matt and resin, ending with cloth on the outside. When this has cured, work overlapping layers of cloth into and over the rabbet on the interior. Finally, sand and paint.

age the areas surrounding the actual break, it will be necessary to rebuild a larger area than is immediately visible. Also, the repair will be stronger if rebuilt from both outside *and* inside the hull, as overlapping can be done without cosmetic damage from the interior.

You must start by grinding away the damaged area, creating a bevel around the perimeter of the hole or fracture. Without a bevel–and one of 8:1 ratio of horizontal area to hull thickness–you will end up with hard spots and a potentially weak joint. This bevel should be made both inside and out, and can be best accomplished with an electric grinder or grinding wheel on an electric drill. Equally, all areas of surrounding gelcoat must be sanded down, as no resin mixture will adhere to such a smooth surface. Once this is done, a mould can be made to conform to the original hull shape.

A number of possible materials can be used for this mould. First to come to mind is cardboard, which is certainly cheap. However, it will not take compound curves. The same is true of plywood. Acrylic sheets of 1/8- to 3/8-inch thickness can be used very successfully, as they can be formed to the hull curves with a heat gun. However, they can also distort and great care must be used. Another possible solution is to use a thin sheet of plastic held in place by light battens. Nothing is perfect, though, and you will invariably have a certain amount of fairing to do.

Patches should be built up with thin layers of glass matching the existing layup as much as possible. Otherwise use, from outside in, a layer of cloth, a layer of mat, a layer of roving, then more mat and cloth until the proper thickness is built up. Using roving close to the surface can result in print-through due to quirks in curing, which is unattractive, though it will not affect the strength of the repair. Each layer should be allowed to cure to a slightly tacky state; likewise, each succeeding layer *on the inside* should overlap the one beneath it. You thus end up with a chemical-structural scarf of great

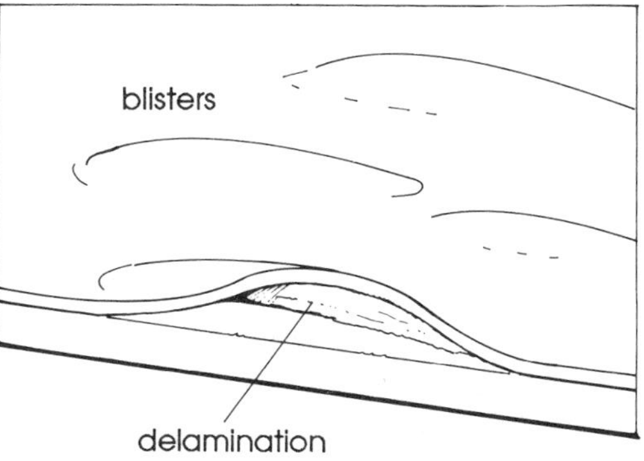

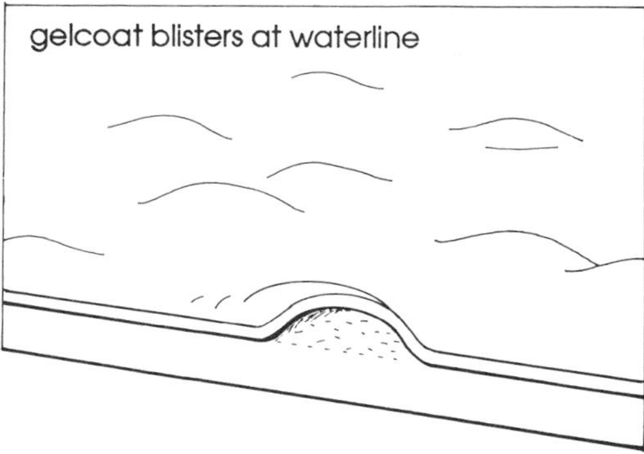

Osmosis, or blistering, is due to moisture trapped in the layup at building time, coupled with the fact that GRP is semipermeable and, under certain conditions, can allow enough water seepage to cause delamination. Any signs of blistering, usually near the waterline, should be attacked immediately. The boat must be hauled and the blisters ground down and allowed to dry out before filling with epoxy compound.

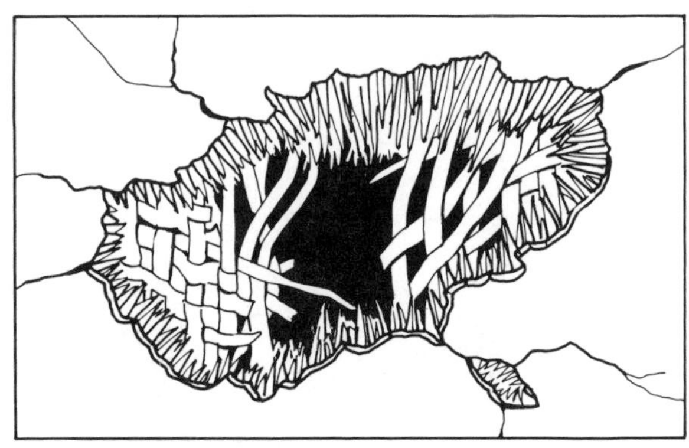

A clinical view of a fracture in GRP. Note the radiating cracks which must be included in the area to be cut out.

strength and without hard spots which might later cause skin distortions.

It goes without saying that directions for mixing resin–either polyester or epoxy–should be followed to the exact letter on the package. Variances in temperature and humidity will have very noticeable effects on both curing times and bonding strengths. Different agents can speed up or slow down curing, and should only be used with complete understanding of their effect.

Cored hulls must be patched somewhat differently, as the core material must be sandwiched between two layers of GRP. Luckily, the core can be formed to the shape of the hull and becomes the mould for interior and exterior layups. The hull should be cut away to contain a regularly shaped piece of core material–Airex, Nomex, balsa, whatever–and the core should be tabbed in place with fiberglass tape and resin. The layup can then proceed in much the same way as for single-skin repair. If the core is only partially damaged, microballoons mixed with resin can be used as filler, and then the covering glass applied over. However, this may cause a hard spot, and it is preferable to replace the core with comparable material, to insure hull integrity.

Obviously, none of the above will give you step-by-step instructions for patching the hole, but the principles are often more important than the individual job. Inasmuch as every repair is unique, understanding the framework should enable you to figure out the best way to solve a particular problem. The most important things to remember:

1. Plan ahead: always figure out how much glass, mat, roving, resin, filler, etc. you will need before starting.
2. Always use fresh resin and catalyst for the strongest bond.
3. Always carefully cut away and prepare the damaged area before even thinking about the patch.
4. Make sure your form or mould is fair before applying any

glass or resin.

5. Allow sufficient time for resin to cure before applying the next layer of glass.
6. Make sure you overlap each succeeding layer on the inside so as to avoid hard spots.
7. Be sure that core materials and resins are compatible before starting. Otherwise you will waste time and money.
8. Try to work in settled weather, and constant temperatures. Variations will make your job harder and longer. Work inside or construct a temporary shed if it will be a big job.

STRESS FATIGUE

When fittings or structural components are attached directly to a GRP hull without proper load-spreading components and bedding, chances are that the natural working of the vessel will eventually lead to stress fatigue. Chainplates, bulkheads, furniture flats, stringers, engine beds and integral tanks must be bonded to the hull in such a manner that no "hard spots" or sharp angles of attachment occur.

This can be assured by the use of overlapping glassing, foam cushions and backup plates of wood or metal, all of which must be installed so as to spread compression and bending loading as much as possible. Additionally, any hard angles in molded surfaces should be inspected for possible stress fatigue. Since these areas are usually found in hull-to-deck joints, and this is certainly the area of greatest stress in a working ship, shelves, top-hat joints and the like are prime candidates for failure. The key to avoiding stress here is to utilize both chemical and mechanical bonds to insure a rigid structure. Any looseness or sharp angles will make for potential problems.

No matter what the angle or where located, the solution is to allow a gap between the material causing the hard spot and the surrounding material–hull and bulkhead, for example. This

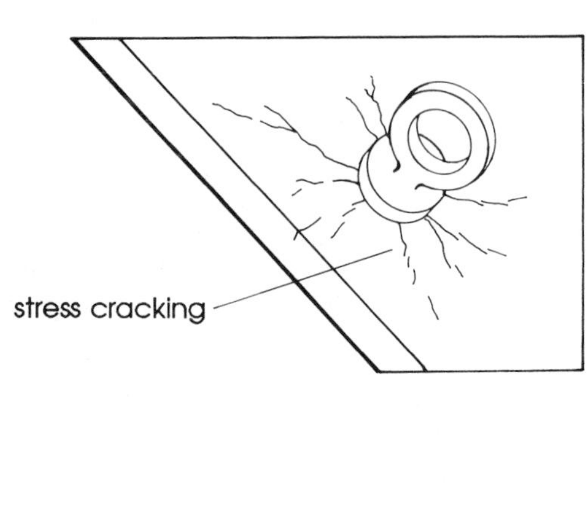

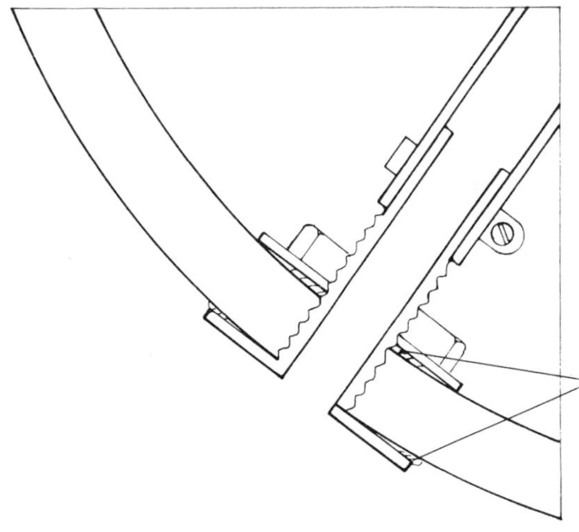

Stress cracking in GRP can be caused by a number of factors: too acute angles in joints without proper foam or core material to absorb stress, fittings and hardware attached without washers to spread loads, pop rivets and other driven fittings under too great a compression load, not enough bedding used and direct bulkhead-hull joining. Care in installation, remembering that GRP does not take kindly to localized stress, is the best solution.

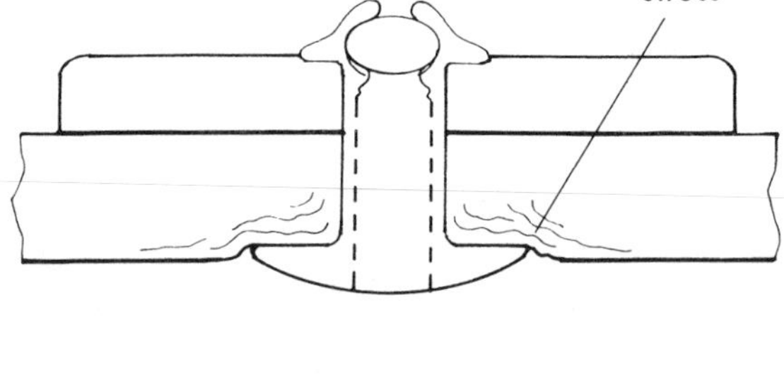

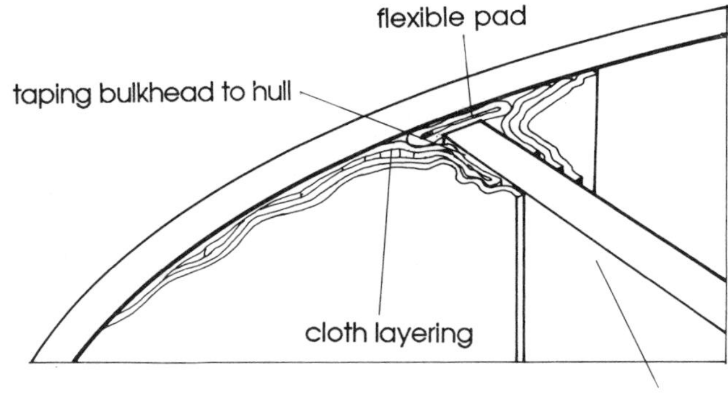

Molded-in stern tubes can cause cracks and delamination in a hull if they are not properly supported. One way to accomplish this is to fashion a wood supporting strut, bonded to the hull and tube by means of overlapping layers of cloth cut to fit; you will literally be strapping it in place. Be sure to cover a fairly large area with the cloth as you wish to spread these strains as much as possible.

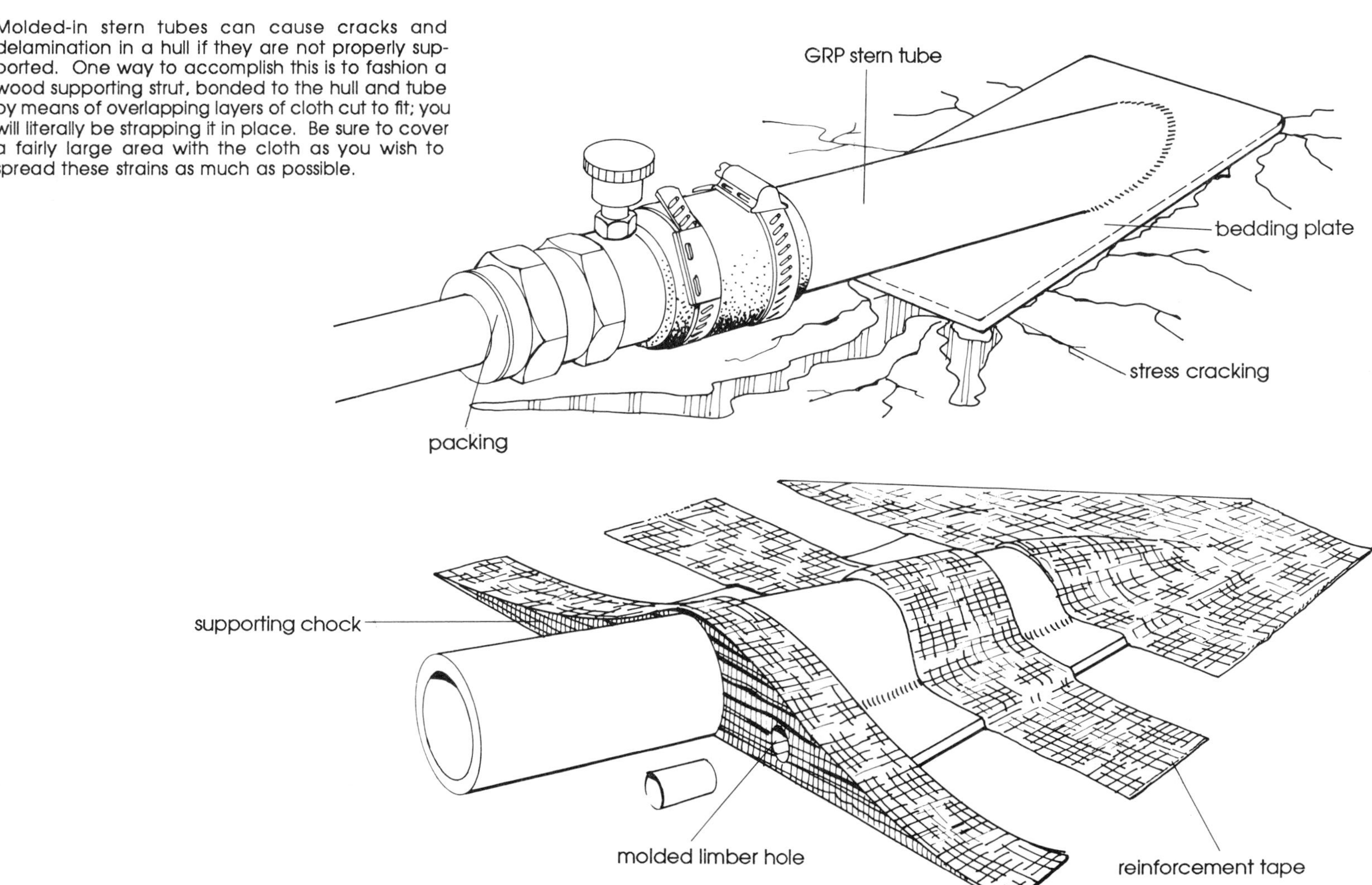

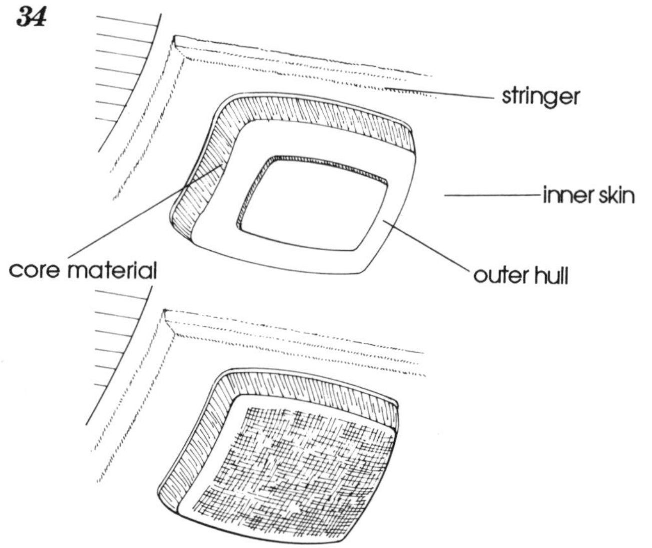

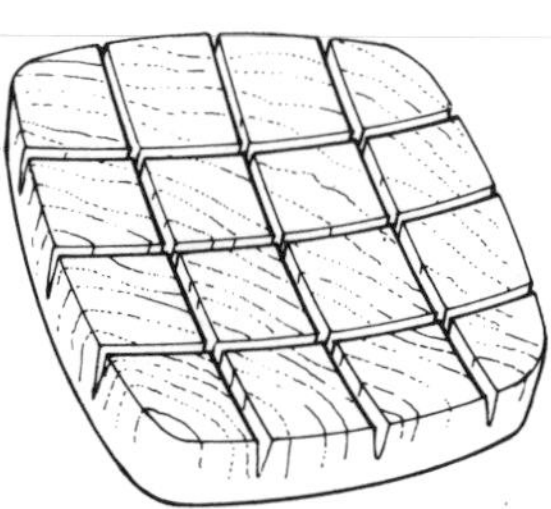

To repair damaged areas of cored hulls, cut out the area from the outside, then locate the center of the interior by drilling. Cut out the damaged core from the inside, allowing a 2-inch overlap between inner and outer skins. Cut a section of core material to fit and groove it as necessary to follow the curvature of the hull. Then bond the core material in place with compatible resin. With the core as a mold form, exterior and interior glass can be layed up with little difficulty, much as one would repair a single-skin hull.

gap can be filled and cushioned with foam, Nomex or cardboard, but it must be a resilient cushion. The point is to support the bulkhead but also to avoid a direct seating of the hard edge against the hull.

All such closures should be glassed with overlapping layers of matt/cloth and resin, at least three layers for small partitions, five layers or more for major bulkheads. Each layer should overlap the one beneath it by at least 1 inch (2.5 cm). The resin should be allowed to cure the tacky stage prior to installing the next layer. Where hull curves are encountered, rather than bunching the cloth, make a series of small triangular cuts on the bulkhead side of the cloth strip to accomodate the tighter dimensions.

Stress fatigue can also occur at deck fitting locations and, in fact, this is the most common place for such failures. This is covered in more detail in the deck chapter.

WOOD HULLS

The amount written on wood hulls is staggering. The number of methods to repair any given break or damage is equally wide-ranging. National customs, types of wood and variances in contruction methods, fastenings and adhesives all play a part and add to a sometimes bewildering variety of choices to be made in wooden hull repair. For anything other than routine repairs, unless you are a master craftsman, it's probably a good notion to let a professional take care of it.

This is not to say that you cannot undertake major jobs, but considering the difficulties prevalent in obtaining good, seasoned wood and of working to the tolerances demanded of good wooden boat construction, a certain circumspection and caution should be observed in evaluating one's skills.

Replacing a plank, for instance, demands first finding wood comparable to the original, seasoning it (lumberyard stock will *not* do), shaping it, cutting bevels, fitting the plank and fastening it in place. All this after removing the original with-

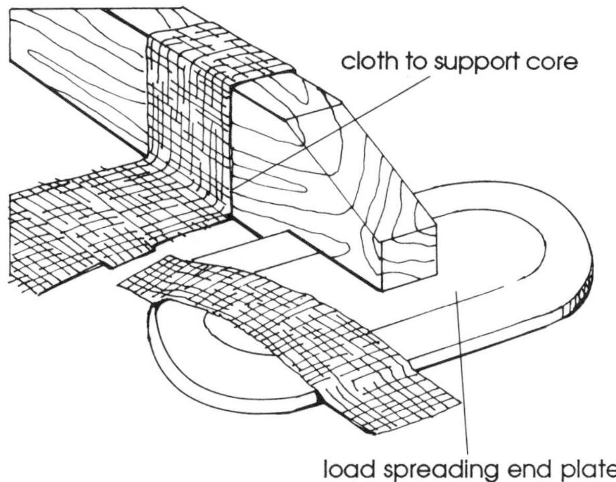

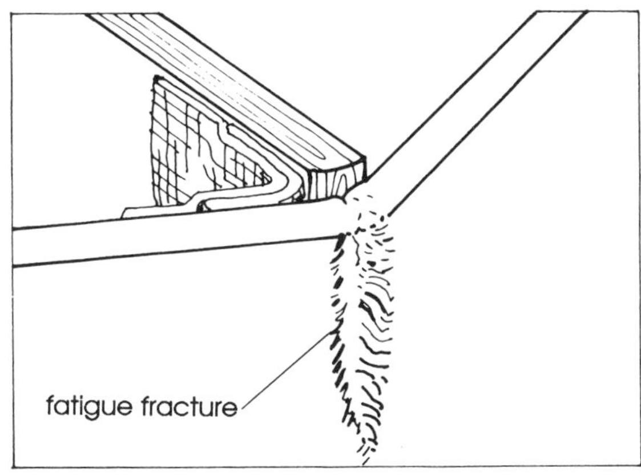

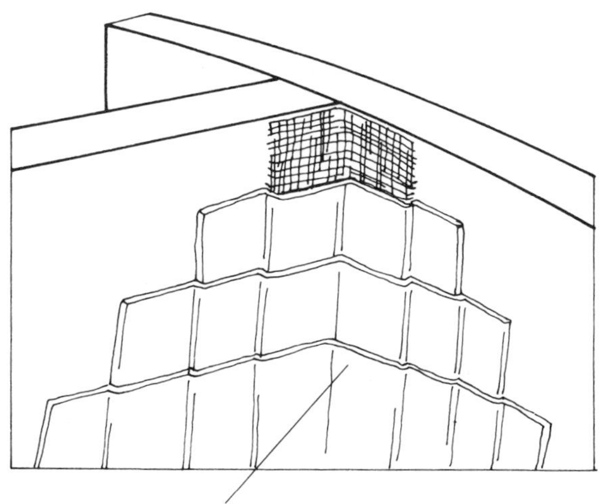

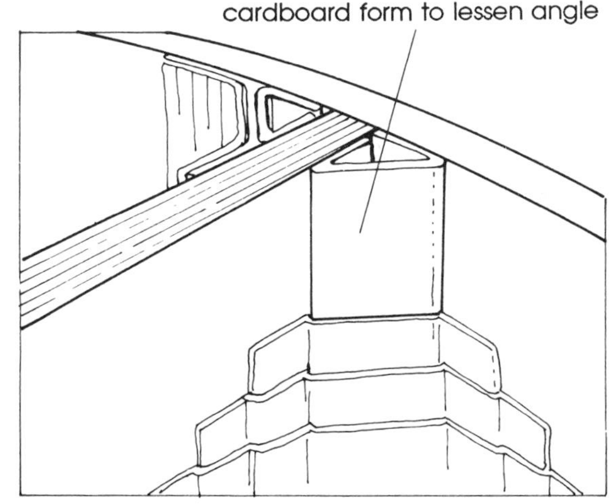

Spreading loads and avoiding hard spots is a cardinal rule in all GRP layup. Here are several ways to accomplish these goals.

out harming the surrounding planks. A pro can probably do this job in a day or two. You may spend several weekends. For those of you who wish to sweat and shove and become proficient, my best suggestion would be to first read a good book on the subject, such as Bud McIntosh's or Howard Chapelle's. Then, and only then, spend some time in and around a good local wood boatbuilder's yard watching. Wooden boatbuilding is not merely an applied skill like laying up GRP. It is a series of fine craft expertises which can only be achieved by constant practice, under knowledgeable guidance.

However, some things can be easily done. Rub rails can be replaced. Individual mouldings and fixtures can be made and repaired. Leaks can be sealed. None of this takes great skill, though it will demand patience and decent tools. Each project on a wood boat is so different that no one method or technique will answer for every need.

The most common problems in wooden hulls are leaks and rot. The first can be solved–providing the planking is in good condition–by the replacement of caulking and seam compounds. The second is more of a problem and relates to the original construction more than to continued maintenance.

Assuming you have located a leak, and it is between planks or, more likely, at the juncture of the garboard and keel or garboard and lowest plank, you will have to haul the boat, strip out the caulking, recaulk–provided you can get oakum–and reseal the seam. Garboard leaks are often due to compression as well as working and there may be permanent twist and distortion present. If this is the case, call in a professional.

Rot comes about mainly because of improper ventilation and insufficient waterways. Frame heels and floors must allow passage of bilge water to avoid stagnant pools which become breeding grounds for rot. Ceilings should allow for air passage and butt blocks should always stop short of billing a bay between frames. Anything of permanent structure which allows for the trapping of stale air or fresh water will eventually start to rot,

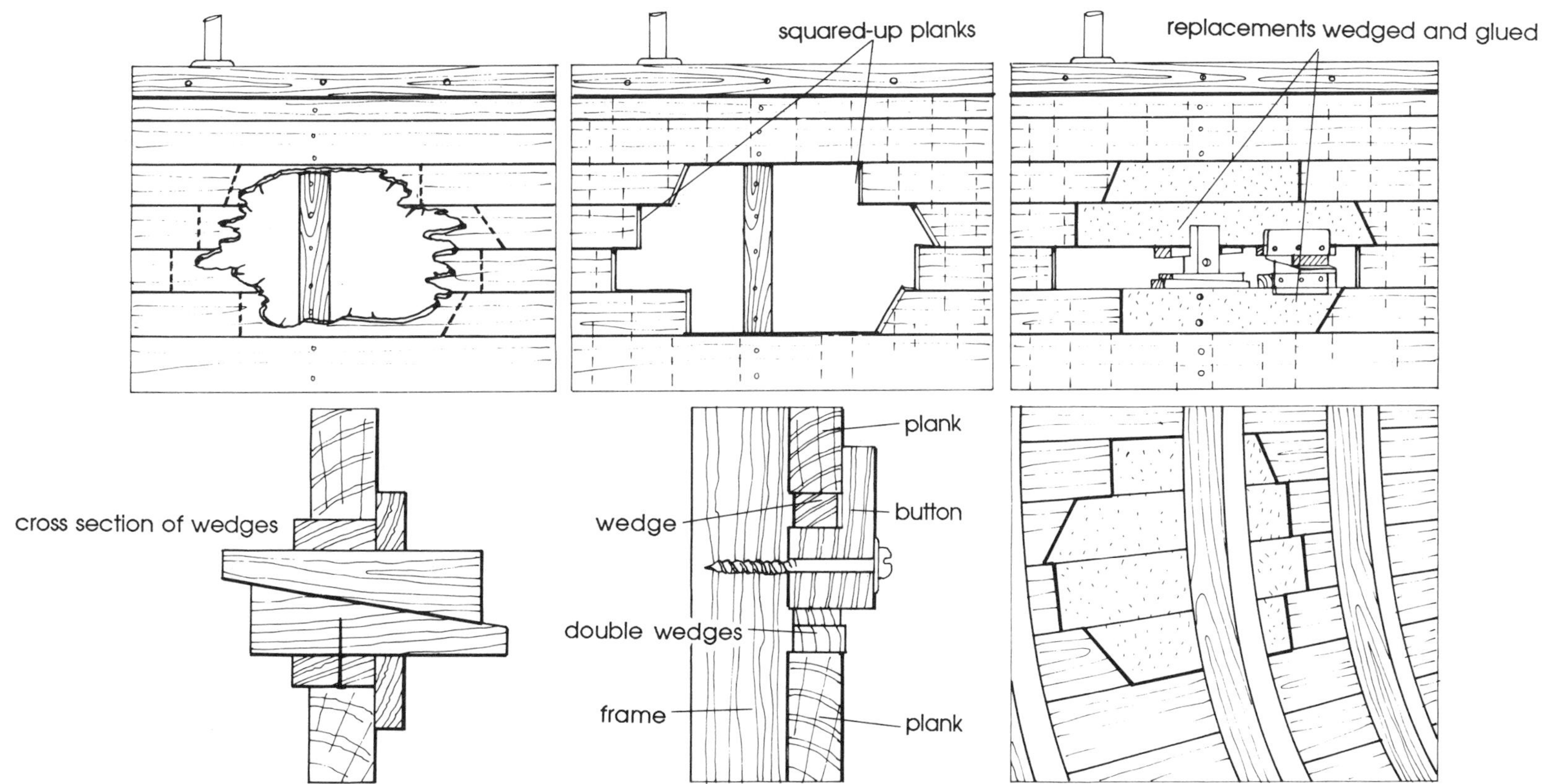

Repairing hull planking, whether strip or carvel, is much the same. Since it is virtually impossible to reuse damaged planks, new wood of the same properties will have to be found. The old planks must be cut out, the ends removed and scarfed where necessary. New planks must be cut to size, beveled, glued and wedged in place in strip plank construction, screwed and caulked in carvel. This is all painstaking work and, if you are inexperienced in boat carpentry, best left to a professional. If you wish to undertake the job yourself, seek the advice of an experienced shipwright, as each hull will present different problems that would be impossible to cover here.

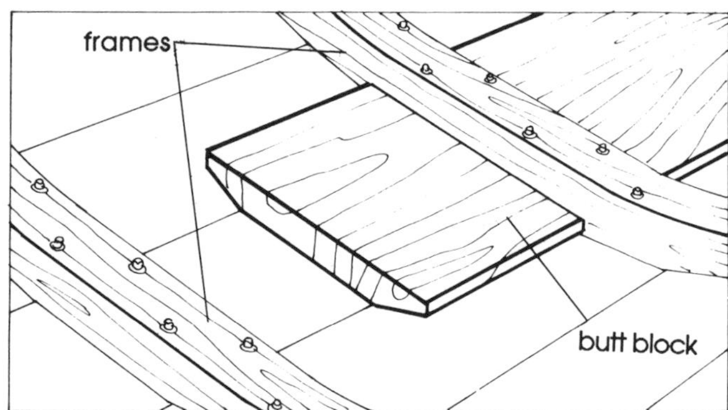

Butt blocks between planks should always be sized to allow for drainage and circulation on all sides. Do not run them from frame to frame as this will do nothing but encourage rot. Paint them with red lead before installing to protect the hidden side.

no matter what the wood type, no matter how good the construction or the fit.

Of course, with cold-moulded construction this will not be a problem *providing all wood components have been saturated with epoxy.* Forget one floor and you will be sure to find rot there after a few years. But repair of cold-moulded construction is a delicate buisiness, though in principle it is no different than GRP layup. However, to get a clean and smooth surface, as well as strength comparable to the original, demands more care and skill in fitting, gluing and scarfing in veneers.

Basic maintenance of wood hulls means keeping the bilges as clean, dry and aired-out as possible, not always an easy task. In warm climates, the water is likely to be filled with teredos. The only way to keep them at bay is to make sure the bottom is coated fully with good antifouling. Even a few square inches of scraped, bare wood can allow entry to these nasty little wood-eating worms. Sheathing the bottom works even better, but the cost, coupled with the fact that very few craftsmen can undertake such a job, makes this an impractical proposition for most.

An especially difficult area is the hull-to-deck joint, where the covering board can allow leaks to penetrate the shelf and cause massive rot. This joint must be carefully and copiously caulked at building and any seams that open should be immediately filled with flexible caulk.

In heavy weather, a wood hull works quite a bit. This is natural and normal. However, going to windward in heavy going can fracture frames. Two solutions exist for this: one is to replace the frame, a major undertaking; the other is sister the original rib with another almost, but not quite, next to it. Since the type of rib depends upon the original construction–steamed, sawn or laminated–the replacement or sister should conform to the original, as laminated and sawn frames are rigid throughout, whereas steamed or bent frames will flex with the hull. Combining the two will invariably put added

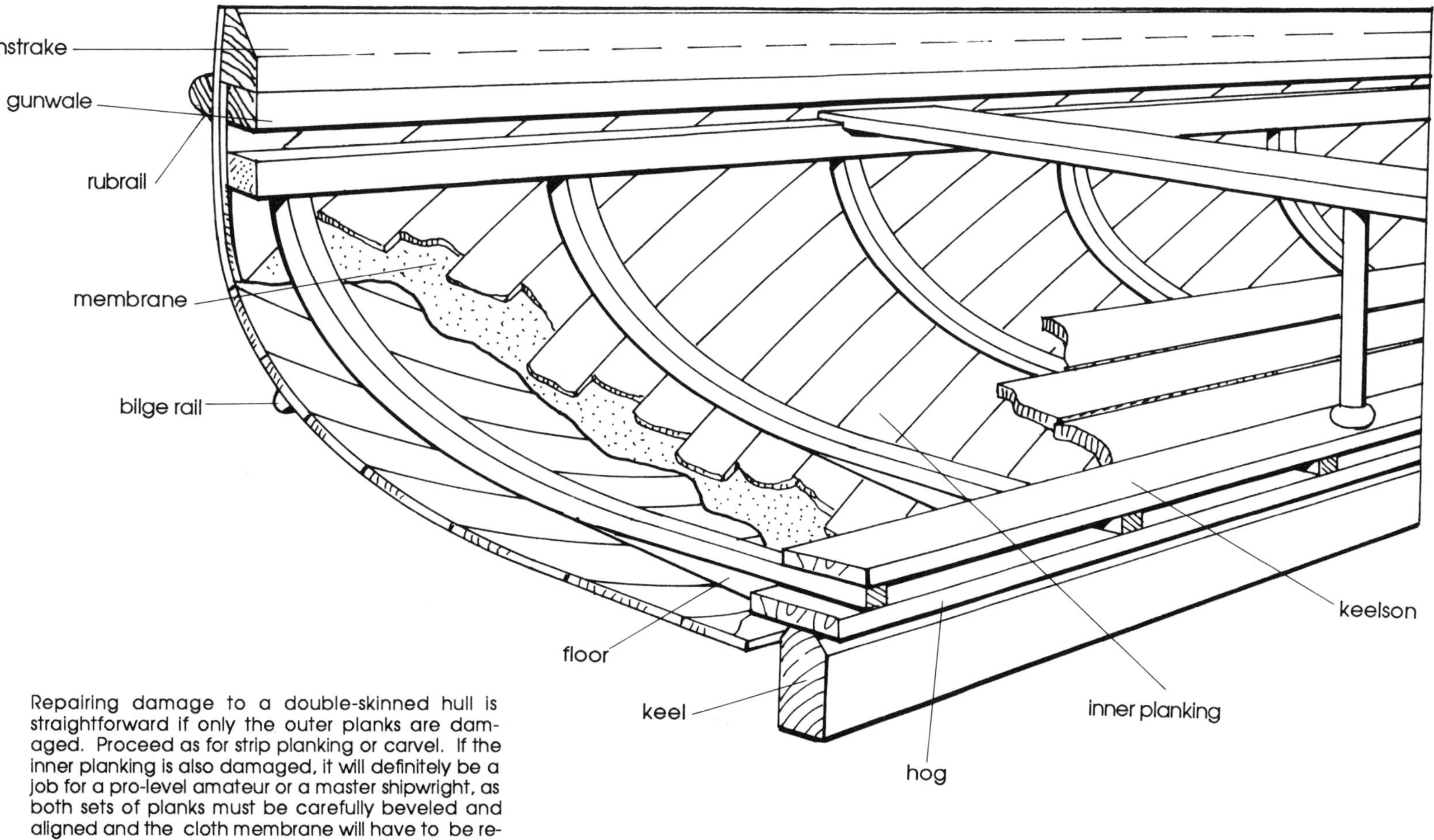

Repairing damage to a double-skinned hull is straightforward if only the outer planks are damaged. Proceed as for strip planking or carvel. If the inner planking is also damaged, it will definitely be a job for a pro-level amateur or a master shipwright, as both sets of planks must be carefully beveled and aligned and the cloth membrane will have to be replaced and made watertight again.

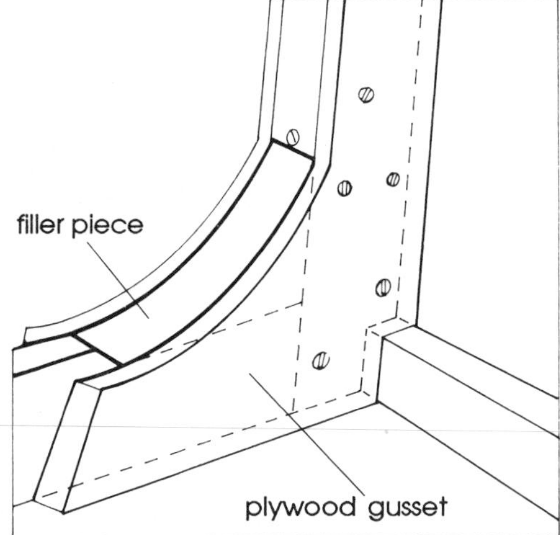

One way to reinforce a damaged frame without sistering is to glue and screw a plywood gusset to both sides of the damaged area extending well beyond the damage on both sides. With these in place a filler piece can be glued on to add fore-and-aft rigidity to the structure.

stress on the hull in that area which may be transmitted to other parts of the structure.

In the period from World War I to World War II it was common practice to combine sawn with bent frames or metal with bent frames. The rebuilding of most of these boats has shown what a mess that can be. Likewise, steel floors will always rust out. If they are not replaced, say goodbye to your yacht. Bronze or Swedish iron floors will last indefinitely, however, and usually will insure a stronger lower structure for the ship.

But most wood hulls are built with wood floors and as long as these are bolted to the backbone and frames, a strong structure will result. This cannot be stressed too much. Screws, lags or nails have no place holding the major framework of a hull together. They are all subject to invisible deterioration and, more importantly, to pulling out and losing their holding power. Only bolts–galvanized or bronze–will stand up to years of mechanical stress and remain in place unscathed. Of course, even these can eventually deteriorate, and it is up to the owner to inspect as many of the fastenings as possible, as often as possible.

This is especially true of keelbolts in sailing vessels. Since without these in top condition, the keel will fall off and the boat will capsize and sink, their integrity is of more than small importance. On the average, say every five years, selected keelbolts should be unfastened and withdrawn for inspection. Unless you have your own crane, this is most likely a job for the yard. But it must be done nevertheless. Not only are keelbolts a source of leaks, they can, if shot, cause a pendulum effect in the garboard and floors, causing twists and racking strains on the entire hull.

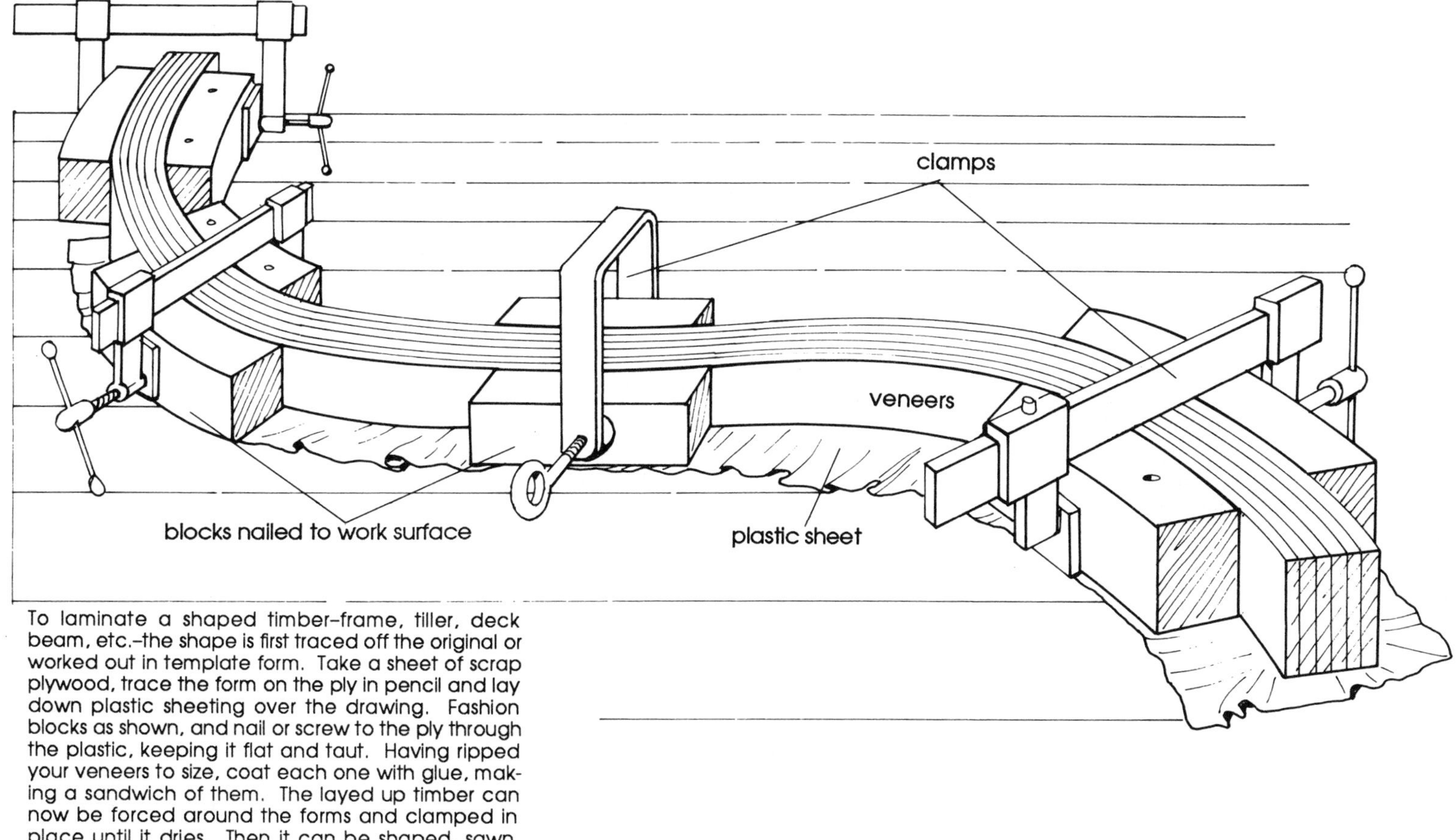

To laminate a shaped timber–frame, tiller, deck beam, etc.–the shape is first traced off the original or worked out in template form. Take a sheet of scrap plywood, trace the form on the ply in pencil and lay down plastic sheeting over the drawing. Fashion blocks as shown, and nail or screw to the ply through the plastic, keeping it flat and taut. Having ripped your veneers to size, coat each one with glue, making a sandwich of them. The layed up timber can now be forced around the forms and clamped in place until it dries. Then it can be shaped, sawn, beveled, sanded and finished to final form.

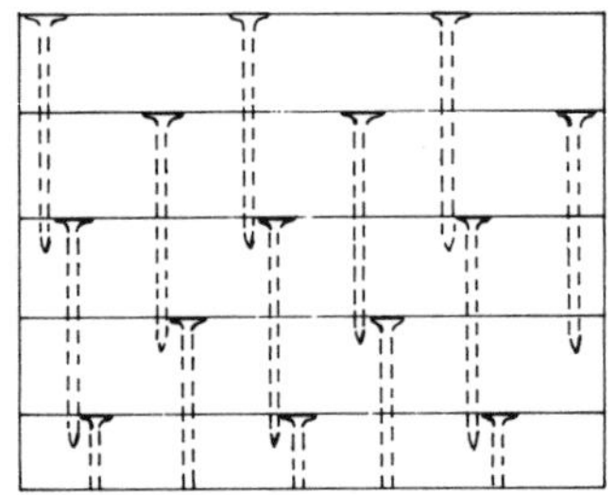

staggered plank fastenings

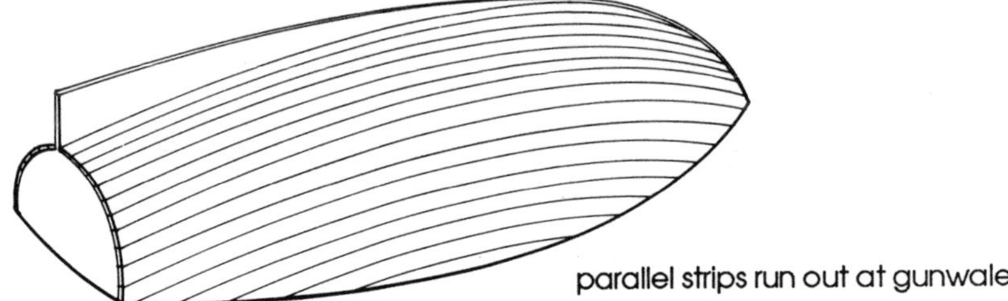

parallel strips run out at gunwale

Strip planking can be a fast and economical method of building one-off hulls of great rigidity and moderate weight. Three methods of building are shown, the second being the most common. Glue or bedding compound is used between the beveled strakes which are edge-nailed, thus providing both chemical and mechanical bonding.

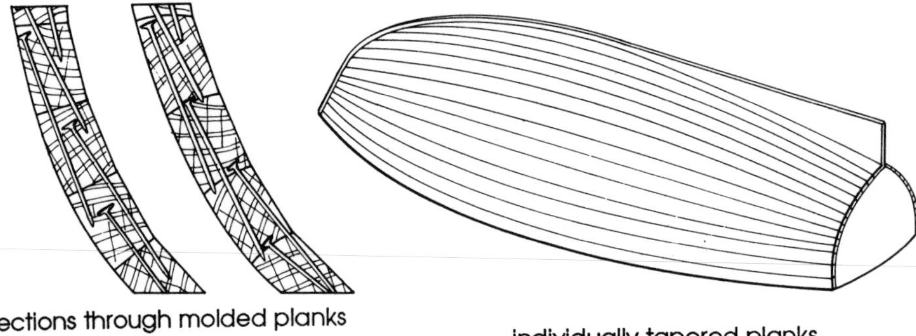

sections through molded planks

individually tapered planks

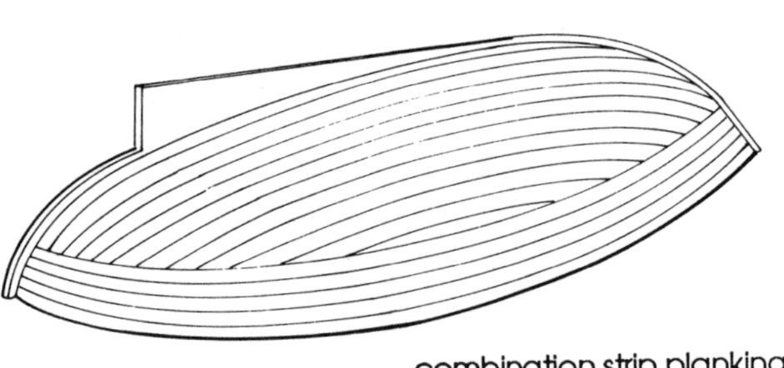

combination strip planking

vertical scarfed joint

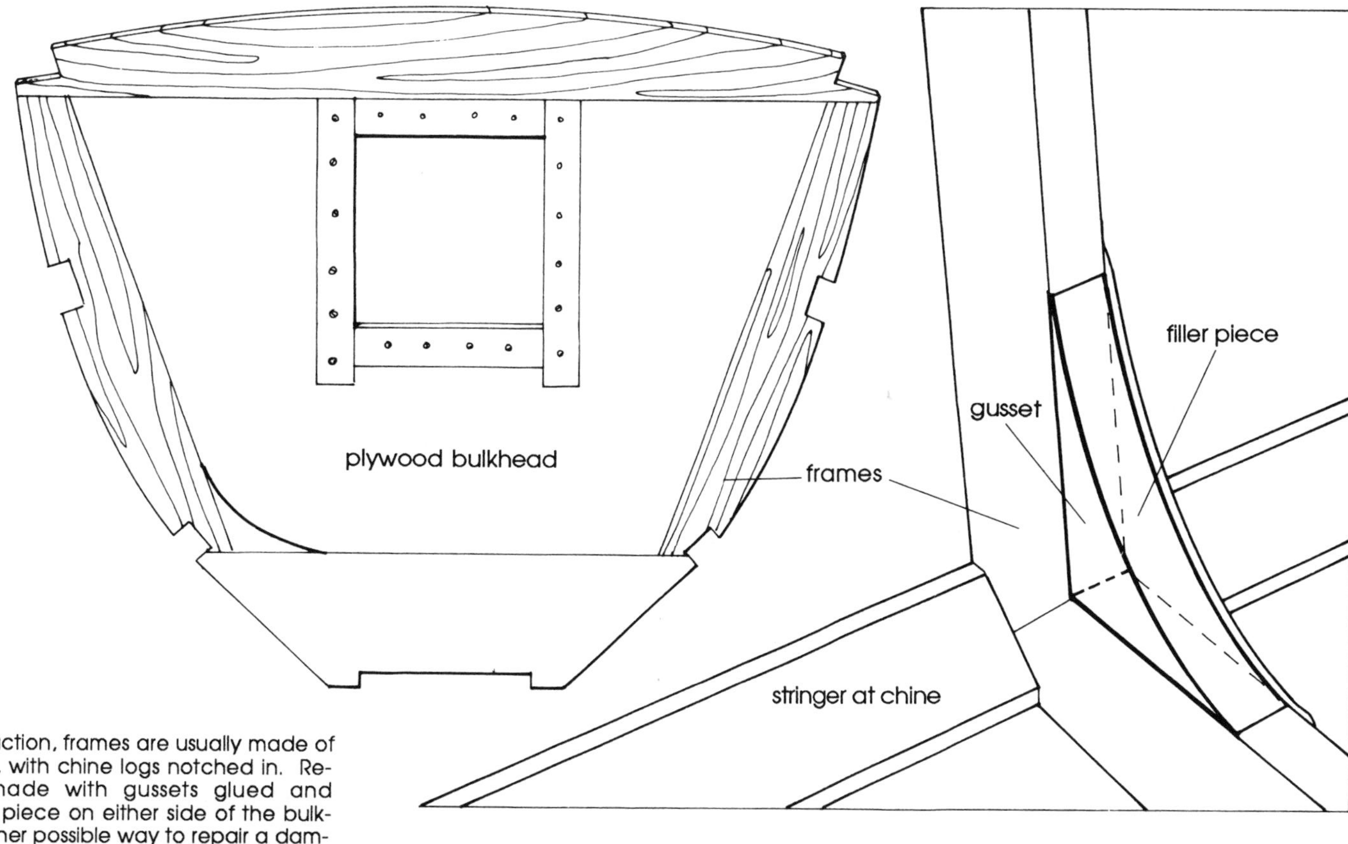

In plywood construction, frames are usually made of ply as a bulkhead, with chine logs notched in. Repairs are best made with gussets glued and screwed to a filler piece on either side of the bulkhead frame. Another possible way to repair a damaged frame is to install a doubler, creating a second partial bulkhead.

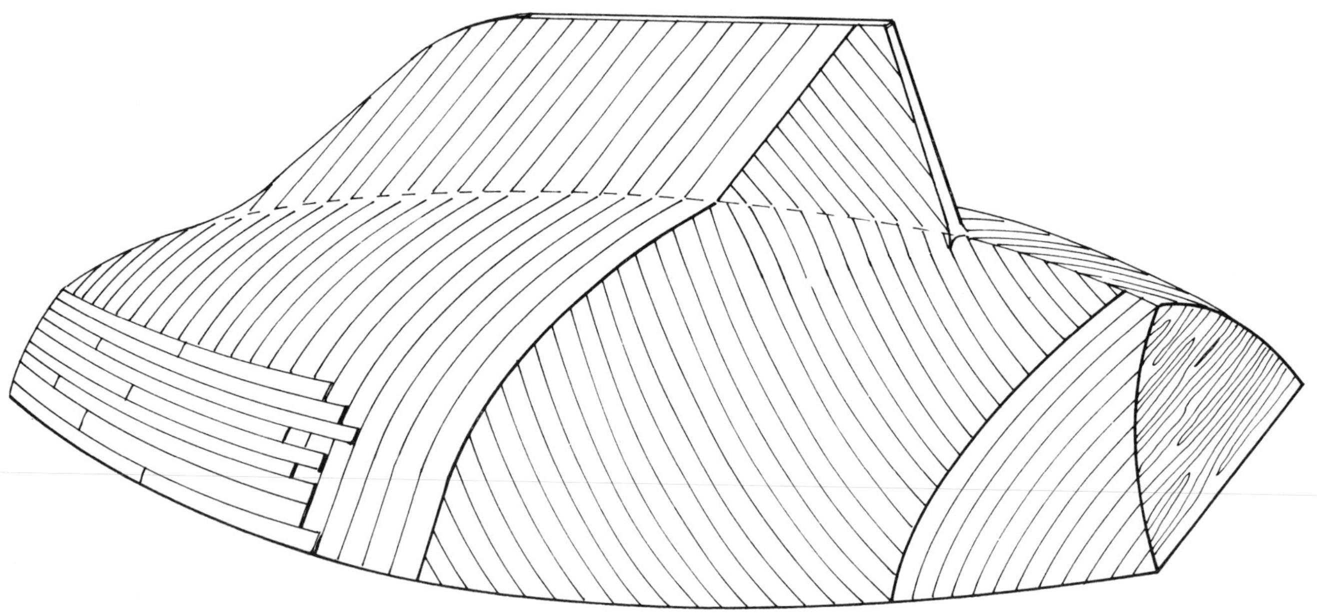

Cold-molded hulls are made up of layers of veneers running at angles to one another, the size of the hull and sharpness of the curves dictating the thickness of the veneers used. The illustrations show how to use a plug as a form for laying up veneers, first on the inside of the hull, then on the exterior. Once cured and sanded smooth, repairs can be painted and will be impossible to detect.

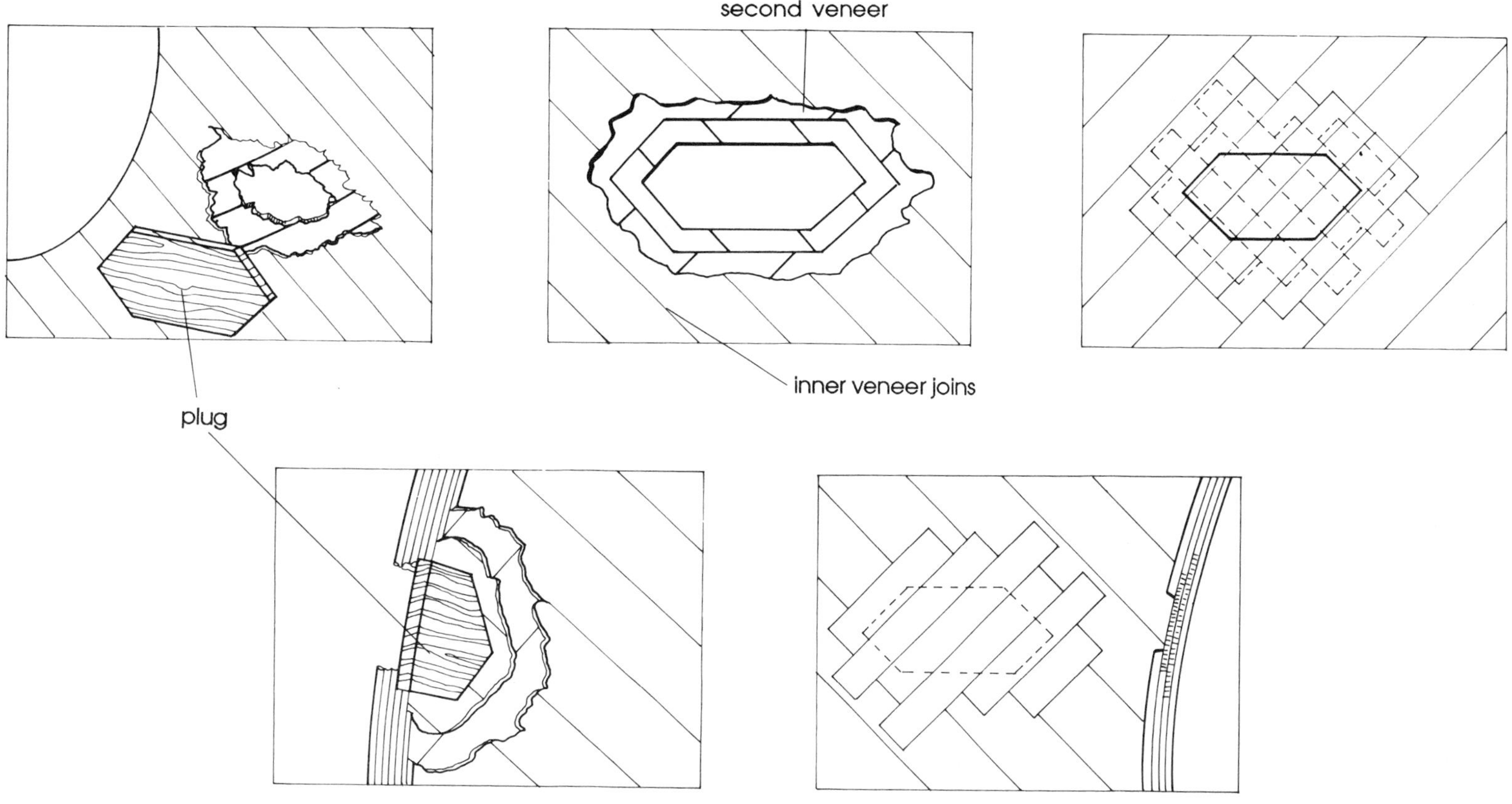
second veneer
inner veneer joins
plug

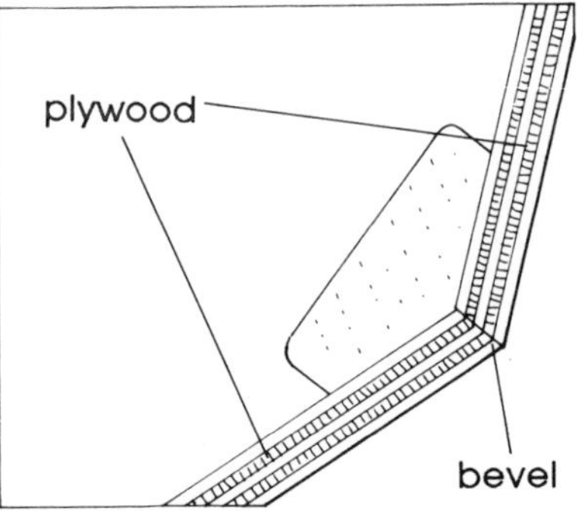

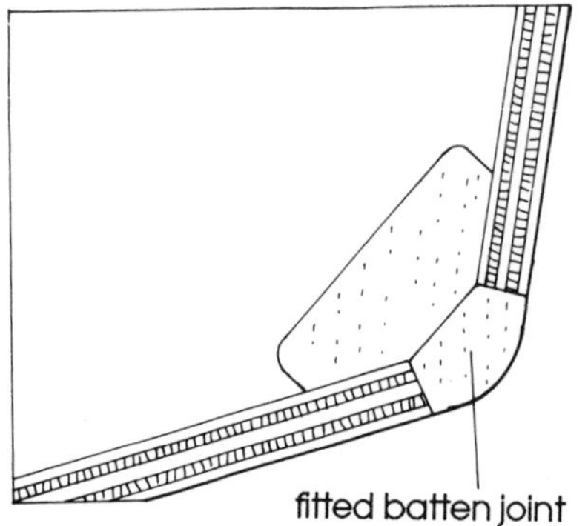

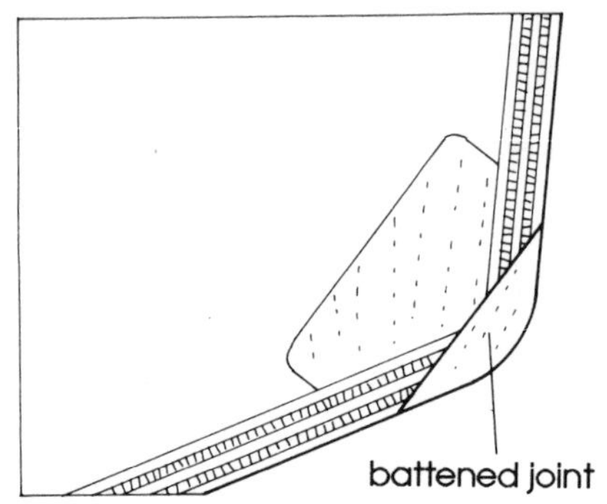

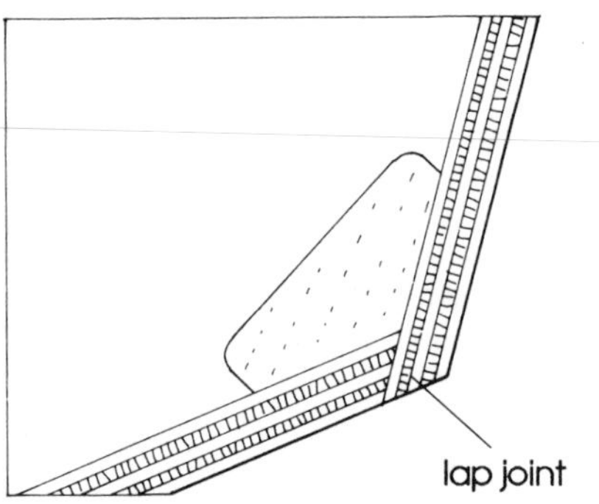

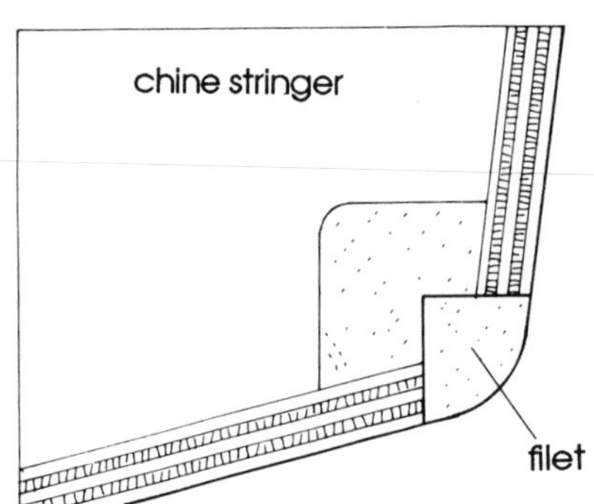

All plywood used in marine applications should be marine grade–guaranteed percentage of voids, waterproof glues, etc. Nevertheless, all edges must be protected from moisture entering to avoid delamination and structural weakening. Here are several ways to do this. In all cases, even those with structural edge protection, edges should be sealed with epoxy, waterproof glue and varnish or paint.

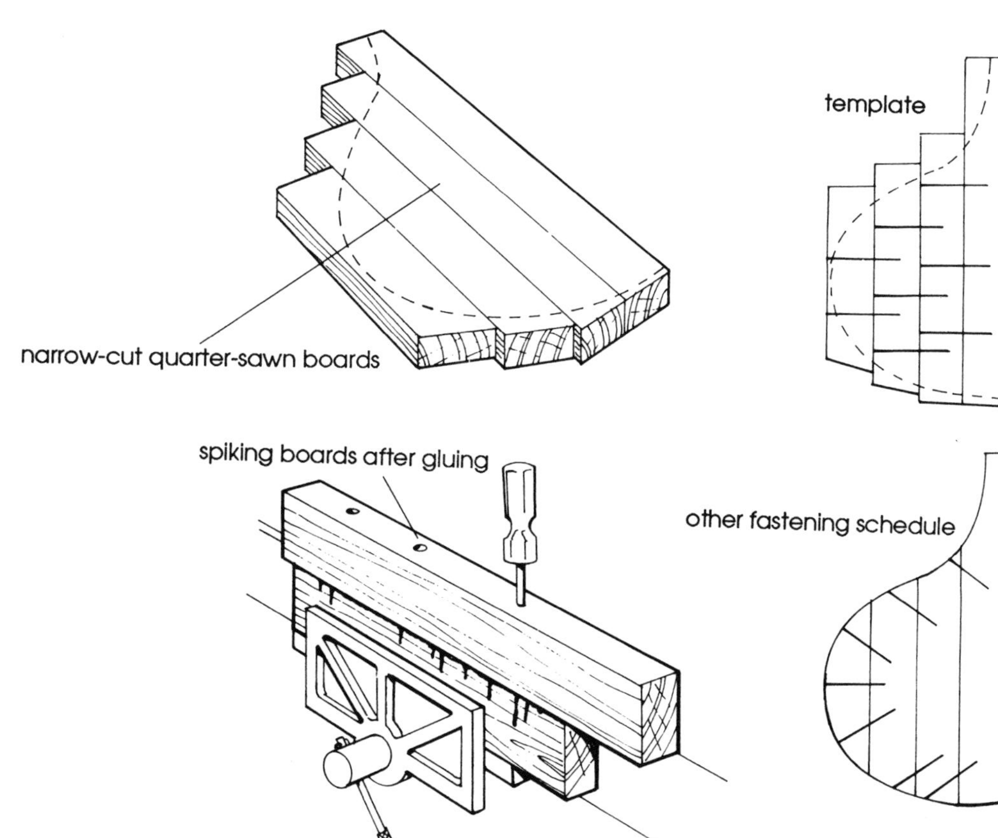

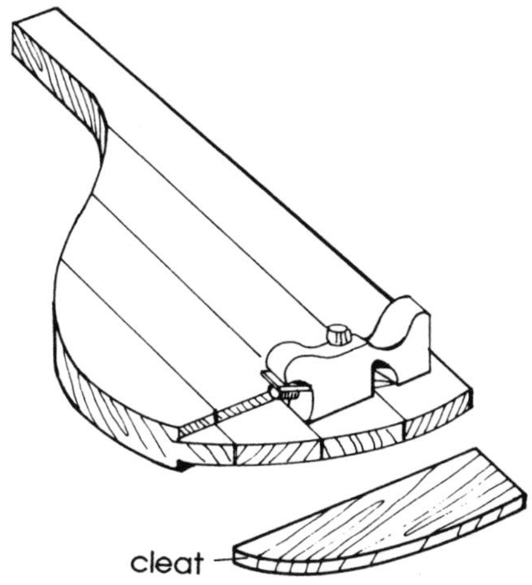

Rebuilding a wood rudder is not as difficult as you might imagine. Use the old rudder as a pattern and use quarter sawn boards (less warping). Plan the fastening schedule before driving the first spike. Cleat the bottom and fair both leading and trailing edges. Trailing edges should be tapered to a fairly sharp edge. Leading edges can be rounded concavely to take the rudder stock or rounded off below the waterline but should still be kept fairly thick for strength and to direct water flow most effectively.

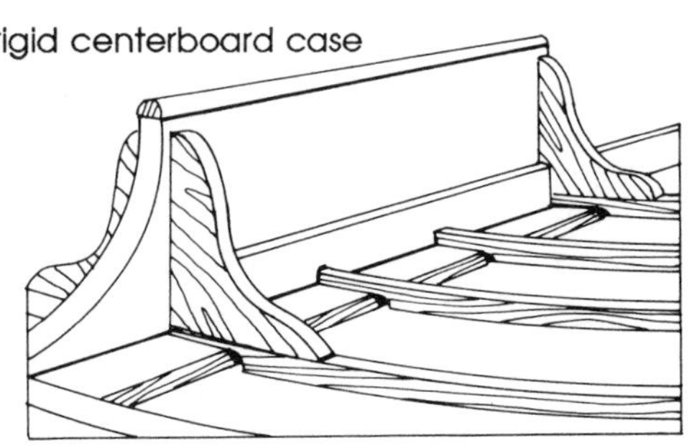

Rigid centerboard case in wood. This drawing shows the various parts and also the potential trouble spots. Once a wood case starts to leak, the only practical solution may be to rebuild it from scratch. Since it is always working, every seam is liable to distortion and fastenings to bending strains. Rebuilding is a major job.

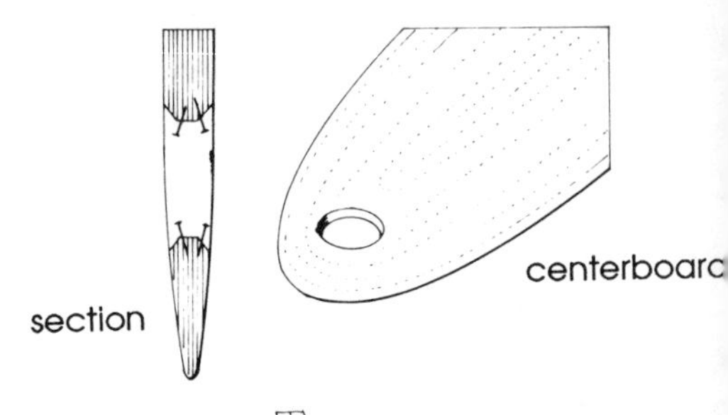

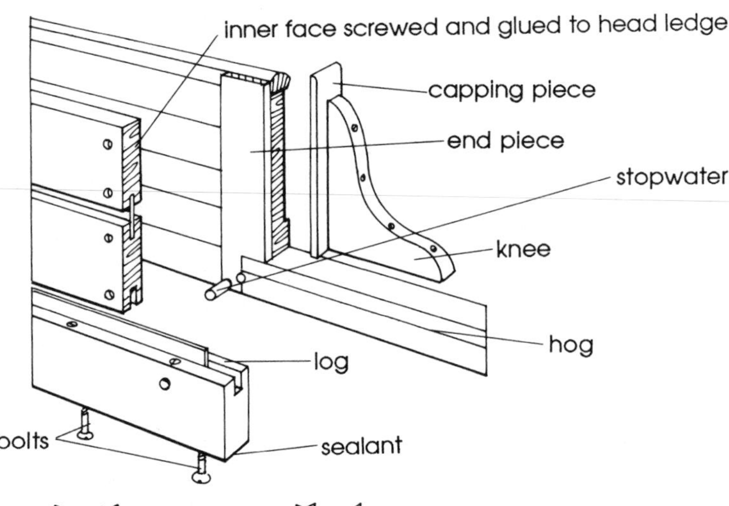

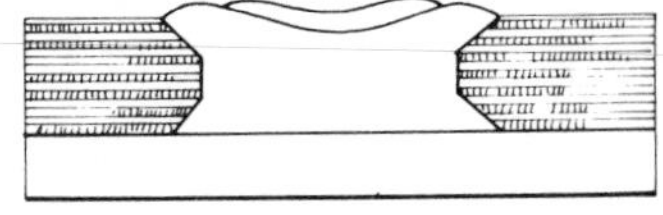

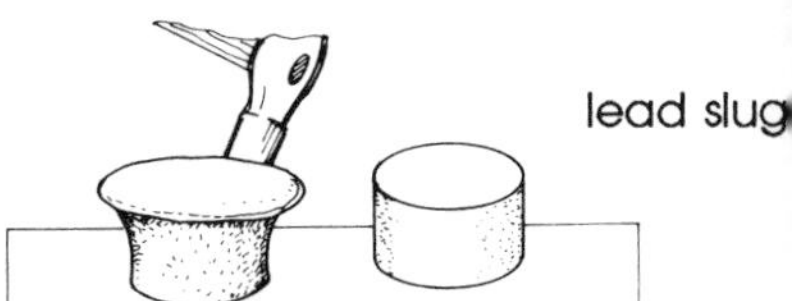

Wood centerboards tend to float up. By fitting a lead insert or slug, the natural buoyancy of the board can be neutralized. Do not pour the lead directly into the hole made in the board. Rather, cast it in a slightly smaller diameter mold and then hammer in place as indicated.

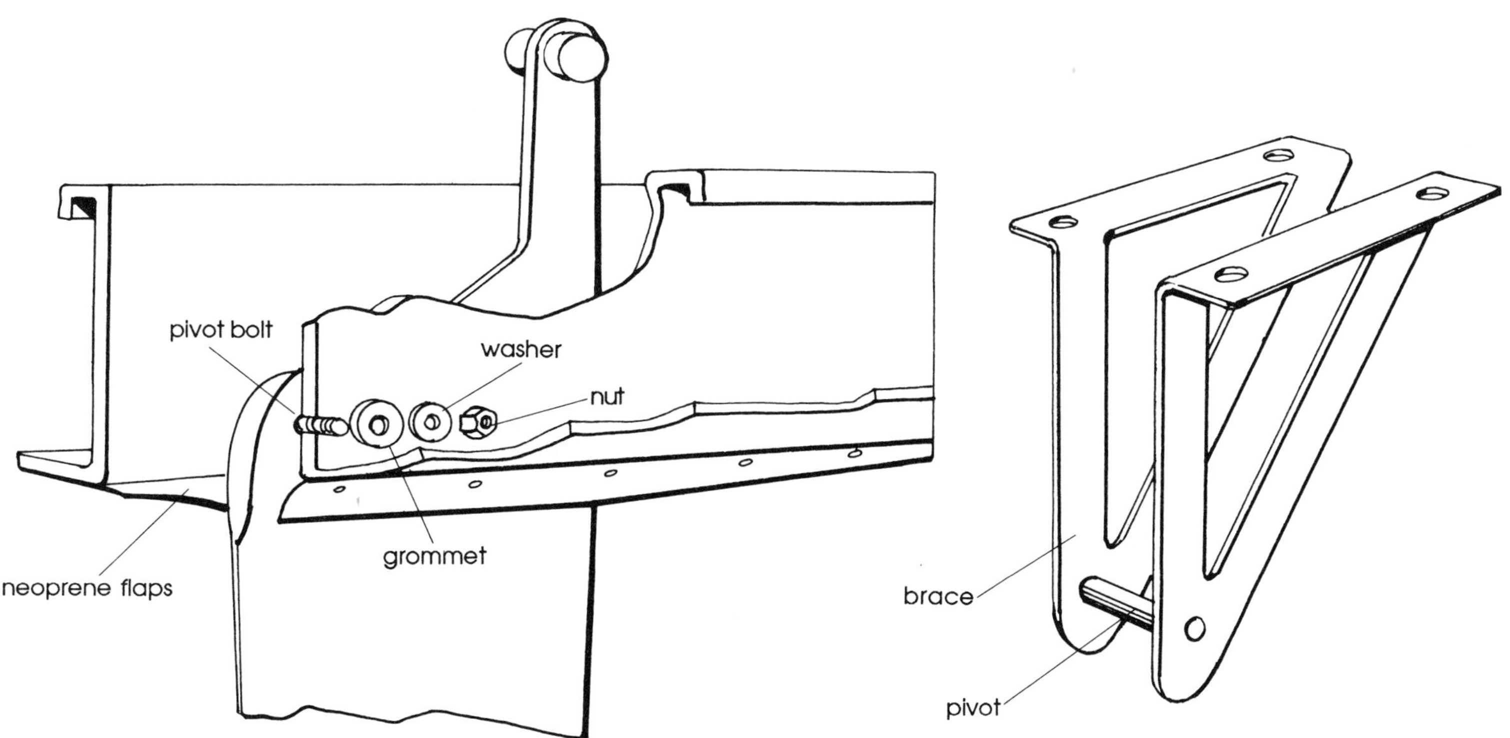

GRP centerboard cases will usually not leak, but careful provision must be made to keep the GRP from crazing. Metal support webs or ample washering are the most common solutions. Note that flanged bushings will keep the GRP from wearing away. Still, structural support is preferable.

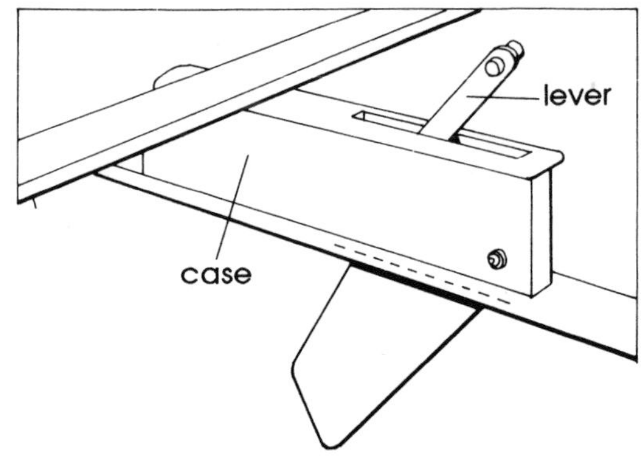

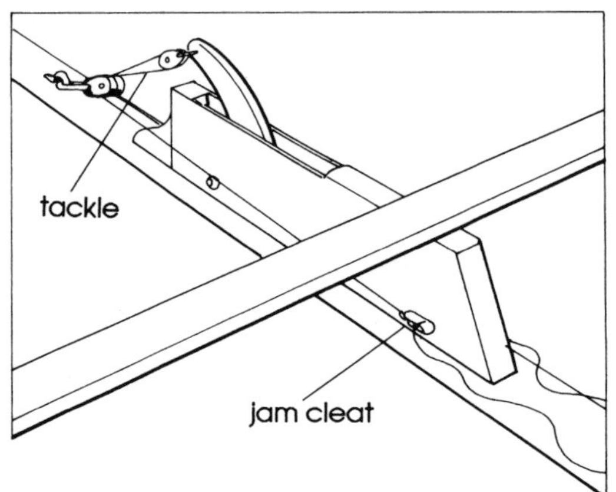

Raising and lowering centerboards can be accomplished in different ways, usually by means of a pulley arrangement or, in smaller boats, with a lever. On larger boats, a winch will substantially aid in raising the board. Daggerboards can be held in place with a length of shock cord and drilled to be kept partially raised with a pin or dowel.

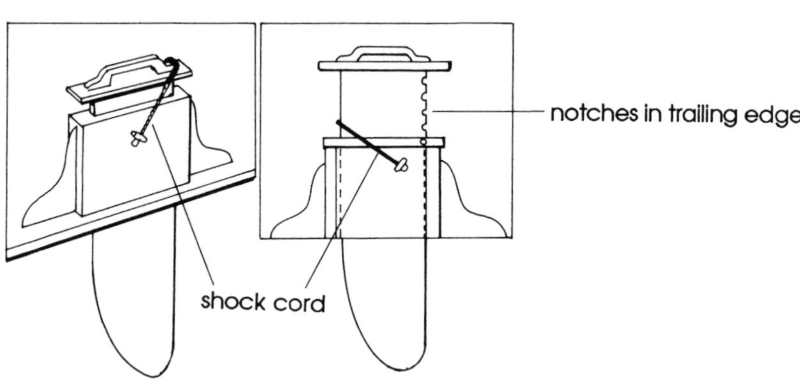

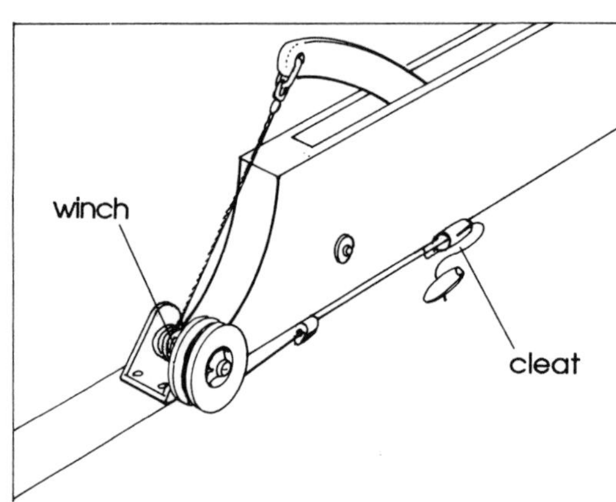

Keel bolts should be withdrawn every four or five years to check their condition. This is a major yard job and should be done in rotation, say one-quarter of the total number every five years. The bolts should be marked and a diagram drawn to indicate position and condition. No other method will really tell you much about their condition, except for X-rays and they are not always reliable, especially with lead keels.

bedding compound
washer

hog
wooden keel
waterproof membrane
water entry
ballast keel

Three typical methods of fitting a fin keel to a sailing vessel. The first is standard wood boat procedure. The other two drawings show bolt and stud methods used for either GRP or cold-molded construction. When nuts and washers are fitted without proper blocking to allow for hull curvature–only bedding compound–leaks can occur.

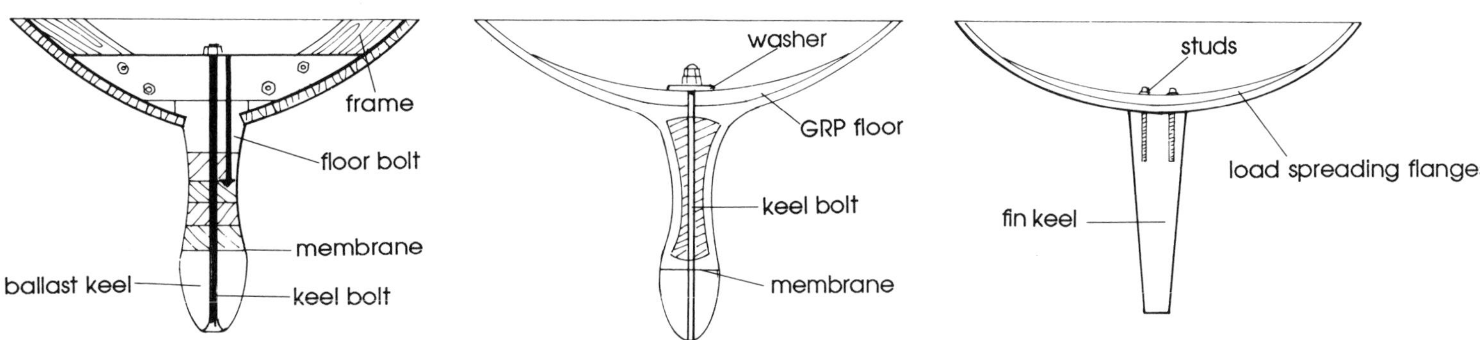

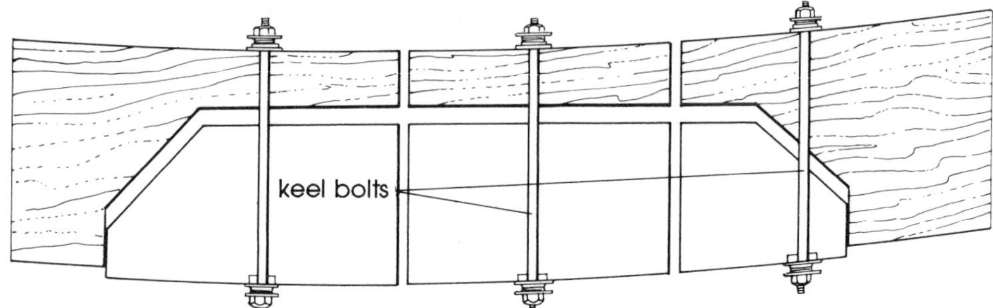

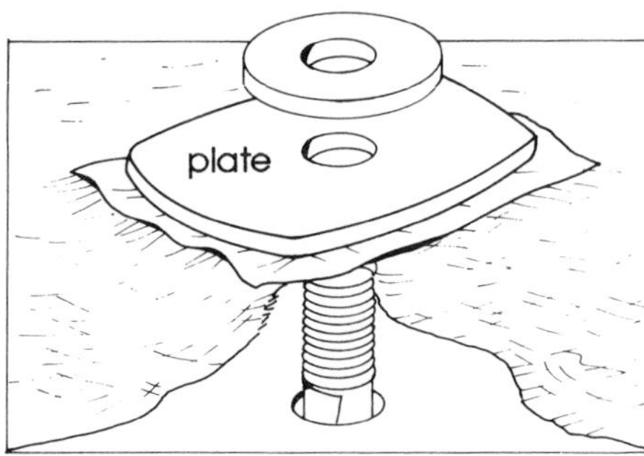

When refitting a ballast keel make sure sufficient bedding is between ballast and deadwood to fill any gaps and seal the wood from contact with the metal. Also use roofing felt between the ballast and wood held in place with bedding compound or hot tar. Tighten lifting bolts before inserting the keel bolts and tightening them.

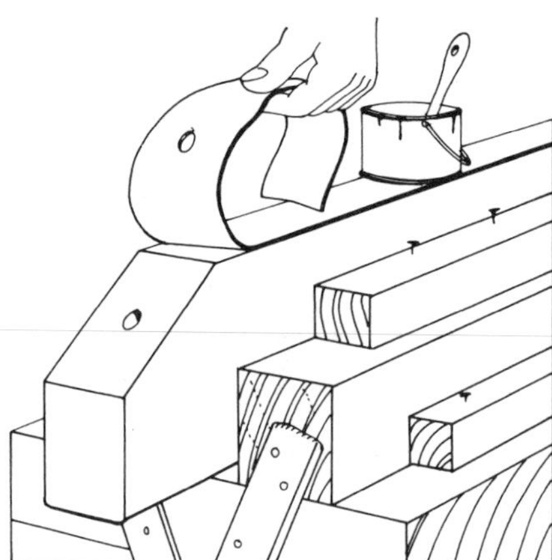

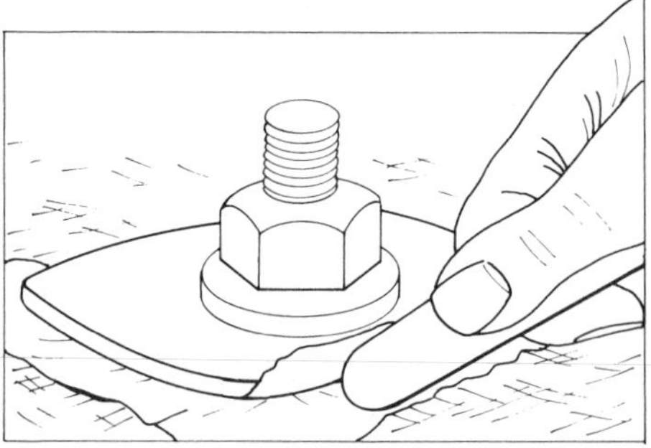

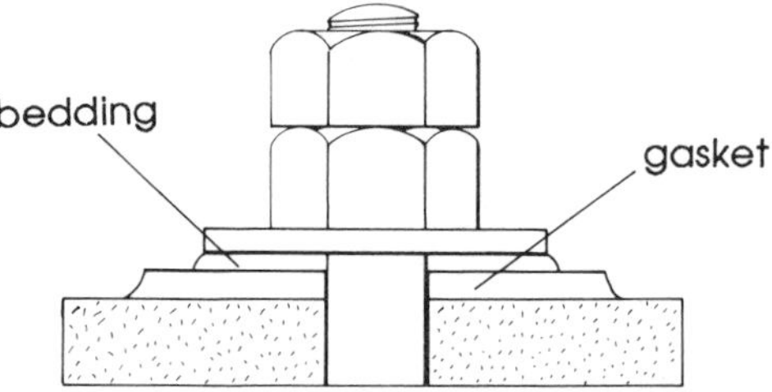

Make sure large load-bearing plates are installed between the washers and the wood when drawing through keel bolts or studs. Even better would be to install a neoprene gasket between the plate and wood.

METAL HULLS

All metal hulls–steel or aluminum alloy or a few of cuprous nickel–will last forever if corrosion and galvanic and electrolytic action are kept at bay. The easiest way to do this would be to keep them on land in a vat of paint. Since this would defeat the purpose of a yacht, some other solution must be found.

The first and most obvious is to keep a hull protected from its watery environment as well as possible. This is done with paint. Navy practice is to chip and paint around the clock. You always see some poor sod hanging on a scaffold with chisel or brush in hand. A yacht can usually do better than this. Steel hulls need protective coatings both above and below water. The paint chapter discusses this in greater detail.

The action of dissimilar metals in salt water–electrolytic action–is exactly the same as a wet cell battery. The action of two dissimilar metals together will create galvanic action. Thus, to protect steel or aluminum hulls, the best bet is to keep anything of a differing metallurgical composition away from the material of the greatest mass. This is not always the easiest thing to do. Through hulls, transducers, propellers and shafts are invariably of a different metal than the hull. The solution is to isolate dissimilar metals as much as possible and to fit sacrificial anodes to all those metals which cannot be isolated.

Isolation can best be achieved through gasketing, usually with neoprene. Anodes, in varying shapes and forms, can be attached to propellers, shafts, P-brackets, rudders, etc. Good examples are stainless steel shafts with bronze props, bronze rudders with stainless rudder shafts and so on. Another possibility is to install through-hull fittings of a neutral–that is, non-metallic–composition. Seacocks are now made of plastic and the higher-end ranges are fully comparable to bronze.

Since metal hulls are more ductile than their wood or GRP counterparts, they will usually bend or distort before they break. Repair can be as easy as pounding the dent back to shape, much like auto repair. When a break occurs, welding to

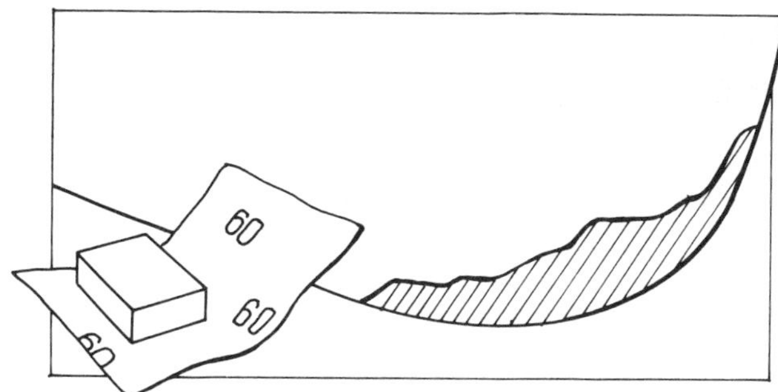

Lead keels are best faired by sanding with #60 grit paper wrapped around a block of wood. For major fairing an electric grinder will speed the job.

original specifications is the answer. With steel this can often be done by an amateur. Aluminum, these days, is usually welded by far more sophisticated machinery than the portable oxy-acetylene welder and should be left to a pro. Aluminum is much more prone to heat distortion than steel and chances are you will make things worse if you attempt the repairs yourself.

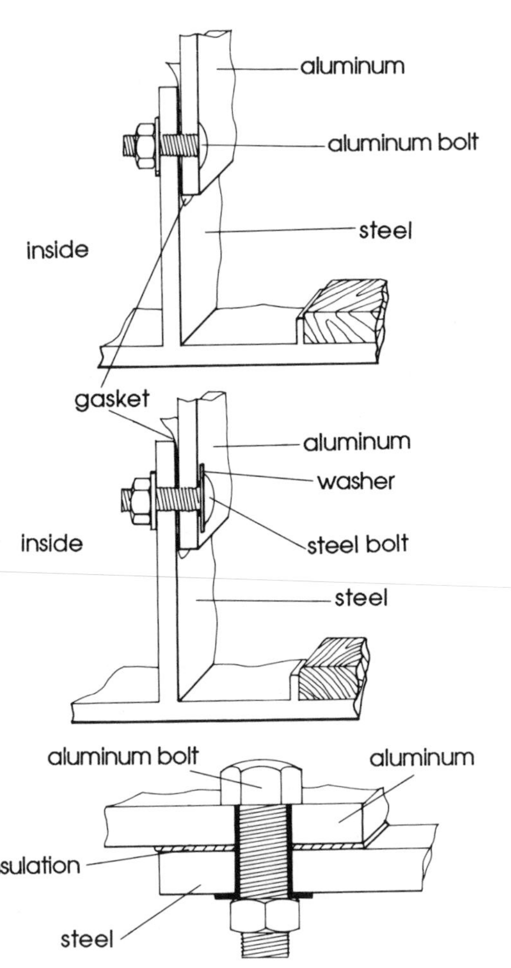

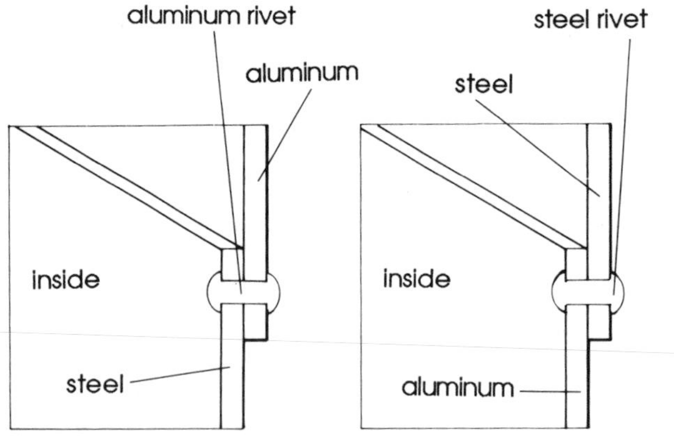

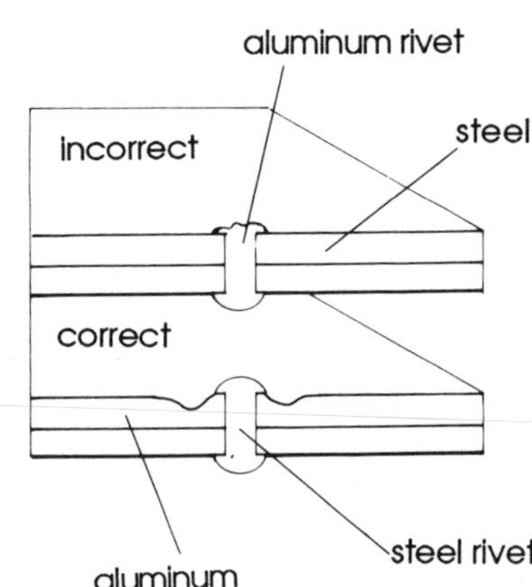

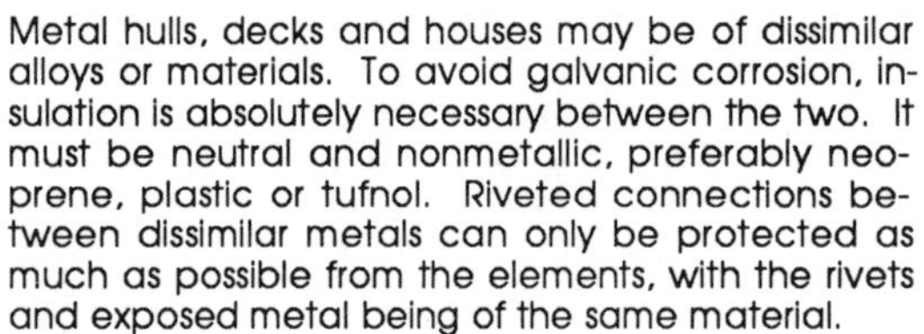

Metal hulls, decks and houses may be of dissimilar alloys or materials. To avoid galvanic corrosion, insulation is absolutely necessary between the two. It must be neutral and nonmetallic, preferably neoprene, plastic or tufnol. Riveted connections between dissimilar metals can only be protected as much as possible from the elements, with the rivets and exposed metal being of the same material.

3
DECKS

While we all spend much time worrying about deck layouts, we spend less concerned with the actual condition of the deck and its attachment to the hull. The first is a matter of convenience; the second a matter of strength, integrity and, just maybe, life and death.

A good and proper deck is one that is tight (doesn't leak), strong (to take a boarding sea), and workable (as free as possible from unnecessary obstructions and with the important fittings at hand). In the days of laid decks with payed seams, if the deck wasn't sloshed down daily, it would leak like a sieve after a hot spell. With the advent of canvas coverings this condition was somewhat alleviated, but it was the development of true marine plywood panels that allowed a first-rate waterproof deck to be constructed. And with GRP, the dry cabin became a real possibility. I say possibility because every hole drilled or cut in a deck–any deck–becomes a potential source of drips and weakening.

Oddly enough, the most watertight deck is in a steel ship, where fittings can be welded, not bolted, to the surface; the result is an *unpunctured* surface, totally free of holes, cuts, anything that demands fillers and sealants, all of which can dry out. Your goal in working on your deck should be to approximate this as much as possible. The fewer openings, the better your chance of a dry cabin with much less chance for the deck's integrity to be breached.

HULL-TO-DECK JOINTS

The most vital area, though, is not a hole near the rail, but the actual attachment of the deck to the hull. In traditionally constructed wooden boats, this was accomplished by means of a heavy shelf beam stoutly attached to the frames, which acted as both support and attachment point for the deck itself. But for

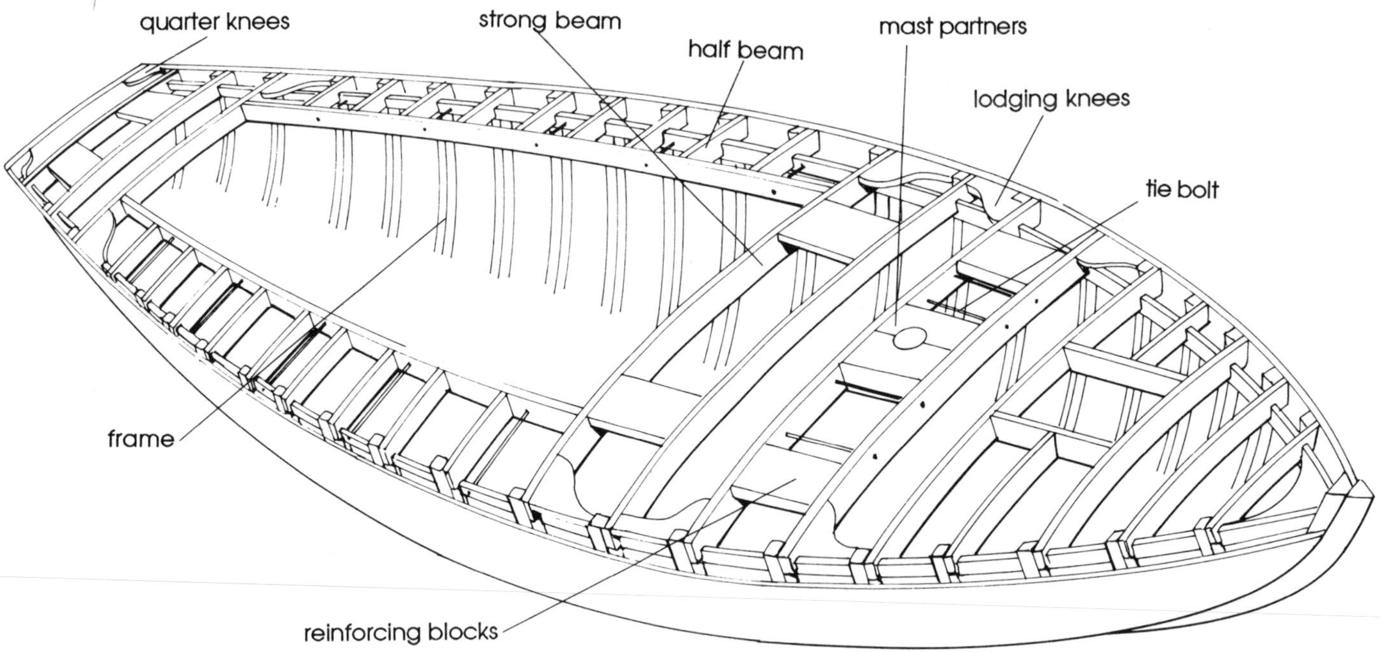

The substructure of a typical deck. Note the extra strengthening at the mast partners and the manner in which all parts interact to create a solid and shape-retaining whole. The best traditional deck construction uses mechanical fasteners, not glue, to obtain the most secure connections between components. Knees and tie bolts keep everything together and assure that shape is retained, even while individual members may flex with the working of the ship. When replacing a complete deck, make sure that the hull structure will be able to stand up to the increased rigidity of ply decking. Greater rigidity imposes all sorts of wracking strains on the entire structure.

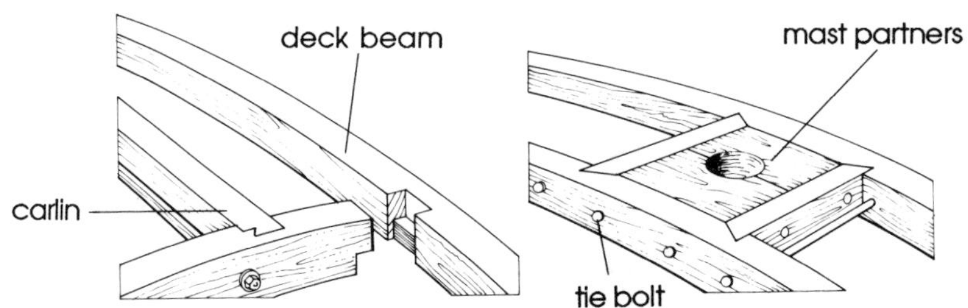

the whole assembly to be strong, each and every part had to be carefully cut and fit with care and a whole bucket of bolts and screws. With the advent of GRP the multipart solution was dispensed with (though not originally; the first GRP boats had traditional wood decks and houses) and a single deck structure could be bonded–either mechanically, chemically or both–to the hull. It is this bond which has been the base of most complaints in GRP construction. Purely mechanical bonds can leak, purely chemical ones delaminate. The best compromise so far seems to be a combination of bolting the hull and deck together with a flexible adhesive sealant, such as 3M's 5200, as the bedding compound; finally, the interior join is glassed over for watertight integrity.

Should your boat have either a mechanically *or* chemically bonded hull-to-deck joint, you can create a combination joint fairly easily. This is no patch job, however. It must be done with due consideration for what you are trying eventually to achieve: the strongest joint possible. If the deck is simply glassed to the hull, you can drill holes on 6-inch centers around the perimeter, making sure they go at least 1 inch inboard from the extreme outside of the deck edge, and through both deck and hull shelf. Occasionally, the deck will rest inside the hull on a flange with the attachment forming a vertical rail, then capped from above. In such a situation, it is best to attach the hull and deck from the outside of the sheer, also on 6-inch centers.

All mechanical fasteners should be of sufficient sheer strength to hold in a major collision. These days, this pretty much means stainless-steel bolts of at least 1/4-inch diameter, backed up by washers and double nuts or locknuts. These must be bedded in a flexible sealant. For a truly tight and professional job, the bolt holes can be threaded with a properly sized tap. A final thought: try to have the bolts just long enough to pass through all glass and hardware with no more than a 1/4-inch over.

Underdeck reinforcement can be chemically achieved by us-

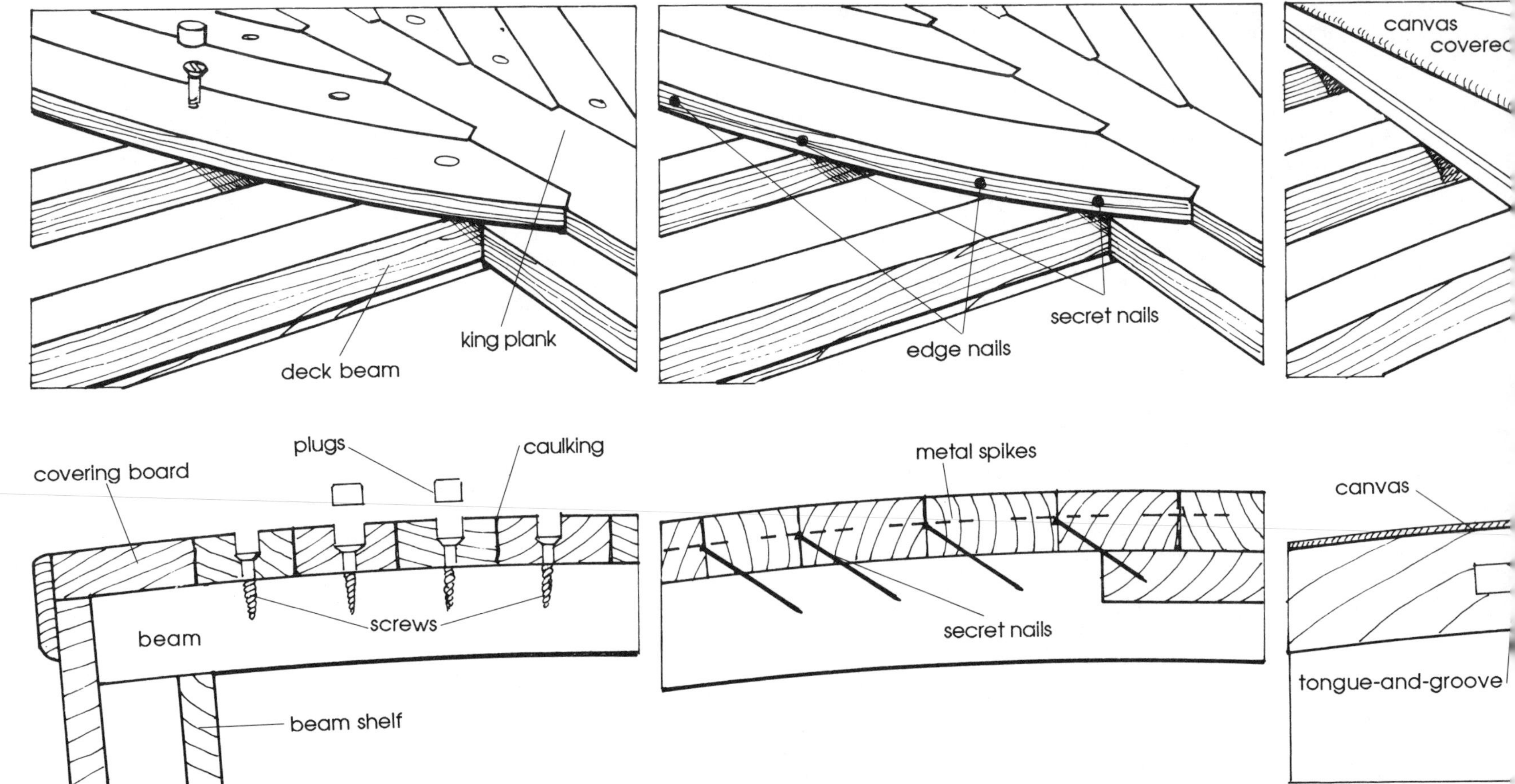
king plank
deck beam
edge nails
secret nails
canvas
covered
plugs
caulking
covering board
screws
beam
beam shelf
metal spikes
secret nails
canvas
tongue-and-groove

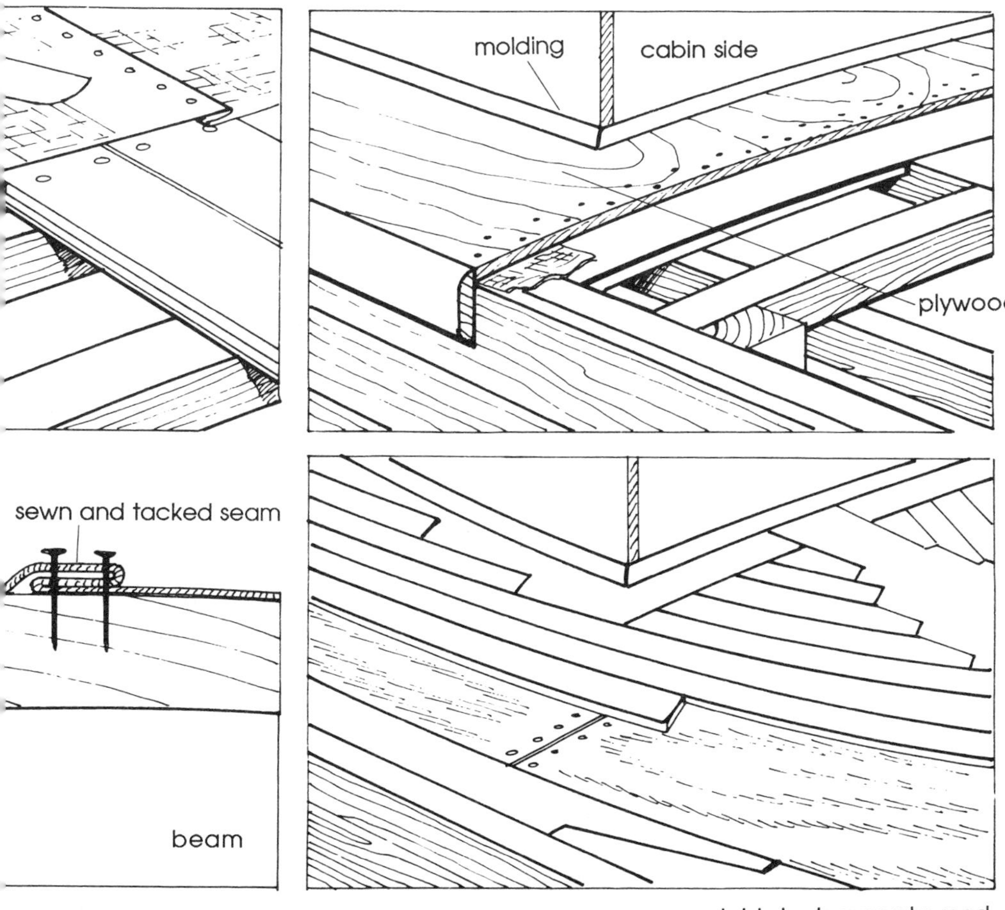

laid deck over plywood

Deck construction. Different boats use different deck construction techniques. 1. Laid decks are most traditional, most time consuming and most expensive to install and maintain. They can either be screwed to deck beams and bunged or secret nailed. 2. Canvas-covered tongue and groove decking is cheap, quicker than laid and reasonably watertight, providing the canvas is properly installed and treated. All tongue and groove decking is subject to expansion and contraction and if too much paint is applied to the canvas, this will lead to cracking and loss of watertight integrity. 3. Most common these days in replacing decks is to use a substratum of plywood covered with either GRP, canvas or planking. This adds to watertightness, cuts down on the possibility of rot and makes for less maintenance.

ing either a combination mat or roving and mat saturated with resin. The glass must overlap the joint by a minimum of three inches either side, preferably more, if you have the working space. A good combination is mat/roving/mat (the weights dependent upon the size of the boat; it's advisable to discuss the matter with your yard or the glass manufacturer). Each should be applied to a thin layer of resin–to hold it in place–and saturated and rolled out. Each successive layer can be applied when the resin has just set and is still slightly tacky to the touch. Since this joint will not be visible after the furniture and liners are reinstalled, it need not look perfect. However, it must be carefully applied! By and large, hard creases should be avoided as resin saturation is not easy. A filet of foam can be used to bridge the glass across the actual 90-degree bend between hull and deck and the above procedure still followed.

HULL-TO-DECK LEAKS

Trying to find a leak in the hull-to-deck joint is one of the great chases of all times. Since water will always follow the laws of gravity, it will run along that joint to the lowest point before dripping. Of course, that spot is always over a berth! The only effective way to trace it back to the source is to use a pressure hose on deck with someone below working backwards from the dripping. This can often be difficult due to liners and furniture. Still, chances are that leaks will occur where fasteners penetrate the deck edge, usually holding stanchions or toe rails in place. Since both of these are flexed constantly, the bolt holes through the deck edge are invariably enlarged. Without sufficient sealant, water enters.

This is of particular concern in balsa-cored decks, as deterioration and rot can sweep through all too quickly. As a general rule, all deck fittings should be rebedded every five years, if not more often; and all through-deck holes should be coated inside with epoxy or polyester resin prior to installation of any deck hardware. One assumes, of course, that hardware will be

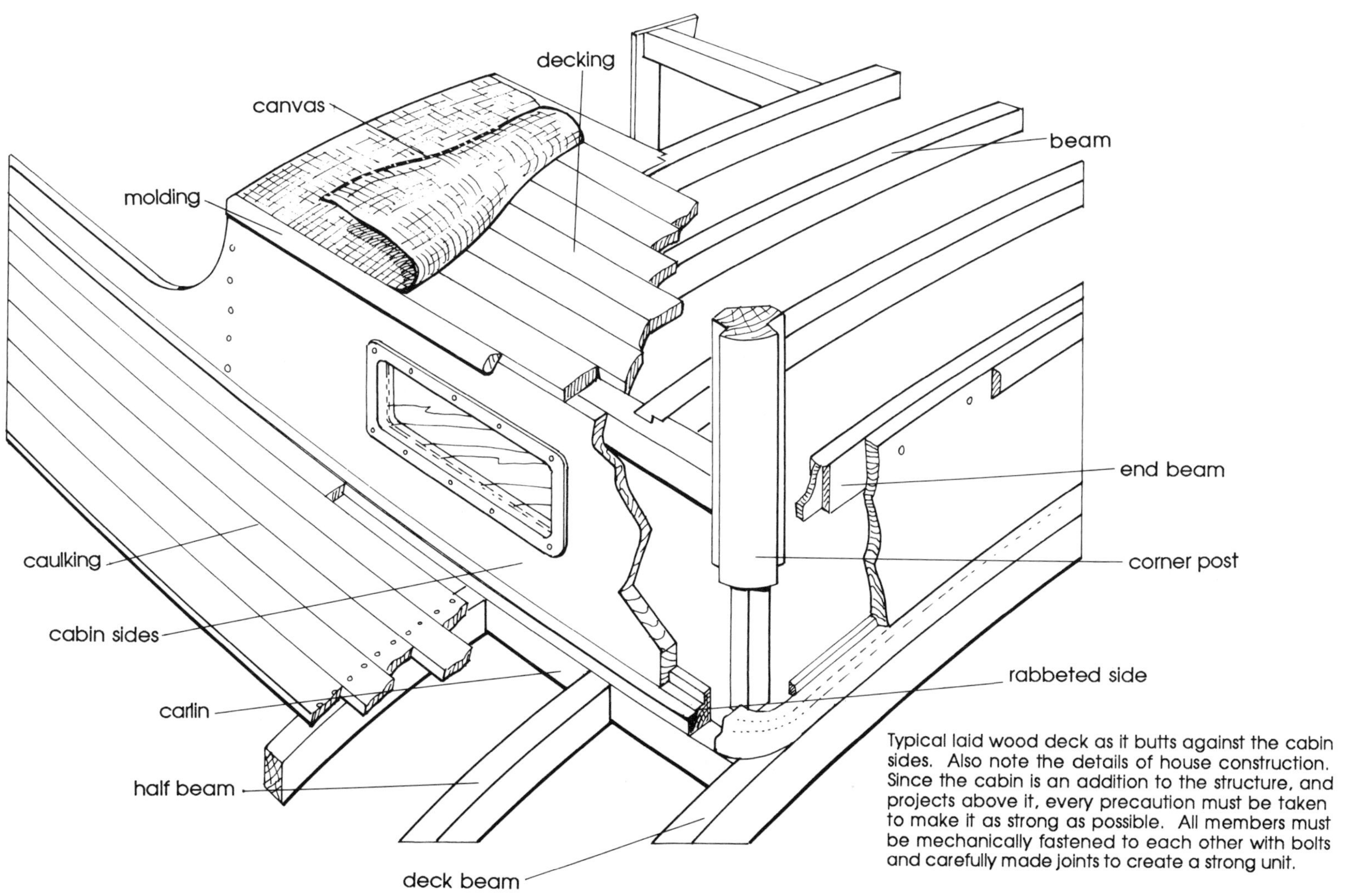

Typical laid wood deck as it butts against the cabin sides. Also note the details of house construction. Since the cabin is an addition to the structure, and projects above it, every precaution must be taken to make it as strong as possible. All members must be mechanically fastened to each other with bolts and carefully made joints to create a strong unit.

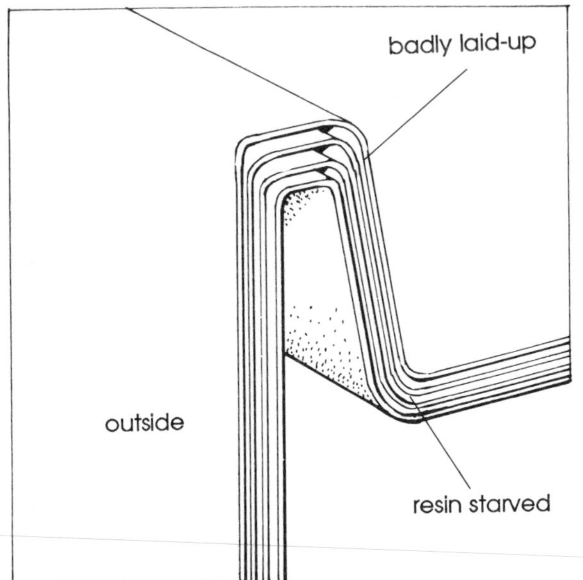

Too much or too little resin in GRP layup will result in weakness or brittleness. Though correct proportions are much a matter of practice, careful and thorough application and full-coverage rolling-out of the mat or fabric will assure sound bonding. Also make sure to follow manufacturer's instructions as to curing times and humidity and temperature control.

backed up with load spreaders–either metal plates or marine ply. In balsa-cored decks this means either substituting solid glass or wood-and-glass for the core, or else using exactly sized metal spacers to run from the underside of the deck glass to the uppermost side of the backing plate. This implies a spacer hole larger than the bolt hole and a gentle touch with the drill. The insert is probably messier, but easier, to install. All cuts must be made from below, and the deck skin cannot be pierced, or the whole point of the exercise will be wasted.

Obviously, the above applies only to those leaks directly traceable to deck fittings. A leak at the actual hull-to-deck join can be a mighty problem indeed. Since this joint can flex, unless the shelf and bonding system is absolutely rigid, once the leak has been located–often behind rubrails–a simple sealant patch will not do. Some sort of combination of glass mat and resin, preferably epoxy in this application, must be worked to seal the leak both inside and out. By merely covering the leak from the inside, it may spread, the water from the exterior being forced further along the seam, unsealed outboard. Another possibility is to use a two-part epoxy patching paste, remembering in all these glass repairs that all gelcoat must be removed and recommended primers will help in making any repair permanent. The epoxy paste, by the way, will be stronger if some shredded glass or microballoons are mixed in, in a 50:50 ratio.

WOOD DECKS

Large numbers of wooden boats remain in use, and increasing numbers of new wooden yachts are being built, though often using anything but traditional methods. Repair is easier in a wood deck, but maintenance is far more time-consuming and difficult.

In traditional planked decks, the seams between the planks were and are the major culprit. Since wood expands and contracts, constant strain is placed upon any caulking compound used to seal the spaces between planks. In the days of working

Fitting canvas to a deck must be done to insure both watertight integrity and smoothness, as well as the best possible adhesion. For these reasons, do not spare the undercoating of white lead and make sure all edges are covered or "framed-out" with moldings or fillets. Do not stretch canvas under houses or major structural members. This will only mean that major structural repairs will be needed when replacing canvas. However, a good, continuous bead of sealant is recommended along the join between uprights and canvas prior to installing any moldings.

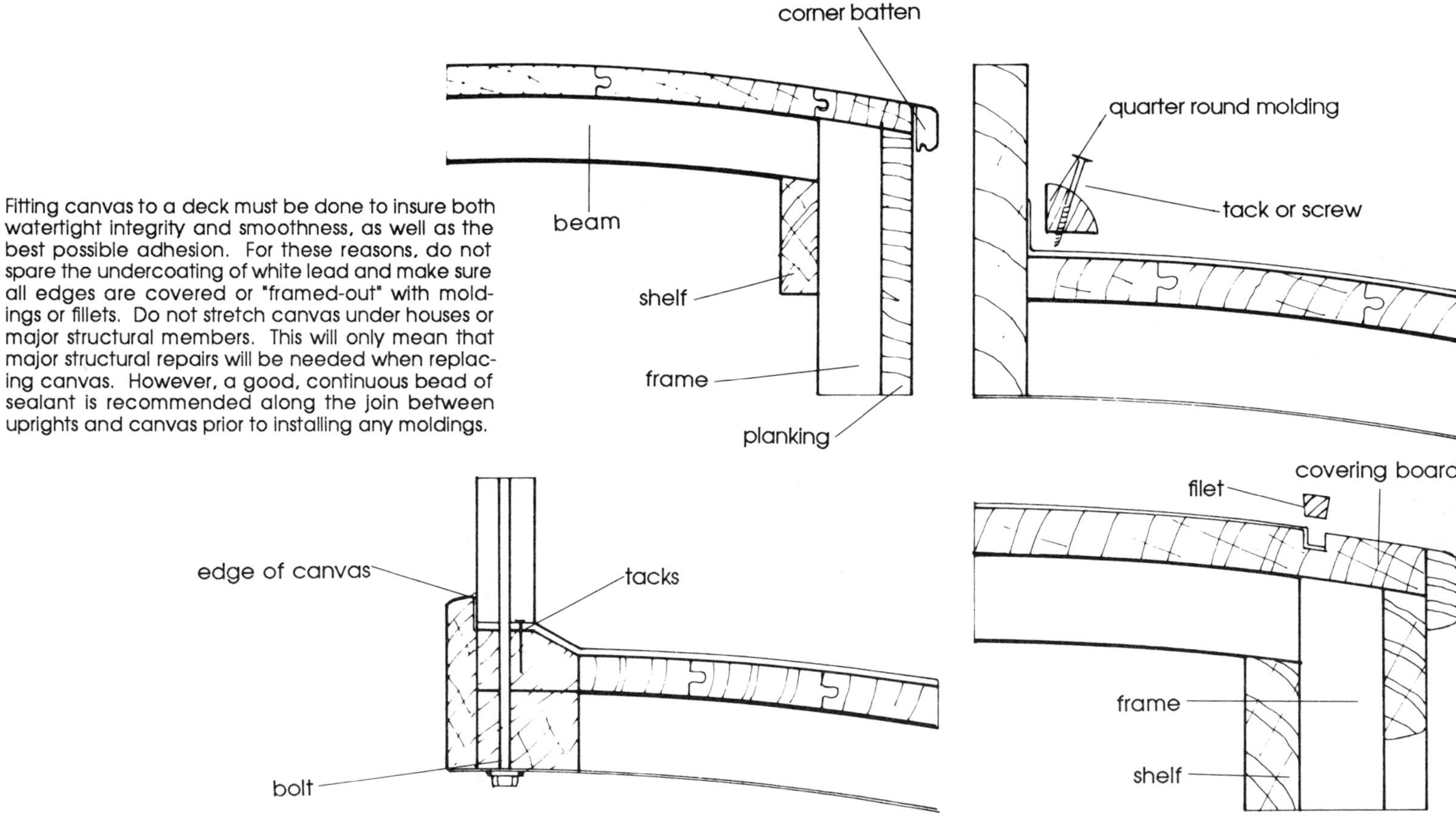

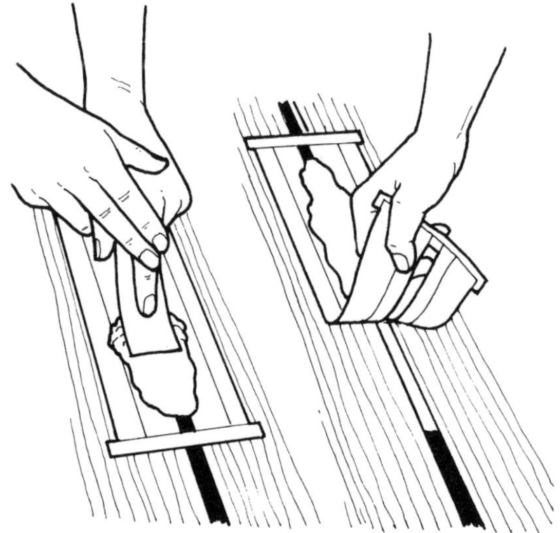

The simplest way to pay out a seam is to mask with common masking tape, press in the sealant, smooth it out and when it has dried, remove the tape. This will not only make for a neater job, but will make for less sanding when the resealing job is finished.

sail, decks were watered down daily, more often in tropical climates to keep the wood swelled and the seams tight. Such action–unless you live aboard–is not possible any longer and a better method does exist. When decks are planked, a v-groove is made by camfering the topmost edges of each plank. Into this goes caulking, followed by a sealant or seam compound. This sealant must be both adhesive and elastic, and it took years of experimentation before suitable formulas were developed. Stockholm tar and pitch work, though they are out of place on a yacht.

Any seams showing signs of leaking–separation between wood and sealant, weeping from below, etc.–must be cleaned out, recaulked and new sealant applied. The groove made by the seam bevels has to be deep enough to hold the caulking securely but not so deep that it creates a weak edge capable of splintering.

Plywood decks have much greater integrity than planked ones. However, they are also more subject to rot, due to voids, butted seams and delamination. For this reason they are usually covered, sometimes with canvas, sometimes with GRP. Sheathing a deck in canvas is actually a simple process, providing you can find the proper material: a medium-weave *untreated* duck. Treated or wax-filled cloths will not be very successful as they will not adhere to the white lead paint used to hold the canvas surface to the deck.

All hardware must be removed, its location marked. Toerails and any deck mouldings must also be removed. The deck must be a clear surface before you go to work. The old covering must be removed and the deck thoroughly and judiciously sanded. Fill any gouges with wood putty and make sure that all joints are level. As in painting, preparation is all. A sealer can be applied, but be sure it will be compatible with any resins or paints you use over it.

The edges, of course, are nailed to the deck and house where they meet or wrap around vertical surfaces. Or they are fas-

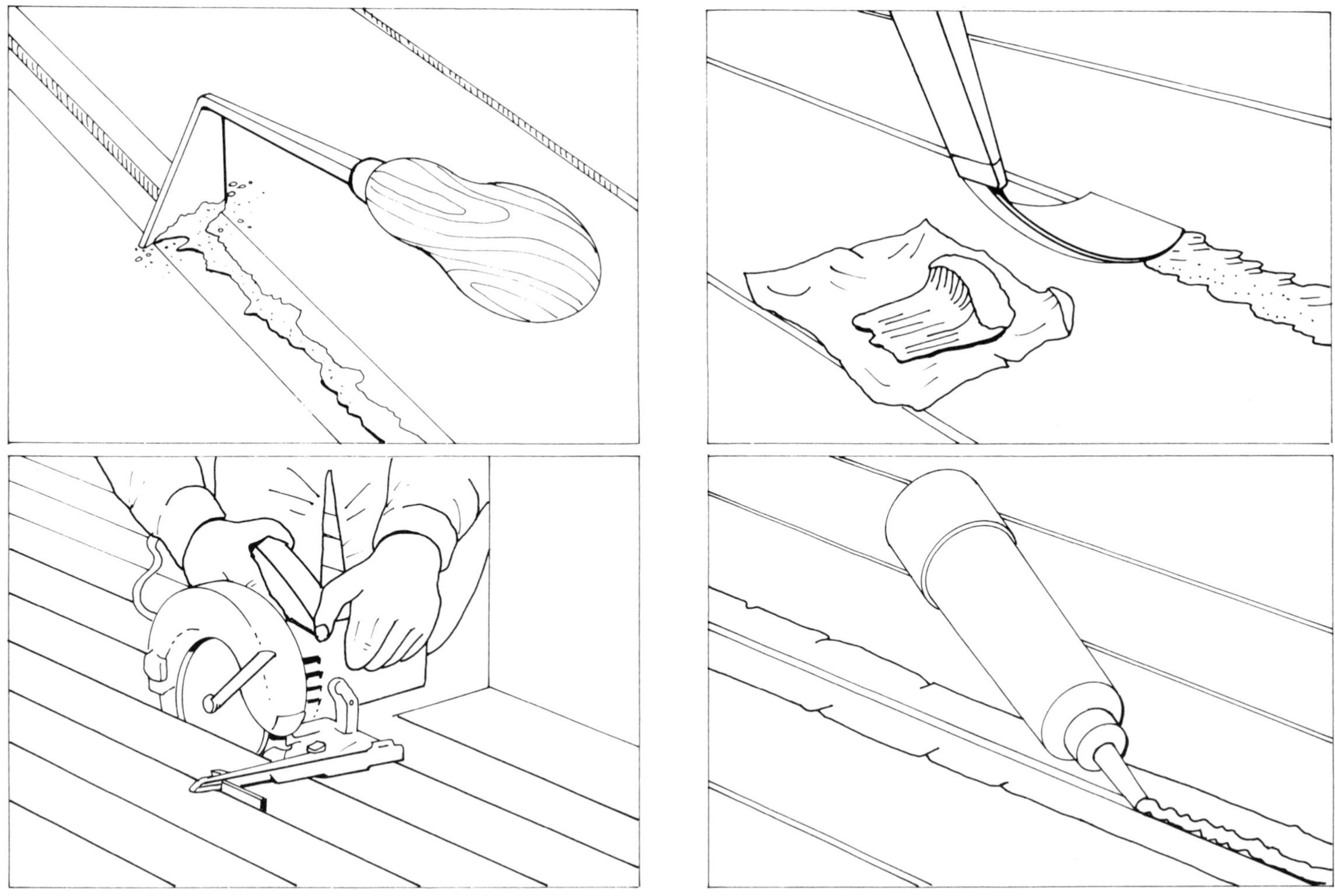

Seam compound will eventually dislodge from any sort of planking. When the time comes to repay the seams, first thoroughly clean the seams out with a hooked scraper or, for the more sure of themselves, use a circular saw (providing the decking is laid fisherman style fore-and-aft). Outline the seams with masking tape to avoid soiling the decking. Then apply the compound, either across the seam by hand or with a caulking gun. Scrape off excess, allow to cure and then sand the entire deck to achieve a level and smooth finish.

tened around battens which are then nailed to deck and house. Any edge over which the canvas passes should be rounded off to minimize chafe. The key is to stretch canvas panels tight over a coat of white lead which will be able to work its way through the canvas weave, holding it to the ply surface. When this has dried sufficiently, a second coat of paint is brushed over the canvas and left to set. If the canvas is a very rough weave, no nonskid need be applied. However, should you have to use a tightly woven cloth, a coat of sand or ground nutshells can be scattered over the surface, let dry and then the excess swept free. A final thin coat will anchor the nonskid material in place.

If you are replacing the plywood or sections of it, make sure all edges of both the cutout area and the new ply are liberally coated with epoxy sealant to lessen the chance of delamination. Also, try to fill all voids you can find in the ply. When butting sheets of ply together, locate the butt over a deck beam and/or carlin. This is the only way you will obtain secure fastening.

GRP sheathing works on much the same principle, though you must have a scrupulously clean surface to begin with. First spread on a coat of resin to both seal the wood and make a holding surface for the glass cloth. Then, with the resin still tacky, stretch panels of cloth over the deck, edge tacking or stapling them in place. Seams can either be butted or overlapped. Work a topcoat of resin over the cloth, rolling it out to make sure of even and complete saturation. When this has dried to a tacky stage, a second layer of glass is a good idea, following the preceding procedure. If you lap edges, these will have to be sanded down and you chance taking away more glass than you might want to.

For finishing, any polyurethane or epoxy deck paint can be used. However, nonskid can be applied over the last coat of resin if you wish, vacuuming away the excess when the surface is thoroughly dry. Follow this with two very thin coats of paint. Otherwise, sprinkle the nonskid on top of the first coat of paint,

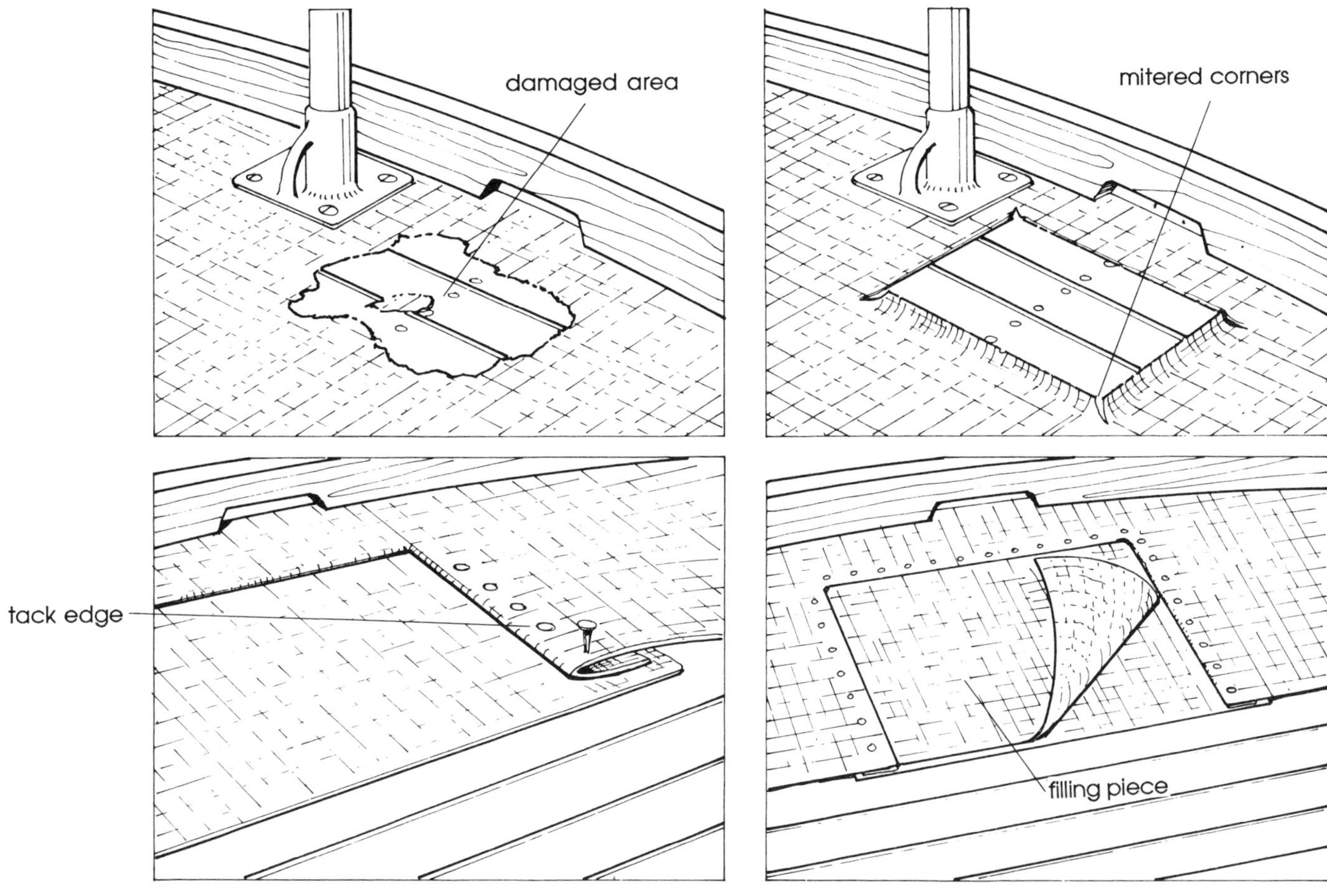

Small tears in a canvas deck can be easily repaired by cutting out a rectangular section around the damaged area, once deck is dry. Fold the cut edges of this under, apply white lead and insert a new piece slightly larger than the cut opening. Tack the edges and insert to the deck. Then apply another coat of lead and top the cut area with a patch sized to the opening. Finally, paint the whole to match the existing deck.

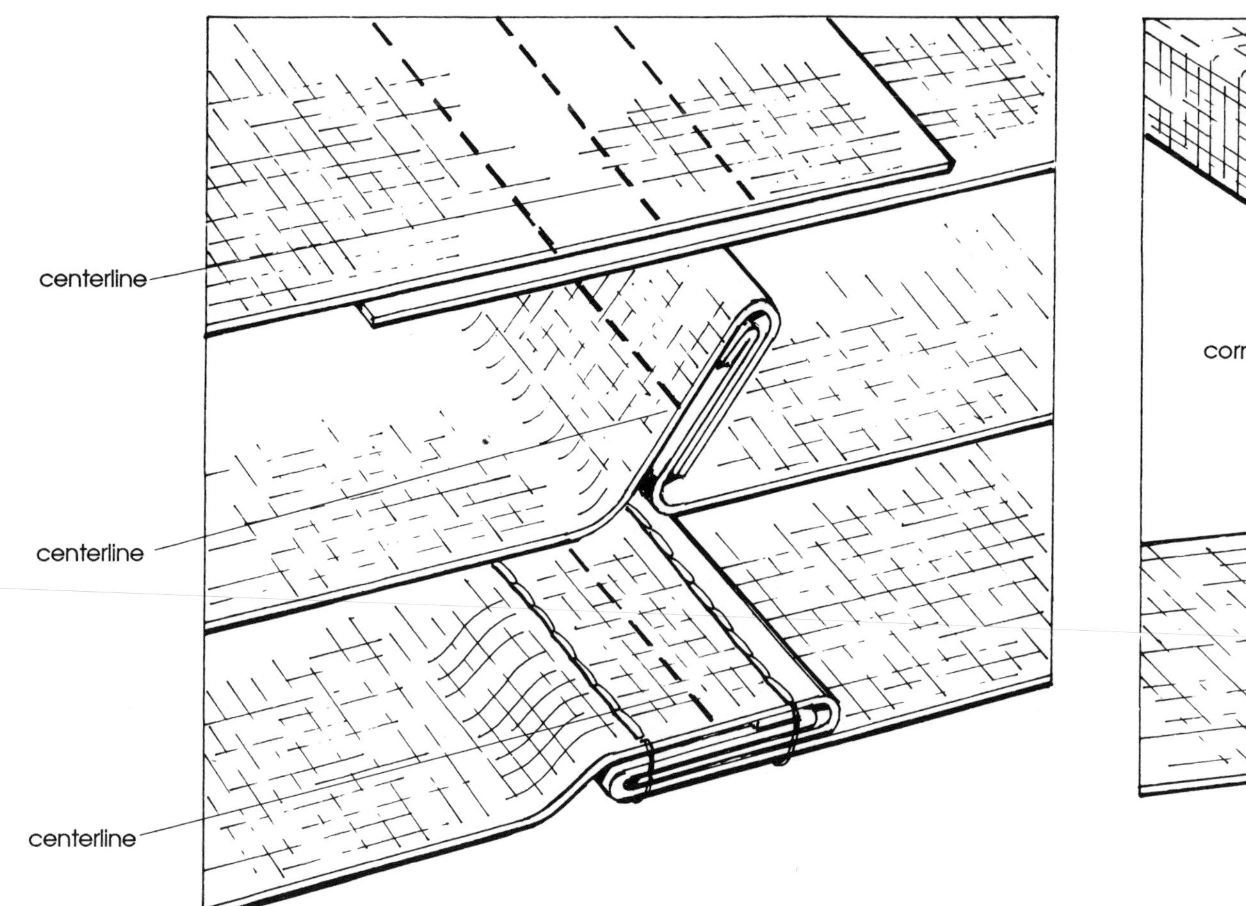
centerline
centerline
centerline
corner fold
tacks

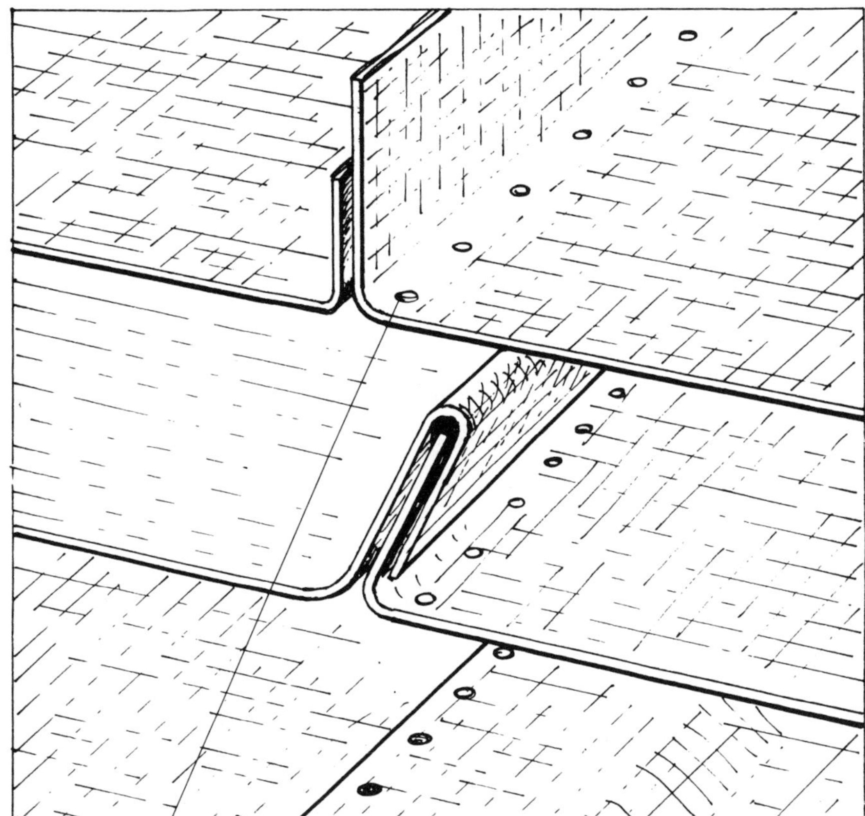

Recovering canvas decks can be done either by butting the canvas together, set in white lead, or by stitching the panels together with overlapping seams. This must be done very carefully, usually with the assistance of someone–a sailmaker–with access to a heavy-duty sewing machine. Another possibility is to tack the seam to the deck without stitching. In any case, try to keep the seams straight, as any unevenness will show up later in buckling and torn edges. All canvas decking should be covered at edges by a molding or toerail to prevent lifting.

covering with a very light topcoat. Mixing the nonskid into the paint is not recommended as it will cut curing times and ofttimes sinks to the bottom of the can, leaving you with uneven coating and the job of another layer of paint, not to mention sanding.

Another good possibility, especially over old tongue-and-groove or planked wood decks, is to cover them with Dynel. A synthetic fabric, Dynel will follow contours better than canvas–glassing over planked decking is not advisable as the movement of the planks will rupture GRP–and will add a certain amount of stability to the wood substratum itself. Procedures are much the same as with glass and resin, but follow the manufacturer's instructions.

METAL DECKS

You will rarely encounter a metal deck except on commercial vessels and the largest yachts. Even then, it may be covered with teak, but the structural part will still be metal. One of the great advantages of metal decking is that it is both monocoque–no leaks–and can have fittings attached by welding, making for more secure cleats, padeyes and such for much less cost than bought fittings. However, every weld is a prime source of corrosion and every metal surface must be kept well and thoroughly painted to prevent deterioration and ugly rust stains.

Another advantage is that sharp corners and rough edges can be easily eliminated with a grinder, assuring a much less dangerous and chafe-free deck area. The price one pays is in weight. In fact, many steel-hulled yachts are fitted with plywood decks attached over wood beams and carlins, all bolted to a steel shelf. This cuts weight considerably as well as retaining the single-piece structure. The only problems will occur at the hull-deck joint and this must be carefully and prodigiously sealed.

HARDWARE REPLACEMENT

Assuming you have marked where hardware originally was, replacement is not much different than installing new deck gear. However, if there is any sign of rot under old fittings, the decking should be cut out and replaced prior to recovering. Ofttimes, especially if the new covering is particularly opaque and you have forgotten to make templates of hardware locations (it does happen), it's best to start from scratch. If you plan on this from the beginning–since it's rare not to be able to improve upon gear positioning–plug all screw and bolt holes prior to recovering. Plugs for larger holes should run with the grain and be full-depth, glued in place with waterproof glue. Screw holes can be patched with wood putty or epoxy, making sure to force the material as deep in as possible from both above and *below* deck.

When repositioning fairleads, tracks, blocks or cleats, wait until the boat is launched, the mast stepped. Only in this way will you be able to calculate real angles based on your use and actual leads. This is especially true of sheet leads and anchor rollers. Also, you will be better able to avoid potential chafe points, unhappy obstacles and a lessening of mechanical advantage.

Cleats, in particular, are often incorrectly mounted. The aft or lower horn of the cleat should be angled out about 15 degrees to the right from the axis made with the base of the winch above or afore the cleat. All hardware reattachments should be bedded with silicone caulk. Personally, I prefer clear silicone as it contains no pigments to mar surfaces and none to deteriorate from ultraviolet rays.

STRUCTURAL REPAIRS

Wood and GRP decks are both subject to rot, even with sheathing, as any hole or break in their integrity can allow rainwater to seep into balsa cores, plywood inserts or sheathing. If this happens, and part of the deck or the beams below

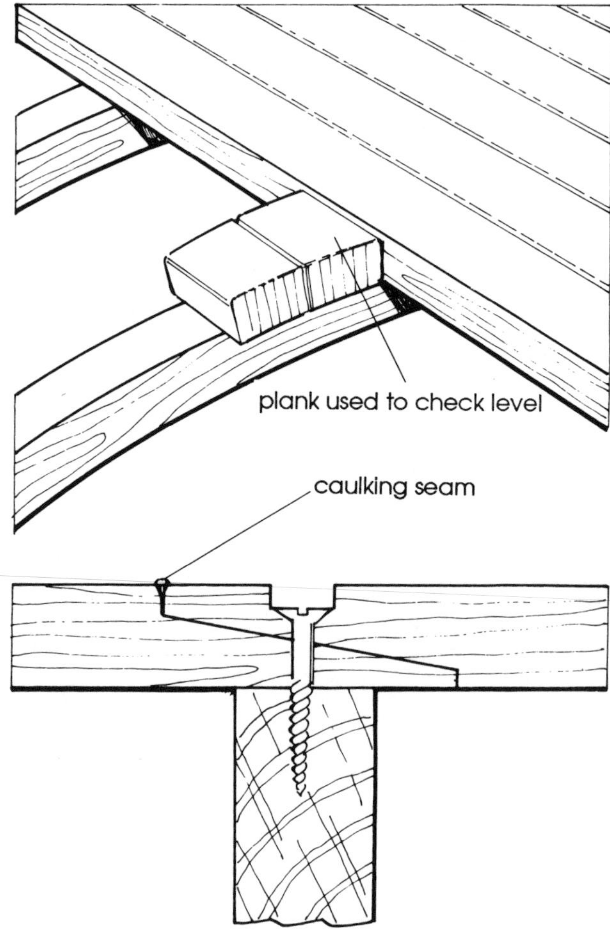

When replacing a laid deck or parts of it, use a spare section of plank to check levels. You will have to bevel the top two-thirds of each edge to allow for caulking and sealant. Plank ends should be centered over beams, scarfed as shown to make a strong and reliable join.

have to be replaced, a major job awaits you. Plywood decks are probably easiest to repair, as the offending rot can be cut out, a new piece scarfed and blocked in place, and the whole recovered. Always cut away the bad piece so that the cut rests midway on a beam and/or carlin. In this way, you can achieve a neat and strong butt joint without extra blocks or complex scarfs. The new piece should be glued and screwed in place with screw heads countersunk and bungs filled with wood putty, not plugs. It is comparatively easy to reglass the surface and grind in the edges flush with the surrounding deck.

Cored GRP decks can be replaced from below if you can assess the extent of leakage and rot. Often the entry point for water will be far removed from the rotted portion of core material. With the headliner removed, the core can be chiseled out, and a new section butted in or replaced by foam or plywood. The original GRP upper surface stays as is. The key to this repair is to saturate all surfaces prior to replacement of the core with epoxy to assure a watertight deck.

4
HARDWARE

Hardware or deck gear consists of attachment points for rigging, line handling equipment, safety devices, and other metalwork. There are three major concerns:

1. That the hardware is solidly and securely attached to the deckworks.
2. That the hardware is kept in working order.
3. That corrosion is kept at bay.

ATTACHMENT

If any deck gear is not secured with the utmost care, it is next to useless and sometimes downright dangerous. When the majority of decks were wood, it was often common practice to screw fittings to the deck. This was fine as long as the strains on the equipment were low. With the advent of stronger, stiffer hulls and masthead rigs, the forces at work increased dramatically. So much so, in fact, that any modern yacht should, as a matter of course, have all deck gear through-bolted with backing pads. The same goes for power boats. Anything which has weight, pull or lines in tension attached to it needs the same treatment.

However, GRP decks and cored decks have not nearly the tensile strength of wood, and reinforcement in the form of backing pads–either of metal or ply–is a requirement. When attaching a new piece of hardware to a deck, first determine the exact position and tape the fitting in place. Try using it for its intended purpose, at least as a simulation. Make sure the lead and clearances are adequate and free. Only then should you drill mounting holes in the deck surface. But be sure to check clearances and surfaces on the underside of the deck too. Quite often you will find obstructions–bulkheads, other furniture, carlins or beams that will disallow any backup plate fitting. The

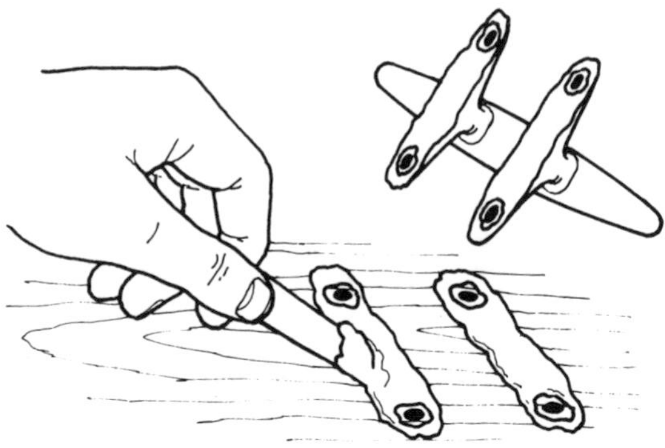

Perhaps the best way to bed a fitting effectively is to coat both fitting bottom and deck where they mate, then squeeze a bead of sealant around the bolt heads before tightening.

holes should be sized to the bolts and the bolts to the fitting. This sounds obvious, but the number of times any old bolt, usually undersized, lying around is used is astounding. Also, the fastener should be galvanically compatible with the fitting.

To be truly precise, any holes through the deck should be threaded with a tap to accept the proper-sized bolts. In addition, be sure to use roundhead bolts with flush hole fittings, flathead bolts with those which have recesses for the bolt heads. Bolts should be bedded in sealant and sized so they project below no more than is necessary. They can be secured with large washers and nuts. Locking capnuts are preferable where the bolt will show below as they will both look better and prevent injury.

In a cored deck, compression problems can arise, as the core material, though dense for its purpose, is not designed to take compression forces. Thus, it must either be cut away and replaced with solid wood or GRP, or tubes of resin-bonded copper or stainless steel should be inserted in the bolt holes. See the Decks chapter for more on this.

Certain fittings need more reinforcement than others. Winches, genoa tracks, mainsheet travelers, turning blocks, stemhead fittings and stanchion bases are all subject to enormous strains. Not only do they require numerous and large fastenings, but the actual surface to which they are attached must be both strong and thick enough to take the strains. Turning blocks and stanchions, in particular, have been known to rip out, causing difficult repairs and serious injury. Here, the backing plates should be slightly larger than the entire structure above and be of marine ply of a minimum of 1/2 inch or an aluminum plate of 1/4 inch in thickness. Make sandwiches between the fitting and the deck, drilling through all so that the holes will line up when all is installed. Then fasten the plate below deck, aligning with the deck holes. These plates need not be glassed in though this additional step will increase watertight integrity. In a wood deck they can be glued with Resorcinol or epoxy. In steel, of course, you will simply weld the

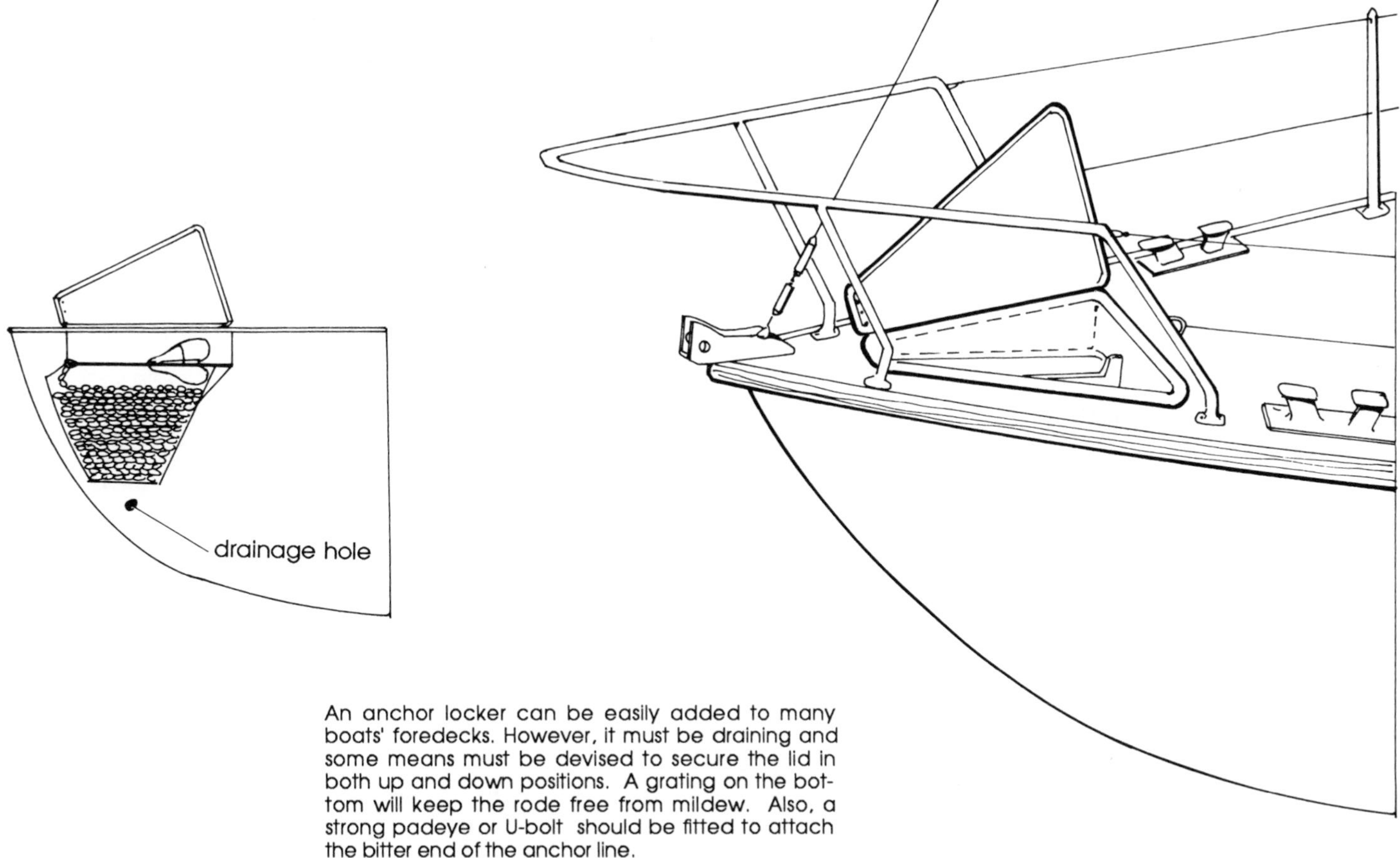

An anchor locker can be easily added to many boats' foredecks. However, it must be draining and some means must be devised to secure the lid in both up and down positions. A grating on the bottom will keep the rode free from mildew. Also, a strong padeye or U-bolt should be fitted to attach the bitter end of the anchor line.

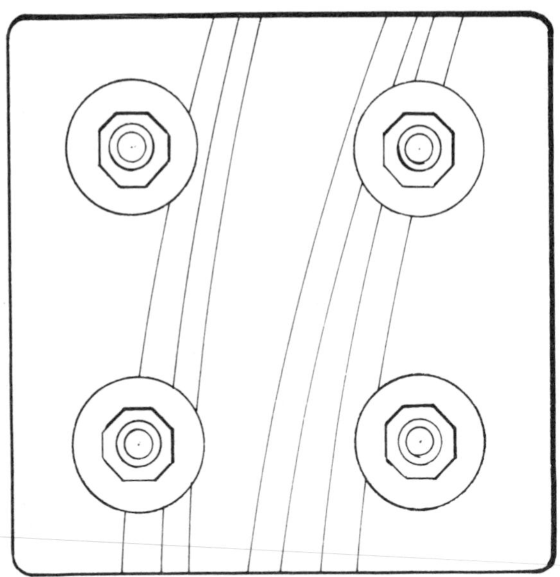

When bedding fitments, tighten the bolts in sequence, each a few turns at a time. In this way the seal will be under even pressure and the watertightness of the join somewhat more positive.

fitting in place or bolt it to a plate (with dissimilar metals) and then weld the plate to the deck. Do not be tempted to do spot welds. A continuous weld is necessary for strength and to prevent the ingress of water underneath, causing corrosion.

KEEPING IT SHINING

All deck gear is subject to constant weathering–sun, rain, wind, dust, grit, snow–all of which takes its toll in corrosion, wear, discoloration and working smoothness. The most obvious sign of weathering is fading and discoloration. With many contemporary blocks constructed from stainless steel and tufnol or nylon or anodized aluminum, and with chocks, bases and winches constructed from aluminum, stainless, bronze or brass, the natural weathering will cause changes in the way they all look. Weather will not, repeat not, affect functioning at first.

No stainless steel is truly stainless. All contain a certain amount of other elements besides steel which give it its hardness, ductibility, strength, and finish. But often, especially in the highly polished examples–rails and pulpits–you will notice, after a few weeks afloat, a brownish splotching. This is entirely natural and can be removed with most any metal polish or ordinary scouring powder. To prevent its return, coating the metal with a good wax or automotive polish will at least keep the corrosion at bay. Note that this is not harmful, just unattractive. Certain spray coatings are available, but in my opinion, none holds up and all eventually peel and flake.

Aluminum, unless it is anodized, will quickly acquire an oxidized coat. This actually protects the alloy. Since almost all deck fitments are used in some way, this coating will wear off and another form. Eventually this will cause wear in the alloy itself. One way to prevent this is to coat all aluminum with a sealant or sealer wax made expressly for the purpose. Anodized fittings will remain unaffected longer, but sooner or later the anodizing will scratch, nick or wear off. Either apply the sealant or have them reanodized–an expensive process.

Brass is often used for chocks and cleats. Frankly, no other hull or deck use is permissible for brass, as it will quickly deteriorate in salt air or when immersed in salt water. Much brass deck hardware is chrome-plated in any case, and this can wear off in time. The only answer, unless you want to polish brass endlessly, is to have the hardware replated. Bronze or gunmetal fittings are somewhat easier to deal with as in their natural state they will acquire a green patina which acts as a surface protector and is quite hard to wear off. Ropes and hands will serve to polish it and keep it smooth. Polished bronze requires even more effort than brass, being harder, and is rarely worth the effort.

Wood cleats, not often seen these days, though still the best possible foil for rope, can be made from teak, locust, lignum vitae or oak. Lignum vitae will wear better than the others and contains so much natural oil that an occasional wipedown with tung oil is all that is needed to keep it glowing. Oak will discolor and needs seasonal scrubbing and oiling. Locust, hard to come by, is quite dense and can use oiling. Teak, the most common cleat wood, is perhaps the least satisfactory in that, though dense, it is brittle and not very strong, and can chip and crumble with time.

KEEPING IT WORKING

All moving parts wear. This is a basic rule of mechanics. Friction and grit will break down most everything sooner or later. The first step in slowing this process down is to wash all moving deck gear with fresh water as often as possible, no matter whether the manufacturer claims it's "maintenance-free" or not. Certain materials are less likely to wear than others, and the movingest hardware are blocks and winches. These are the pieces that need the most careful choosing, especially as they are amongst the most expensive. Good blocks will last a lifetime with care, but they must be carefully made from

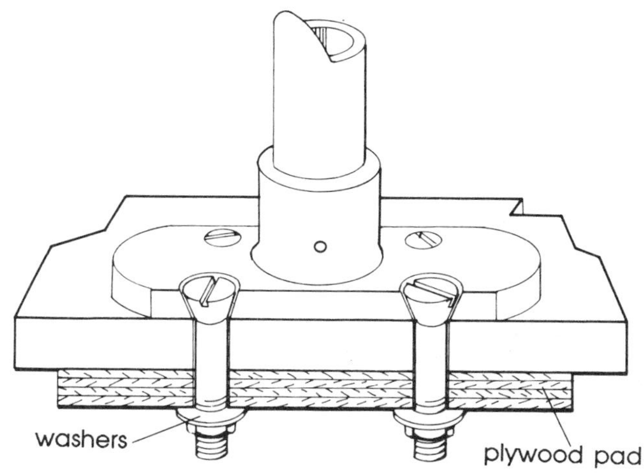

All deck fittings should be through-bolted with a backing pad of ply or metal. Stanchion bases are particularly susceptible to shocks, as well as to the working of the ship. Use neoprene washers as well as bedding compound to assure watertightness. Make sure backing washers are large in area.

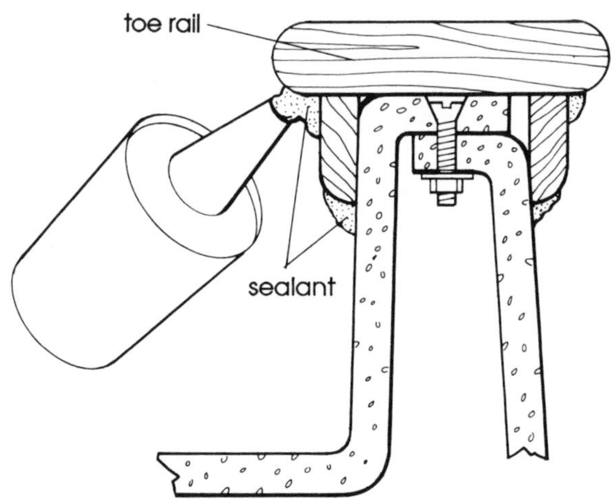

Toerails and overlapping joints are prime candidates for leakage. Running a bead of sealant the entire length of the rail or lap will make a good temporary repair. However, the cap or rail should be removed, when time allows, and the entire fitting rebedded.

the best materials.

Wood-shelled blocks are certainly beautiful and, if you have a character yacht, they can add to the aesthetics of the ship. However, they are heavy and demand massive maintenance in terms of scraping and varnishing. However, the sheaves will most likely be stainless or bronze. Be forewarned: bronze, as mentioned above, is a whole range of metals and it will not wear well over time unless kept very well lubricated. Stainless is far more durable but can become brittle and sharp edges can ruin good lines.

Glass-filled nylon and tufnol (which is a laminate of linen and resin) are among the most durable sheave materials and are least likely to damage rope. Furthermore, they need no lubrication and can be replaced, should this become necessary, for a very small cost.

Ball-bearing blocks will run more smoothly than dumb sheaves on a spindle. They also cost a great deal more. The bearings must be hosed down regularly and lubricated each season with clean grease after a *thorough* cleaning with spirits or kerosene (paraffin). Any grit in the bearings will cause fast wear, unevenness and eventual nonfunctioning or freezing.

Winches are much more complex pieces of equipment than blocks and demand regular care, no matter how often one uses them. Since they all contain gears, and anything more than a simple single-speed winch will invariably contain a series of ball or needle bearings, the same precautions taken with ball-bearing blocks are appropriate, only more so. Considering the cost of winches, this is nothing to be taken lightly. Yet many yachtsmen rarely, if ever, service their winches, despite the enormous strains and wear and tear, not to mention exposure to the elements, they receive.

At the beginning of the season, all winches should be disassembled, cleaned with a good grease-dissolving solvent and regreased with an appropriate lubricant. This can be a natural substance such as lanolin or one of the Teflon compounds or lithium grease. Personally, I prefer Teflon, as it does not break down in salt air, is comparatively "greaseless" and will not stain sails or ropes. Any sealed bearings, of course, remain that way. Since all metals corrode in contact with salt water, make sure all salt is thoroughly washed off before greasing. Otherwise, salt granules will be driven into the gears, scarring them and accelerating wear. Also note that any grit will do likewise, only faster.

At the end of the season, a hosing down with fresh water and a protective coating of petroleum jelly on the exterior parts including the drum can save much springtime heartache.

TRAVELERS

Most modern auxiliaries are equipped with travelers to control the mainsail. Other than winches, travelers probably get the hardest workout of any dynamic piece of deck equipment. Constant banging, pulling and heaving can wear them down in little time if neglected. Like winches, they must be carefully cleaned with fresh water and kept lubricated. The same recommendations apply. End stops should be replaced if they show the slightest signs of distortion or cracking. If the mainsheet assembly happens to fly off the traveler when gybing in heavy air, all hell can break loose, not to mention the possibility of serious injury and loss of the rig. Any control lines should be checked seasonally for chafe, especially around sheaves. All fasteners should be tightened and bearings should be inspected for wear or distortion.

STEERING MECHANISMS

All steering arangements consist of a rudder manipulated either directly by tiller or indirectly by a wheel linked to the rudder mechanically or hydraulically. Tiller-to-rudder steering, depending on where and how the rudder is connected to the hull, is straightforward and demands maintenance to bearings (lubrication), stuffing boxes (tightening and repacking) and at-

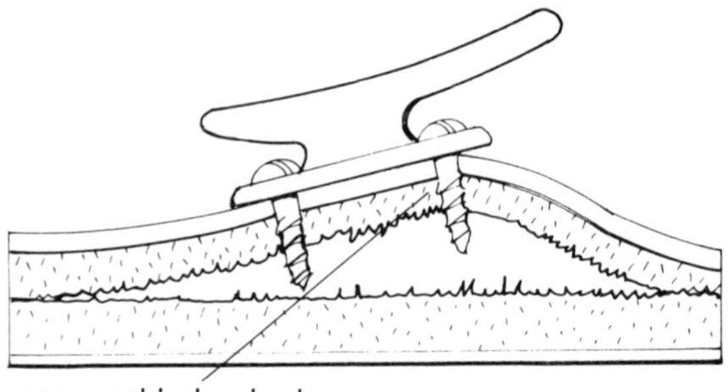

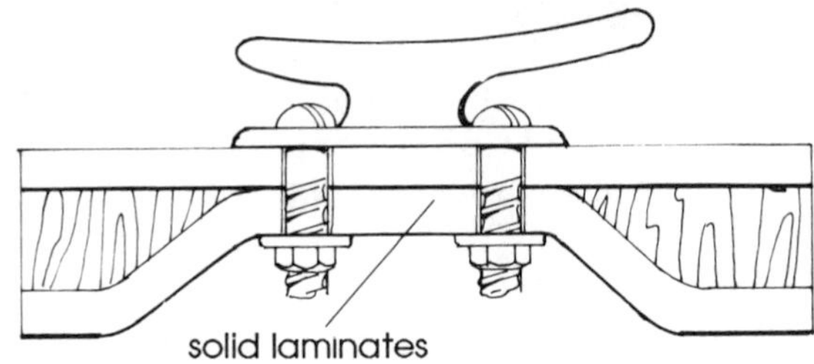

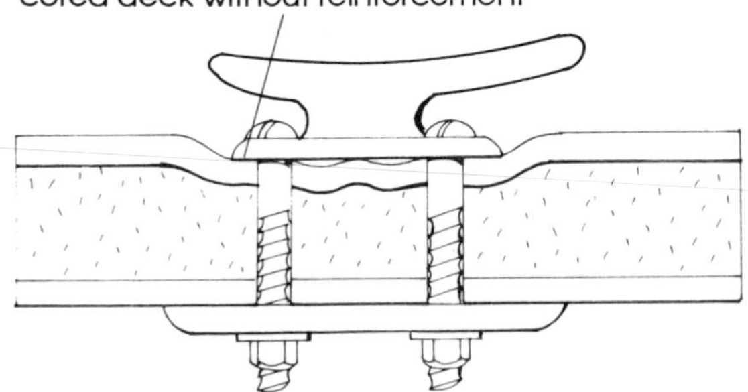

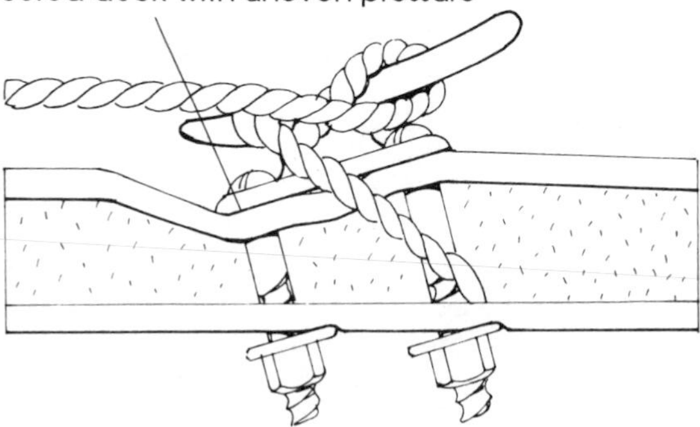

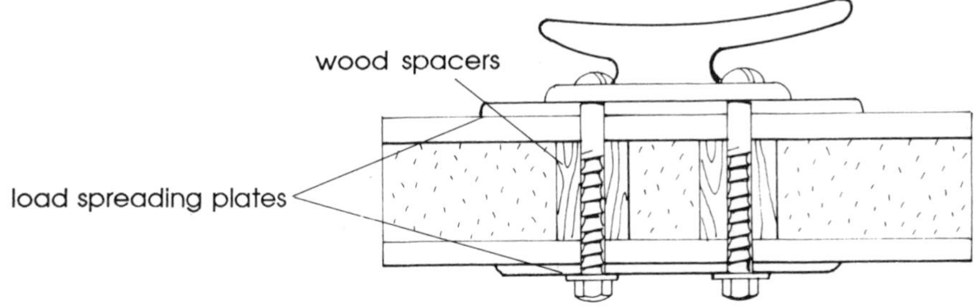

Through-bolting fittings to a sandwich deck can be tricky. Screwed-in, they are sure to pull out. Cutting away the core material and adding a solid GRP core is one solution. Another is to use spacers as well as top and bottom load-spreading plates. Whenever you work through core, make sure the holes or cuts are carefully sealed with epoxy to insure against moisture penetration into the adjoining core material.

tachment hardware (tightening bolts and screws).

Wheel arrangements vary and, broadly speaking, fall into four catagories: cable/quadrant, gear, push-pull (rod or encased cable) and hydraulic. Most important to the functioning of all these is a regular check on moving parts (lubrication), making sure connecting hardware is secure and without sloppiness and play, constant surveillance for wear and, in hydraulic systems, making sure there are no leaks and that hoses are sound and securely clamped. The illustrations and captions cover each system in greater detail.

MISCELLANEOUS HARDWARE

Little things mean a lot, especially when ship's systems depend on them. Witness filler caps for fuel and water. It goes without saying that each should be separately labelled and on opposite sides of the yacht. Caps should be permanently fastened to their receptacles with a light chain, wire or nylon line. The threads should be lightly greased with a nontoxic–in the case of water–lubricant such as Teflon, and the gaskets should be pliable and tight-fitting. If not, replace them. Any leakage will cause bad-tasting water or contaminated fuel and potential engine damage.

Hinges are subject to violent blows, tearing stresses and sudden shock. Make sure all are well screwed or bolted in place, that they align and that no cracks have appeared. Should any hinge pins bend or distort, replace them immediately. If there is no need for removable pin hinges, peen the ends of the pins to secure them permanently.

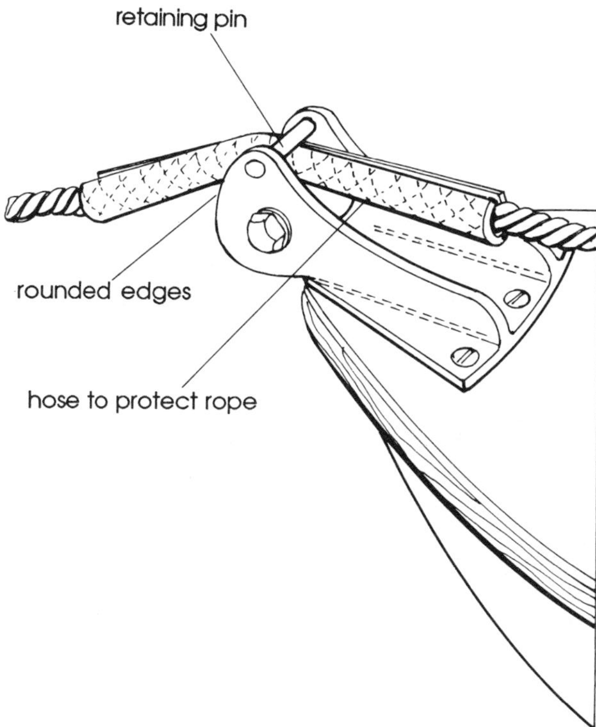

Whenever rope passes through a stemhead roller, make sure chafing gear is affixed in place. Also, add a retaining pin–one of the quick release types is perfect–to the cheeks of the roller fitting. In anything but a dead calm, the chances of the rope jumping the roller cheeks and chafing on the rail are more than even.

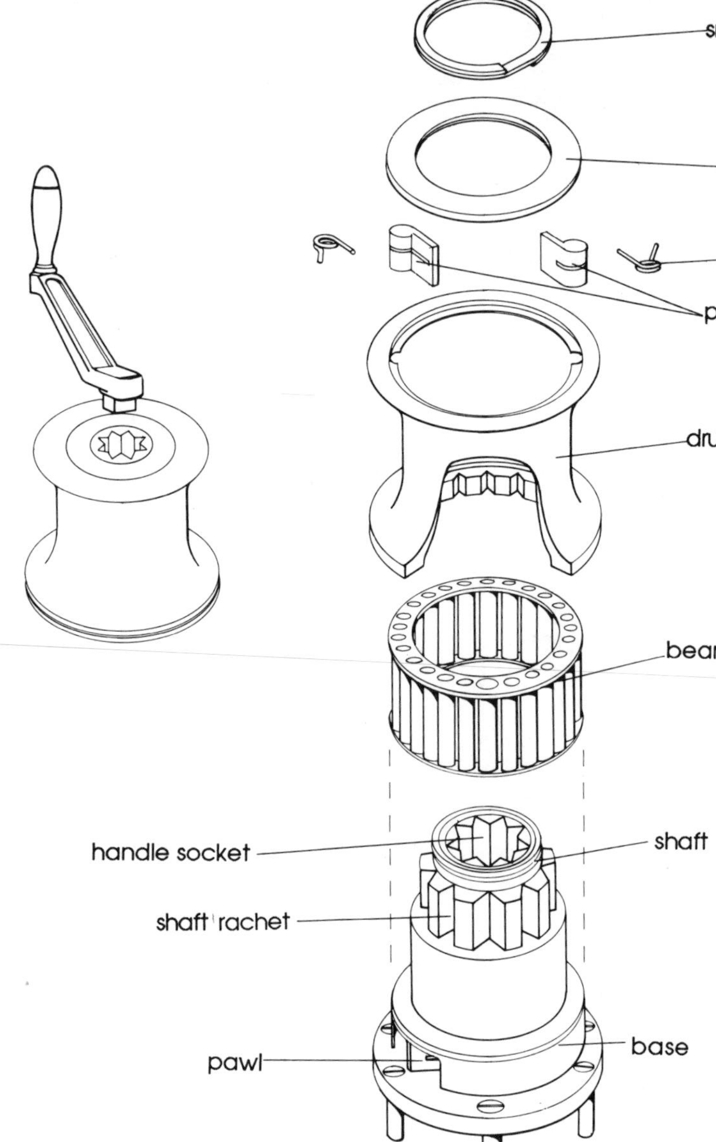

Deck-mounted winches take enormous strains and must be through-bolted with properly sized bolts. Since all winches–all mechanical equipment, in fact–are corroded by salt air and collect dirt internally, each winch aboard should be periodically disassembled and cleaned, then recoated where appropriate (see manufacturer's manual) with heavy-duty waterproof grease. Teflon or lithium are both excellent. Be careful to note the pawl alignment and orientation when taking the drum off, as the winch will only work if these are reinstalled in proper sequence. Spare springs and pawls for each winch should be carried aboard at all times.

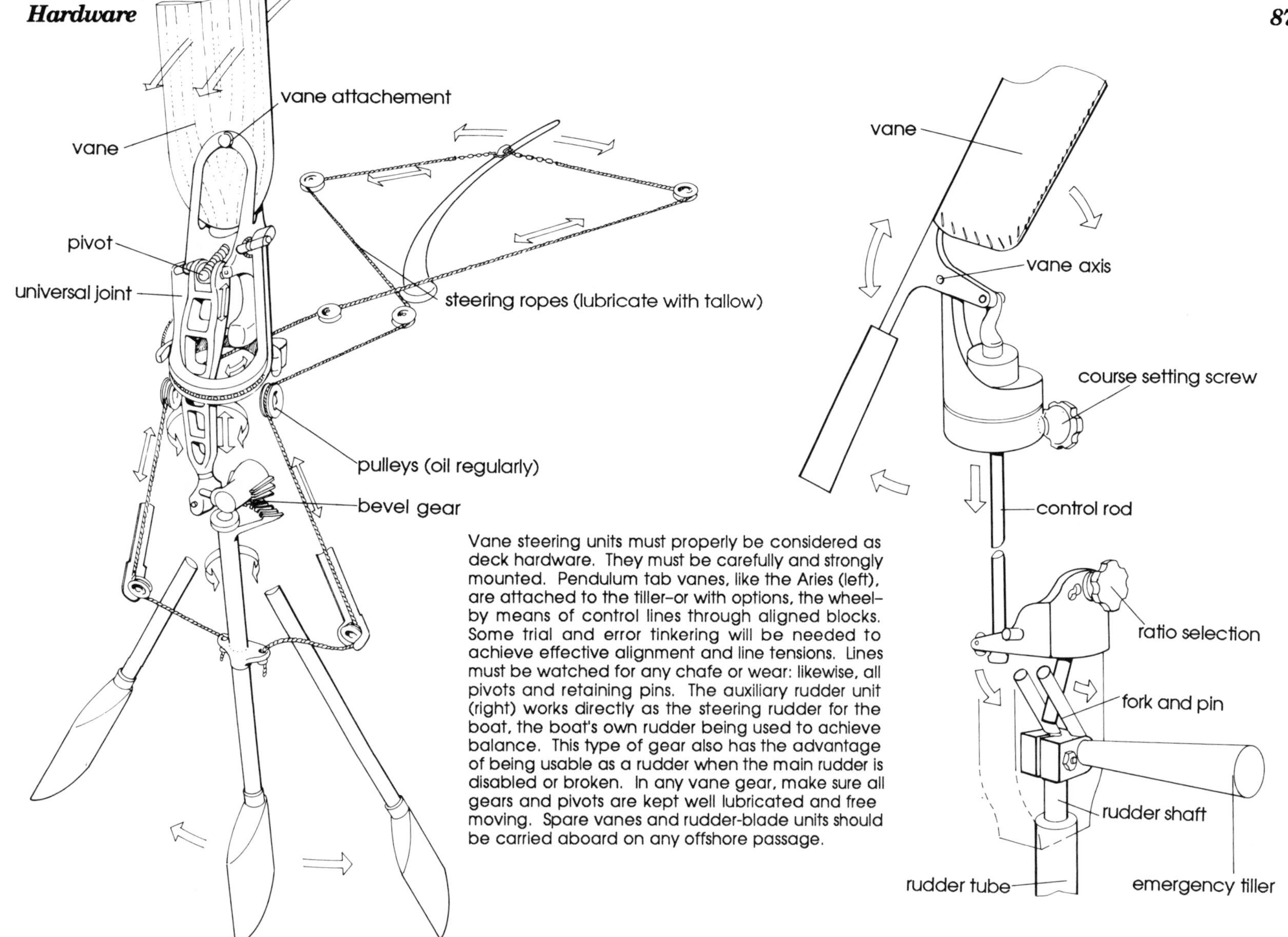

Vane steering units must properly be considered as deck hardware. They must be carefully and strongly mounted. Pendulum tab vanes, like the Aries (left), are attached to the tiller–or with options, the wheel–by means of control lines through aligned blocks. Some trial and error tinkering will be needed to achieve effective alignment and line tensions. Lines must be watched for any chafe or wear: likewise, all pivots and retaining pins. The auxiliary rudder unit (right) works directly as the steering rudder for the boat, the boat's own rudder being used to achieve balance. This type of gear also has the advantage of being usable as a rudder when the main rudder is disabled or broken. In any vane gear, make sure all gears and pivots are kept well lubricated and free moving. Spare vanes and rudder-blade units should be carried aboard on any offshore passage.

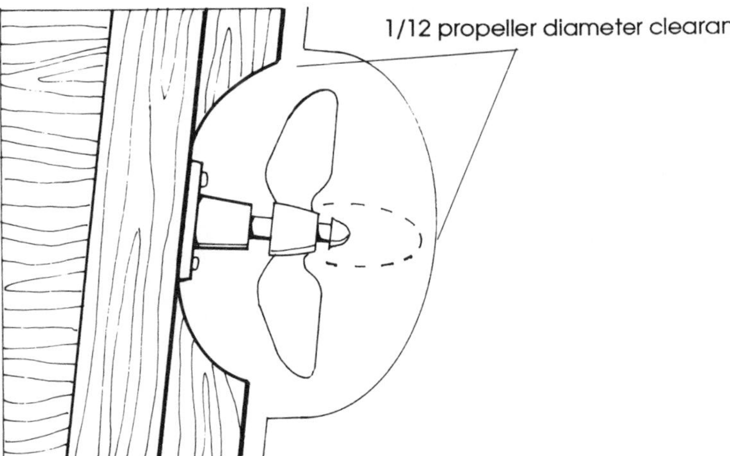

Rudder clearance from the propeller must be adequate to allow for efficiency. Ideally, most cutout will be in the deadwood. Cutting the rudder away will decrease response dramatically.

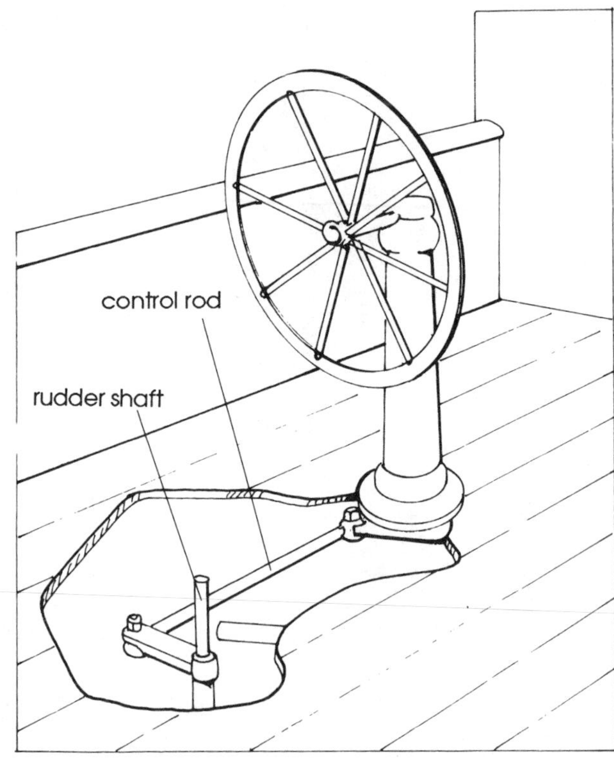

Rod steering is subject to the wear of all mechanical systems. Make sure connecting bolts are tightened and all moving parts are kept greased.

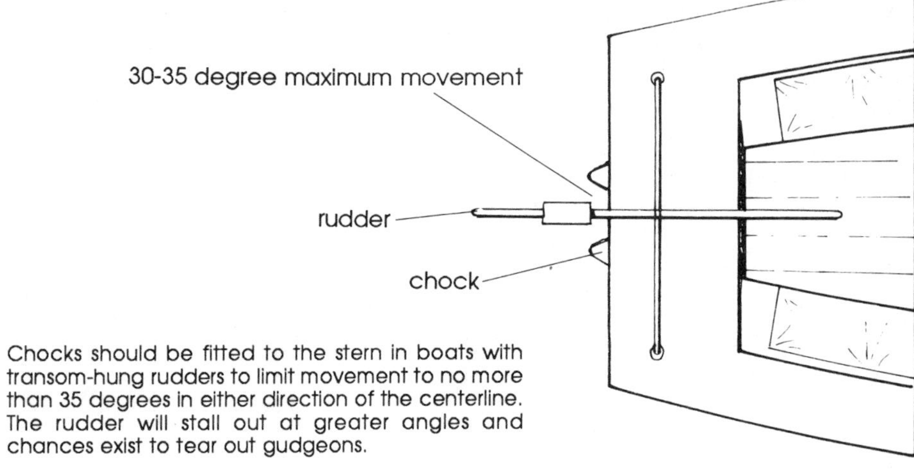

Chocks should be fitted to the stern in boats with transom-hung rudders to limit movement to no more than 35 degrees in either direction of the centerline. The rudder will stall out at greater angles and chances exist to tear out gudgeons.

Transom-hung rudders are held in place by pintles and gudgeons. Make sure all bolts are tightened and, for added security and to avoid having the rudder float off, drill through the protruding shafts of the pintles and pin with cotters.

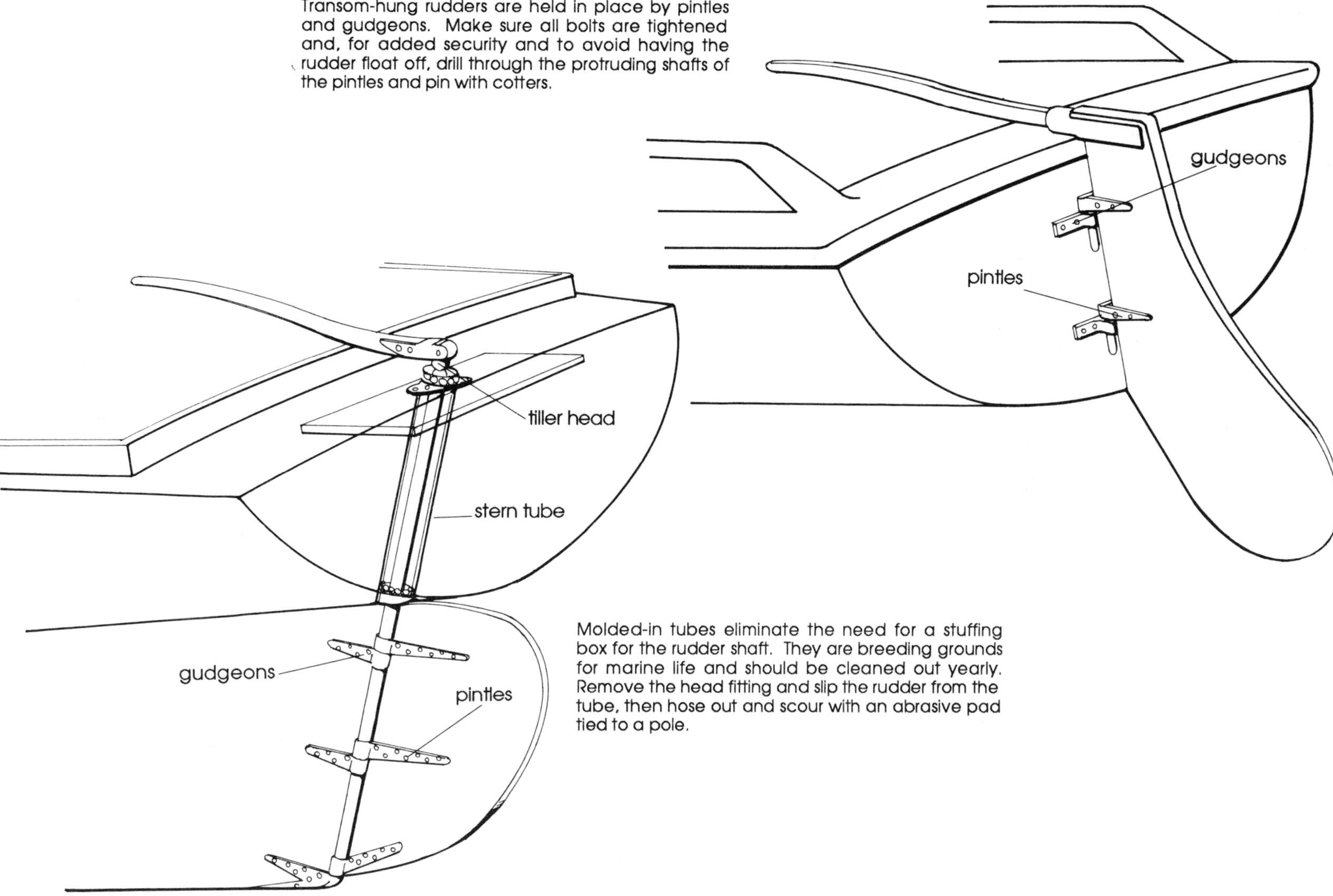

Molded-in tubes eliminate the need for a stuffing box for the rudder shaft. They are breeding grounds for marine life and should be cleaned out yearly. Remove the head fitting and slip the rudder from the tube, then hose out and scour with an abrasive pad tied to a pole.

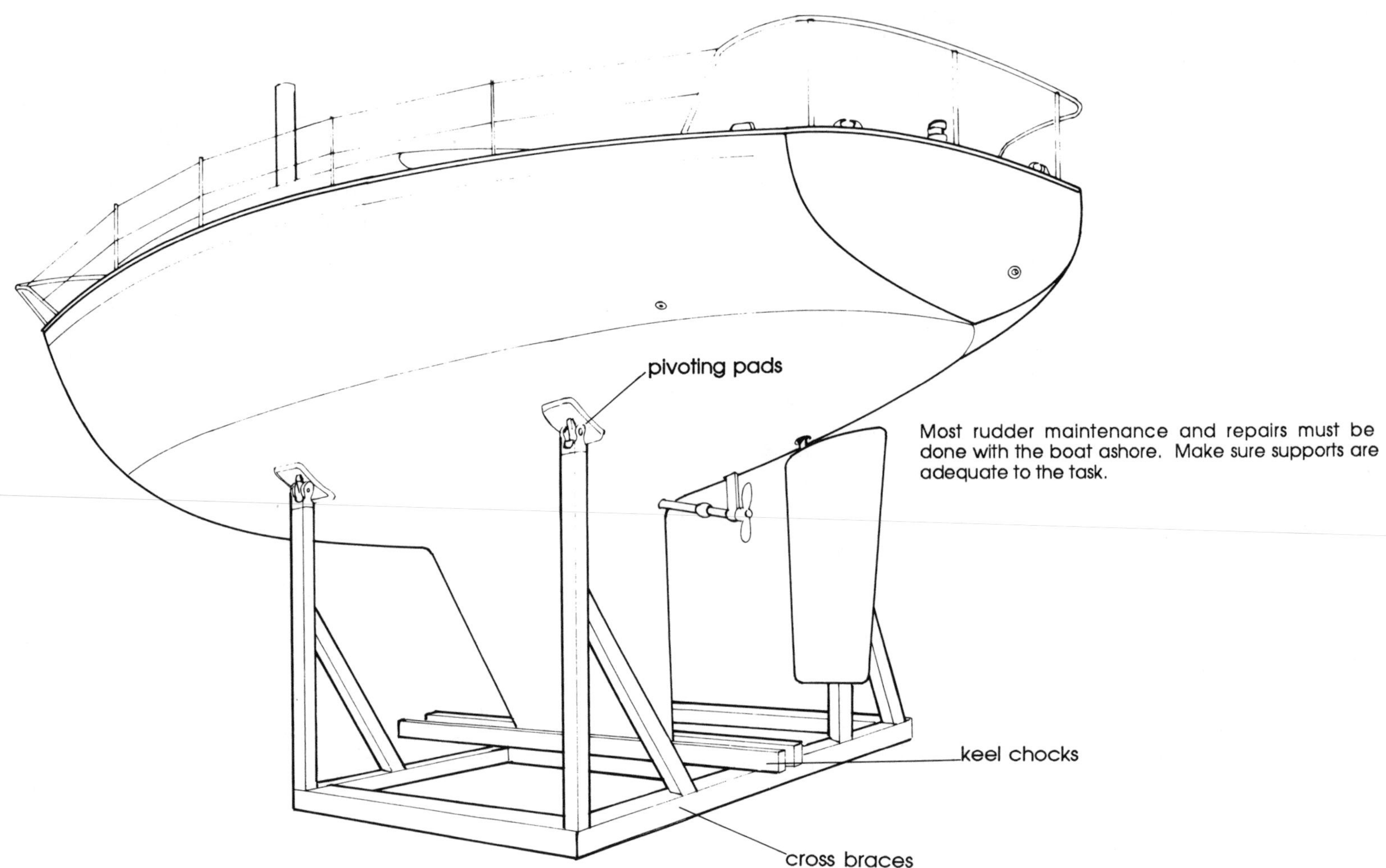

Most rudder maintenance and repairs must be done with the boat ashore. Make sure supports are adequate to the task.

Hydraulic steering systems are simple in concept, complex in design and manufacture. Check the level of hydraulic fluid in the reservoir regularly and inspect the hose runs for leaks and the connections for tightness. Major repairs are best left to a professional.

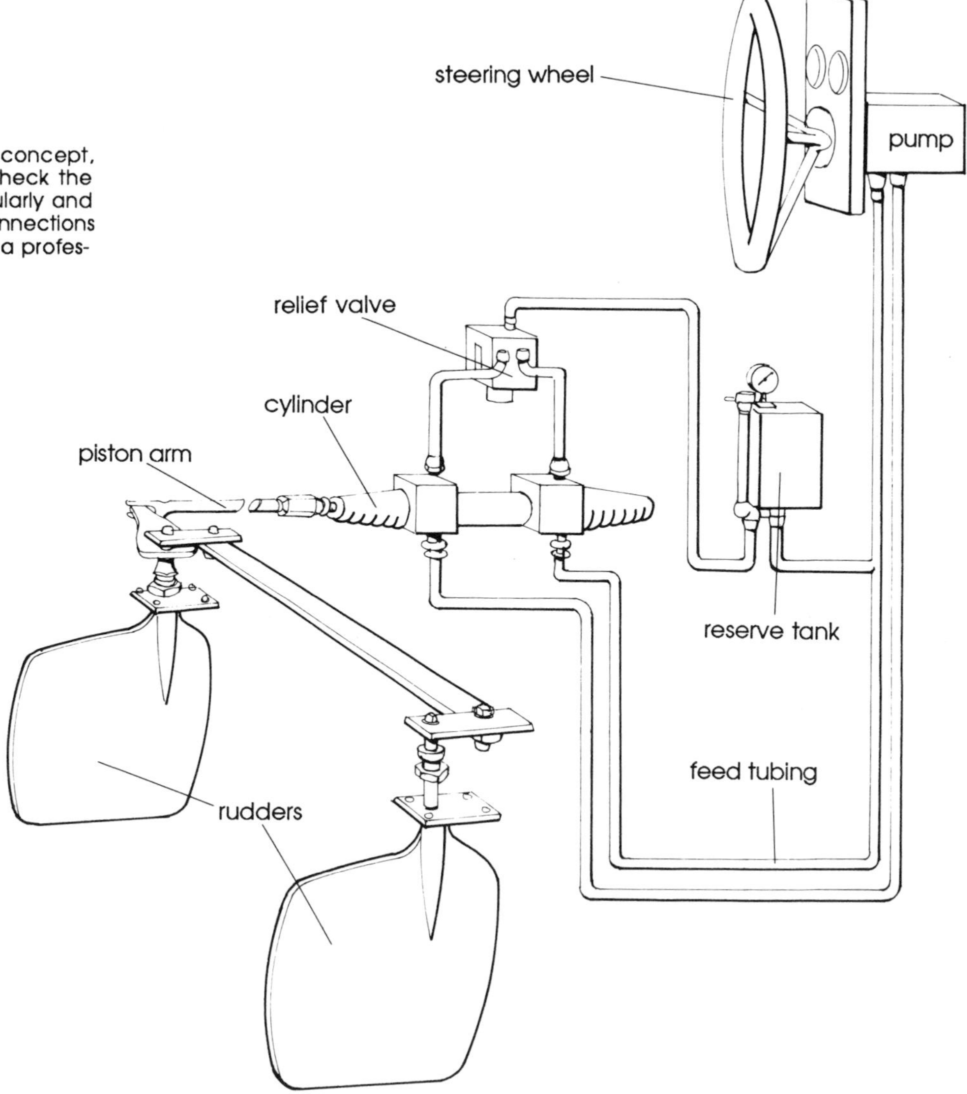

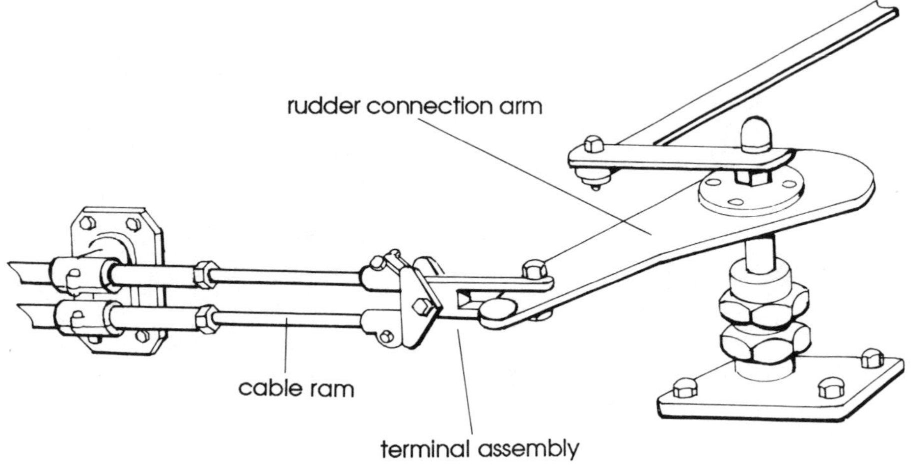

Rack-and-pinion cable connections at the rudder-post are the most vulnerable part of the system. Grease them regularly and tighten all connections.

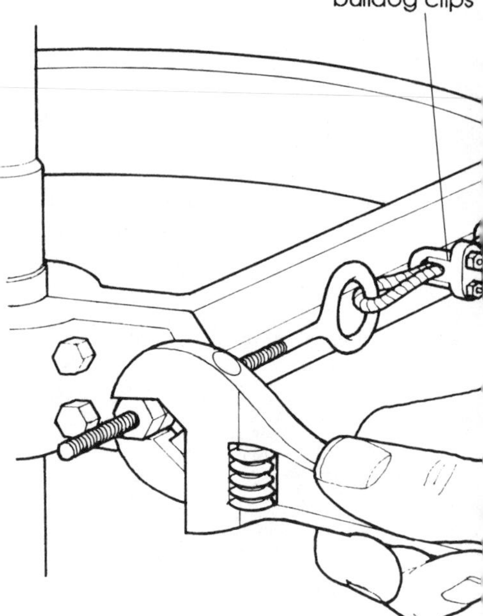

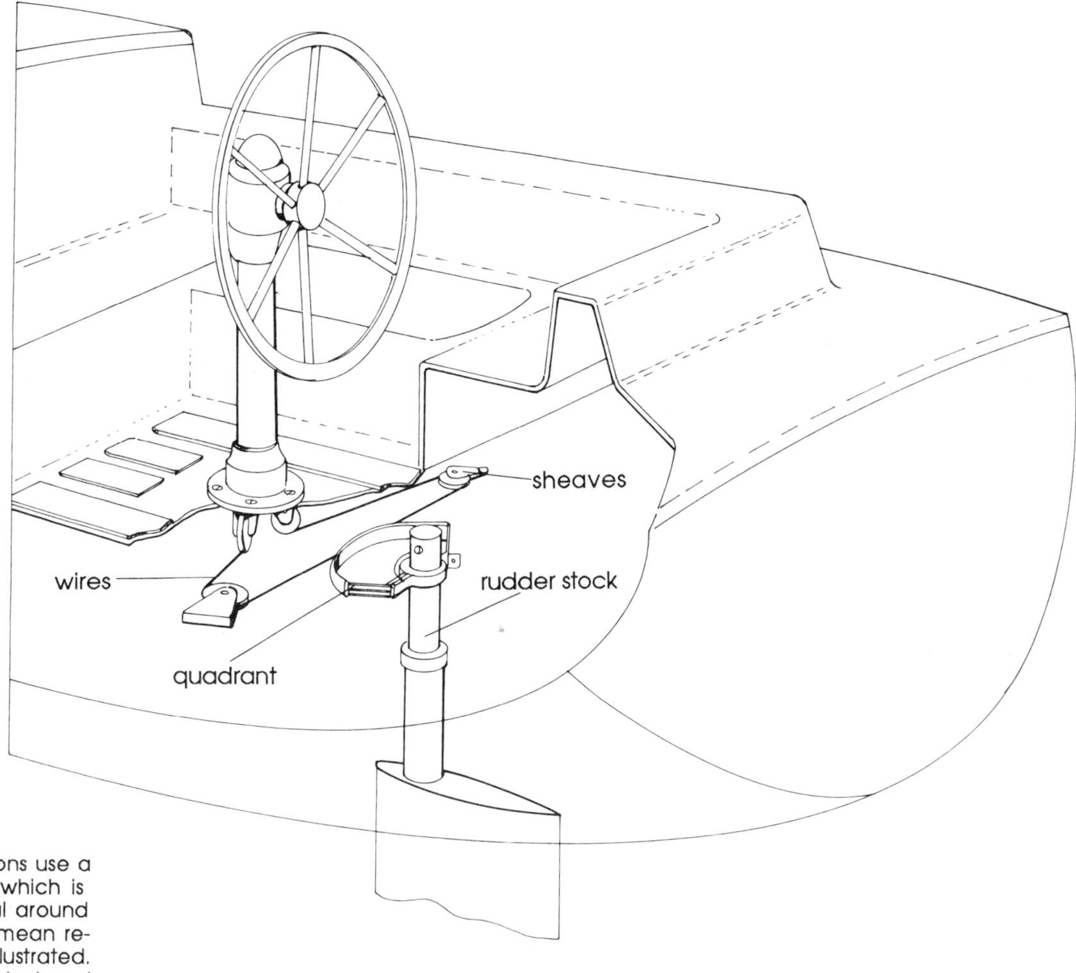

The majority of pedestal steering installations use a quadrant attached to the rudder stock which is turned by wires running from the pedestal around sheaves. Any broken strands in the wires mean replacement. Keep the wires tensioned as illustrated. Also, make sure sheaves are kept lubricated and that they are firmly bolted to bearing members of the hull. Finally, check to see that the quadrant is firmly keyed to the rudderstock; tighten key bolts if necessary.

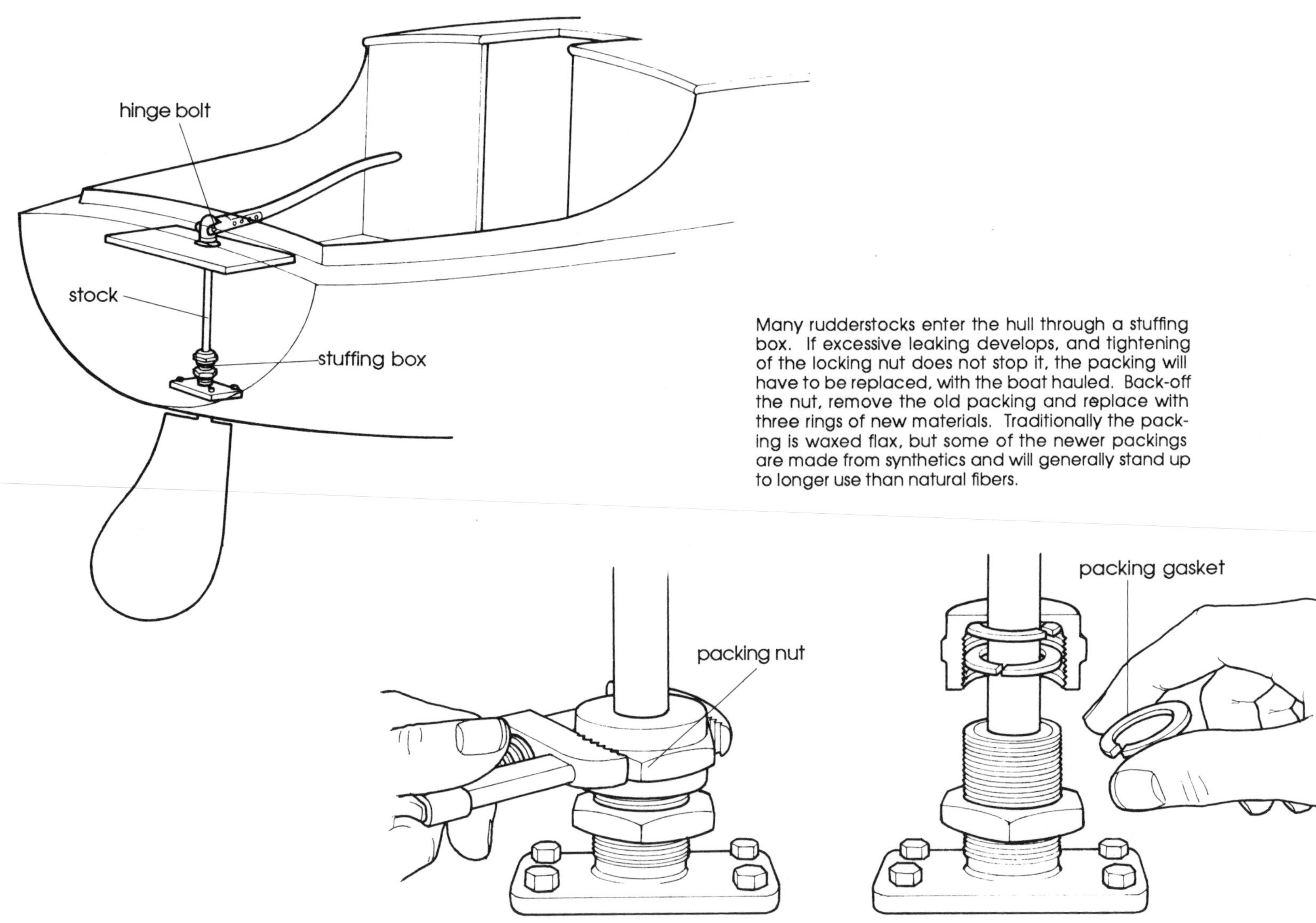

Many rudderstocks enter the hull through a stuffing box. If excessive leaking develops, and tightening of the locking nut does not stop it, the packing will have to be replaced, with the boat hauled. Back-off the nut, remove the old packing and replace with three rings of new materials. Traditionally the packing is waxed flax, but some of the newer packings are made from synthetics and will generally stand up to longer use than natural fibers.

Worm gear steering is the most long-lived and reliable type existent. However, since it is subject to constant friction, all moving parts should be coated with grease monthly, including pivot points and all bearings. Also check the mount bearing for any looseness or play and tighten the lag screws yearly. Racking strains are high and every turn of the wheel will apply prying forces to all mounting hardware.

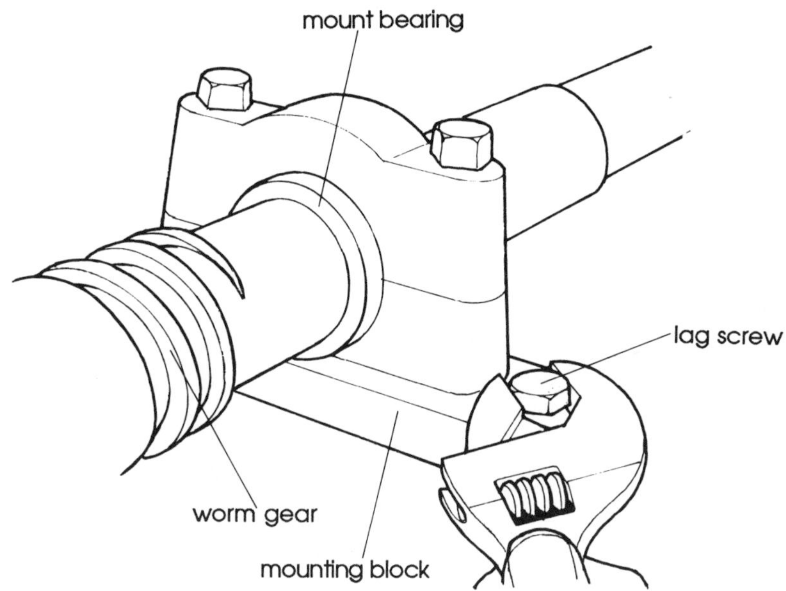

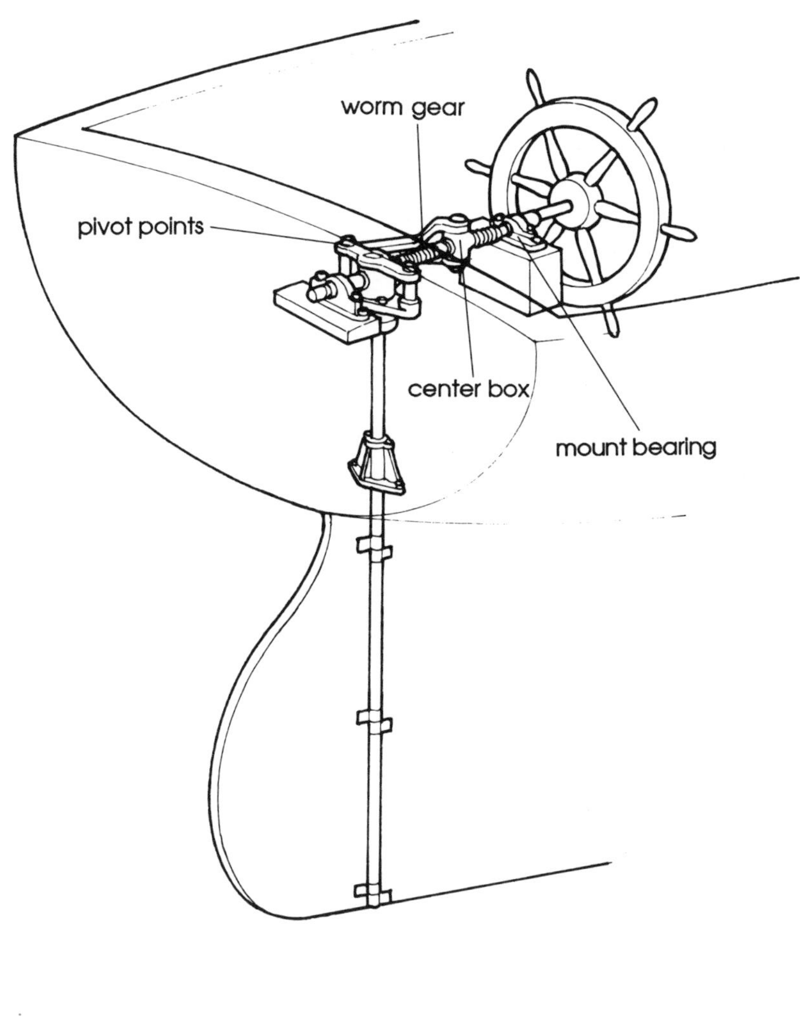

5
PROPULSION SYSTEMS

Under this category I class all engines and their attendant gear and accessories: ignition systems, fuel supply and tanks, filters, transmissions, controls, shafts and propellers, generators, struts and mountings. Though there are few stalwarts who use nothing but sail and/or oar power, most of us have an engine aboard, be it an outboard or an inboard gasoline or diesel powerplant.

All internal combustion power units are subject to countless maladies. First, they are made of metal, and all metals corrode. Second, invariably there are electrical components that get affected by the damp. Third, they use petroleum products as fuel, which can be adulterated and contaminated with impurities which can wreak havoc on the engine.

DIESEL ENGINES: GENERAL

The majority of yachts will probably be fitted with diesel engines. They are heavier than gasoline (petrol) engines of the same horsepower and more reliable. Unlike gasoline engines, they do not rely on an electrical ignition system which is subject to malfunction from the mere existence of a marine environment. However, the quality of the fuel, which is injected under high pressure into the combustion chamber, is far more critical. Since the injectors that perform this task are comparatively fine tolerance devices, any impurities in the fuel supply will likely cause clogging and possible damage to the injectors.

Since pressures build to a very high level in diesels, proper lubrication is vital to the smooth running of the engine. Engine oil levels should be checked before starting the engine for the first time on a given day. Oil should be changed and filters renewed every 200 to 250 hours of running time. If you don't use the engine frequently, change oil prior to launching, at mid-season and as winterizing. A good general rule is that the faster an engine's running speed in revolutions per minute, the more frequently the oil should be changed. Consult your owner's manual.

Air is a necessity for any combustion, in especially large quantities for a diesel. Make sure vents are large enough, air filters likewise. The warmer the ambient temperature, the more air will be needed. Many high-speed engines will require more air faster, and some provision may have to be made to accommodate this requirement–either extra vents or a blower with flame arrestor.

The majority of small diesels are raw-water cooled. For this cooling to be successful, all water piping must be kept clear and free of impediments and clogging. Likewise, the pump must be working properly. Quite often the impeller–with neoprene blades–will be damaged or the blades stripped off by even a small bit of grit entering the system. A spare impeller or two should always be carried. Since the water pump is usually located at the front of the engine, this is one of the easiest repairs to make. Raw water will have corrosive effects if left standing, and all raw-water cooling systems should be flushed with fresh water at least twice yearly, more often if possible.

After a certain point scaling will occur internally. This can be partially flushed out by running fresh water through the engine in reverse, under pressure, then draining the entire system. Commercial cleaning solutions can be used (most are a mixture of oxalic acid and water) then flushed out with a solution of bicarbonate of soda. Best is to connect both inlet and outlet hoses to a common tank, flush the cleaning solution through, let it stand a couple of hours, neutralize it with the soda solution, then flush out the whole works with fresh water. It is a messy and time-consuming job, and is best left to the yard unless you are feeling particularly energetic. Wear protective clothing and rubber gloves as oxalic acid, even in a highly diluted form, can be irritating to the skin and dangerous to the eyes.

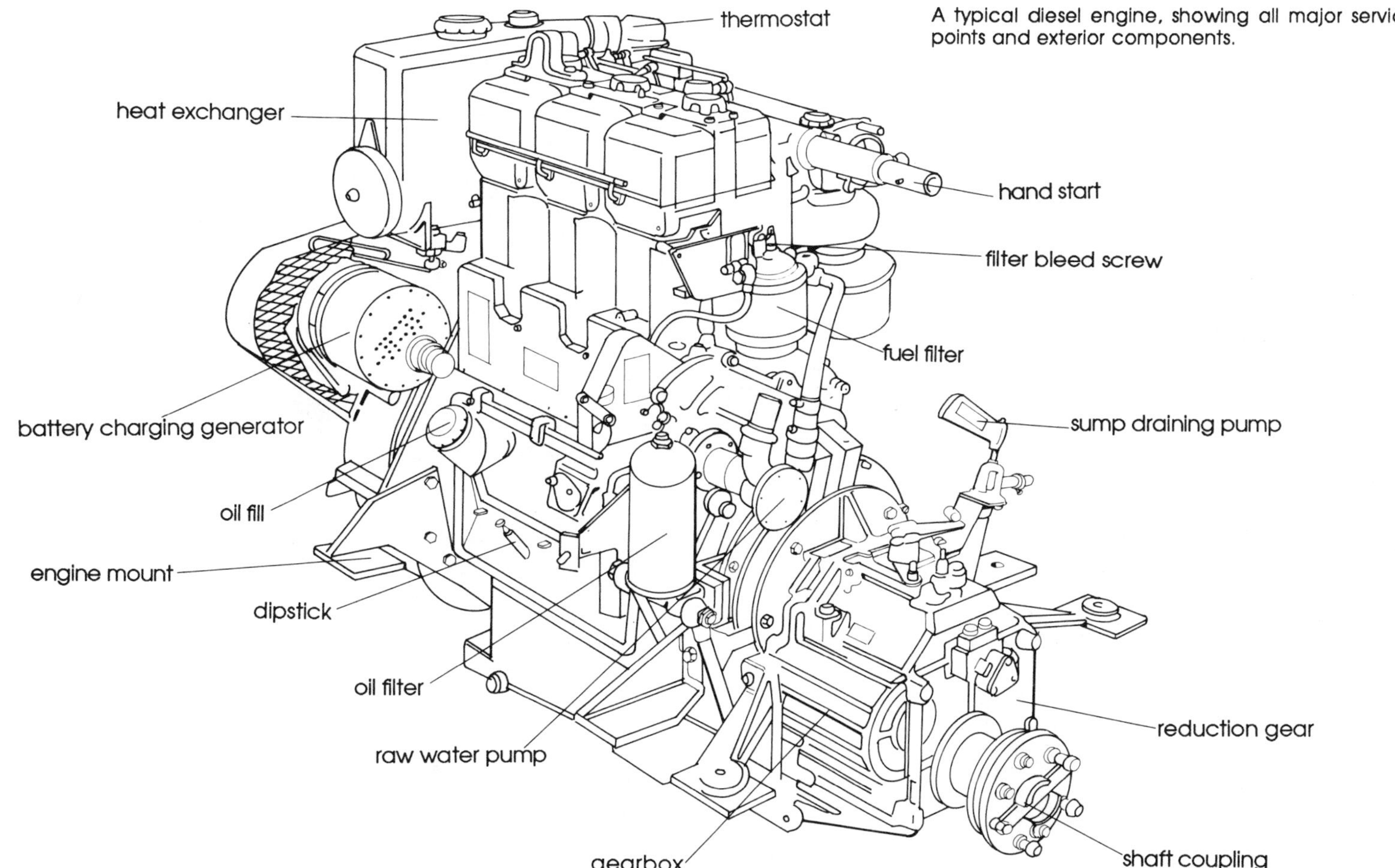

A typical diesel engine, showing all major service points and exterior components.

A typical gasoline engine, showing major external components.

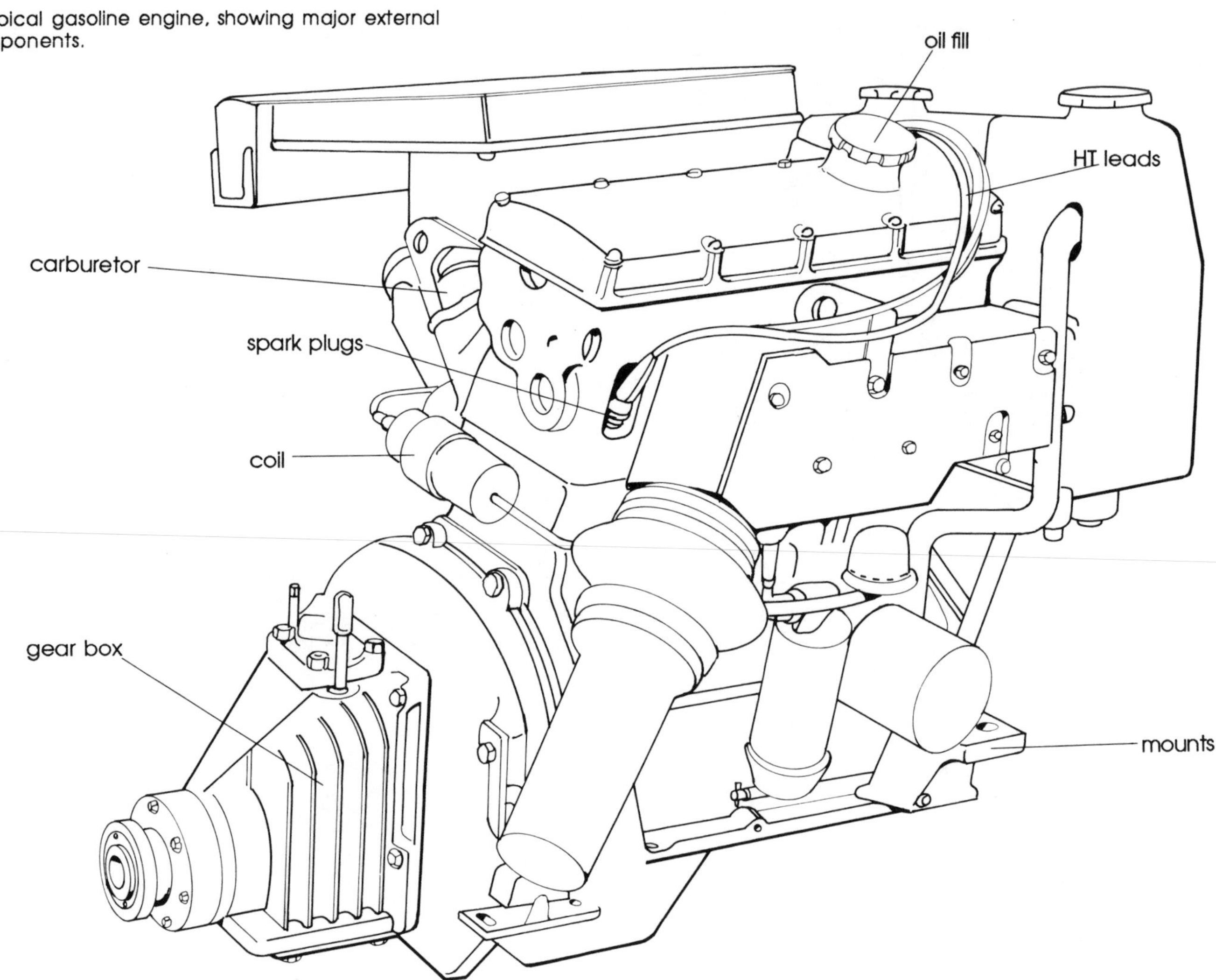

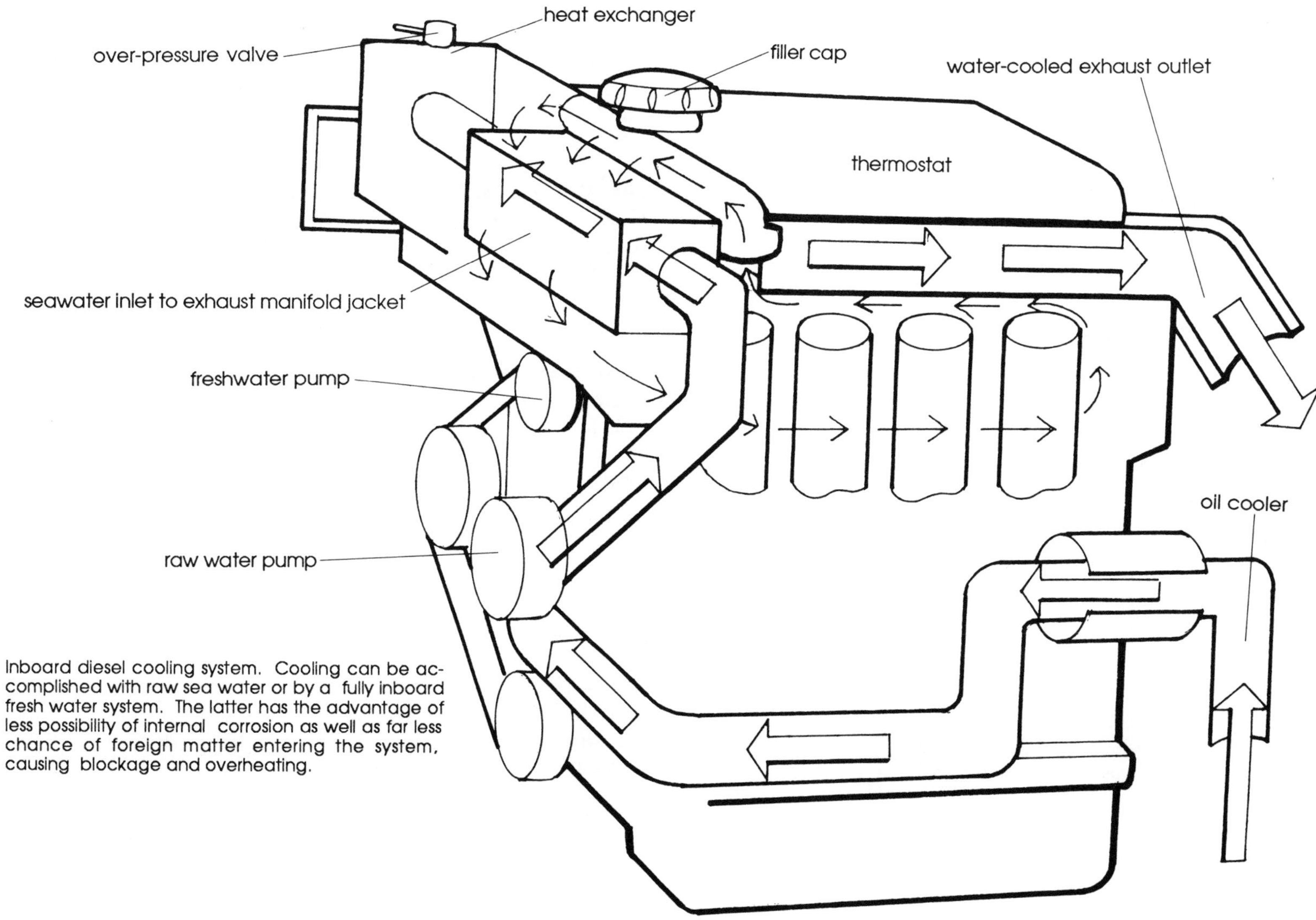

Inboard diesel cooling system. Cooling can be accomplished with raw sea water or by a fully inboard fresh water system. The latter has the advantage of less possibility of internal corrosion as well as far less chance of foreign matter entering the system, causing blockage and overheating.

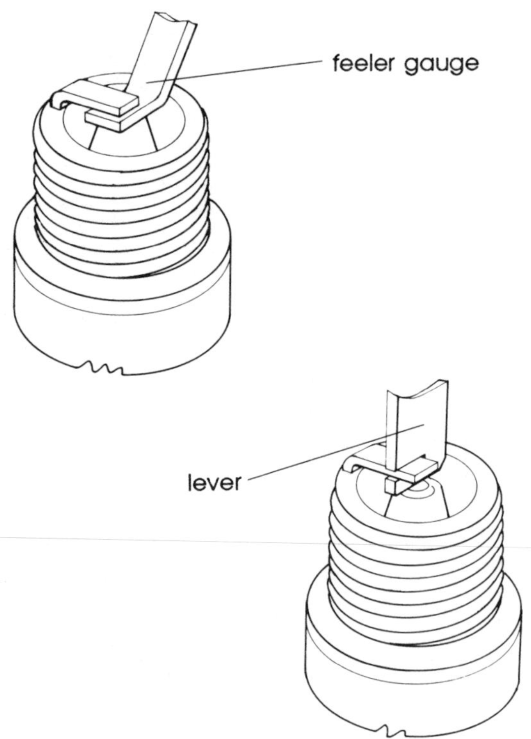

Spark plugs must be correctly gapped to run properly. Before installing any plug, use a feeler gauge to gap it to manufacturer's recommendations for the conditions you expect to run under. If you use the engine at low speeds for long periods, such as trolling, use a hotter plug to burn off impurities in the fuel and avoid fouling. The reverse is true of fast running.

Water flow is controlled by a thermostat. A spare should always be kept aboard, for when this little piece of equipment goes, nothing will suffice except a replacement. Be sure you get an exact replacement, as anything else will not work or fit and you'll be left drifting.

GASOLINE (PETROL) ENGINES: GENERAL

Gasoline-powered engines also need air and clean fuel to operate properly. However, unlike diesels, they have a far more complex electrical system to contend with. As with all things electrical in a marine environment, dampness and salt air will take their toll. What with points, spark plugs, distributors, timing, cables and such, every likelihood exists for a short, current drain or power blockage. Luckily, most of the problems are much the same as with an automobile engine, accentuated by the marine environment.

In addition, gasoline engines use a fuel with a very low flashpoint and one which evaporates, forming a highly explosive, heavier-than-air gas. All engine rooms *must* be fitted with nonsparking blowers, and these must be run for at least five minutes prior to starting the engine. Do not smoke during this period or during any refuelling or maintenance procedures. Having seen both boats and owners blown to bits at fuelling docks, it is a vice to be viewed circumspectly around gasoline.

As with most marine engine installations, major jobs should best be left to a marine engineer. However, certain items can and should be checked regularly, just as you would with your car. Always check the oil level before departing on any voyage. At the beginning of the season and, preferably, at midseason, change the oil and oil filter(s). See that linkages are lubricated regularly with good-quality waterproof grease.

Always carry spare spark plugs. One of the most common causes of engine failure is fouled plugs, due to overheating and contaminated fuel. Plugs should be chosen with an eye to the type of service expected of them: hotter plugs for trolling and slow speeds, less so for faster speeds and lighter loads. They must be gapped as per manufacturer's specifications. Newer plugs are nongapping and the initial choice is therefore more critical. Carry a plug wrench socket aboard and make sure it fits your plugs, as several sizes are available.

At the beginning of the season, check all leads and electrical cables and replace any with cracks or chafed and worn insulation. Have the carburator cleaned and adjusted and the timing adjusted at least every two years. Points ought to be checked every 100 hours of operation and replaced if any signs of wear appear.

Since gasoline engines run at much higher speeds than diesels, lubrication is vital. Choose engine oils as per manufacturer's recommendations, but make sure that the viscosity rating is compatible to your climate and the type of operation the vessel is most likely to undergo. At higher speeds, over a prolonged period, a thicker oil will be needed to stand up to temperature increases and faster moving pistons and shafts.

Please remember that all tanks should be located far from the actual engine and that all hoses carrying fuel should be of approved type and double clamped. Tanks must be properly vented and strapped down. Any leakages are cause for immediate stoppage of the engine. They must be isolated and repaired before restarting. You court explosion otherwise.

Like all gasoline engines, high temperatures and over-choking can cause vapor lock. If this happens, disconnect the spark plugs and turn the engine over a few times, then let it rest. Reconnect the plugs and restart.

FUEL SYSTEMS

All engines need fuel, and all tanks, hoses and pumps needed to deliver fuel to the engine encompass "fuel systems." Most modern fuel systems have both static and dynamic components: tanks, hoses and filters (though not all) are static; pumps, carburetors and injectors are dynamic. For all to work

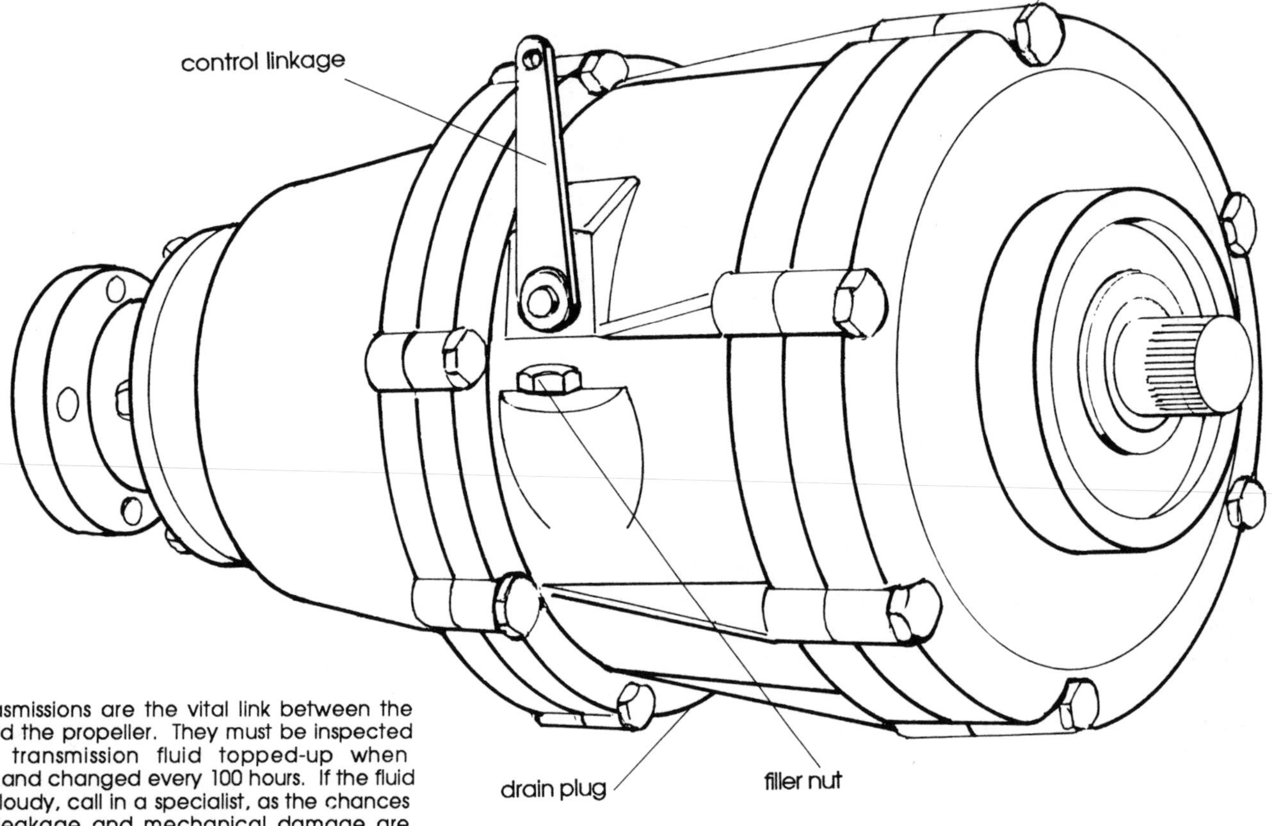

Marine trasmissions are the vital link between the engine and the propeller. They must be inspected regularly, transmission fluid topped-up when necessary and changed every 100 hours. If the fluid appears cloudy, call in a specialist, as the chances of water leakage and mechanical damage are serious matters. When draining any crankcase, open the drain plug first, then the filler nut. The partial vacuum will keep the fluid from gushing out all over the place.

effectively, the fuel introduced into the system *must be clean.* No grit, no water, no sludge must be allowed to penetrate the system defenses.

The most effective defenses against the ingress of these impurities are the fuel filter and water separator. Most engines come equipped with a single filter; occasionally a second in-line filter will be installed. However, if one wants really clean fuel to reach the engine–and in diesels especially, this is vital to protect injectors from damage–one will install a series of multi-element filters and a fuel/water separator along the supply lines. All filters ought to be bolted to structural uprights near the front of the engine, so as to be visible, as well as keeping any weight off the fuel lines.

Fuel lines–copper piping in older boats–should be approved type, guarded neoprene fuel hose. Copper is prone to vibration and fatigue fractures. Other metals are prone to corrosion. All fuel line terminations should be double clamped with stainless steel clamps. As well, a fuel shutoff valve should be installed between the tank and first filter, accessible from the deck, to isolate the engine in case of fire.

Tanks can be made of many materials. For diesel fuel they should not be of stainless steel, as this is subject to pitting and corrosion in the presence of diesel oil. All tanks should incorporate baffles to prevent surges, and must be padded and securely fastened in place against anything the sea can throw. Without this precaution, chances are all too prevalent for breaching the hull or severely damaging structural components. All tanks must be securely chocked in place. Bearers must be broad enough and securely bolted or glassed in place and all supports and straps should be heavily padded. A ruptured tank is an unmitigated disaster!

ENGINE BEDS, MOUNTS AND COUPLINGS

Any engine, gas or diesel, must be securely mounted to the hull by means of bolting the mounting feet to engine bearers

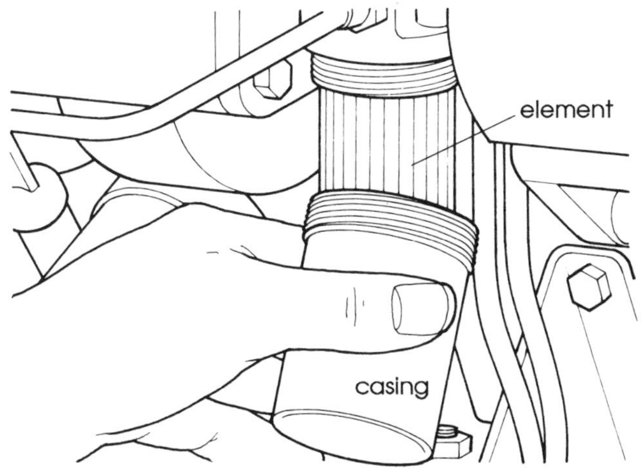

Gasoline filters do not have to separate water from fuel, but enough impurities exist in most available gasoline to make regular replacement necessary after 100 hours running.

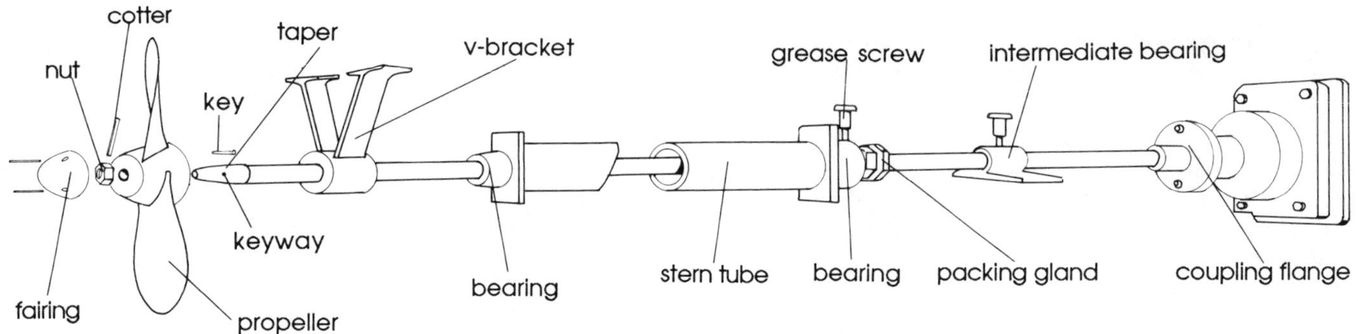

Inboard drive trains are simple things but certain precautions must be taken to avoid leaks and insure smooth running. Make sure all clamps are seated and tight. If the packing in the take-up nut is worn, replace it with the same size flax and tighten the take-up nut to allow for as little water seepage as possible. Do not tighten to the point of crushing the packing. This will only allow increased leakage and possible shaft wear.

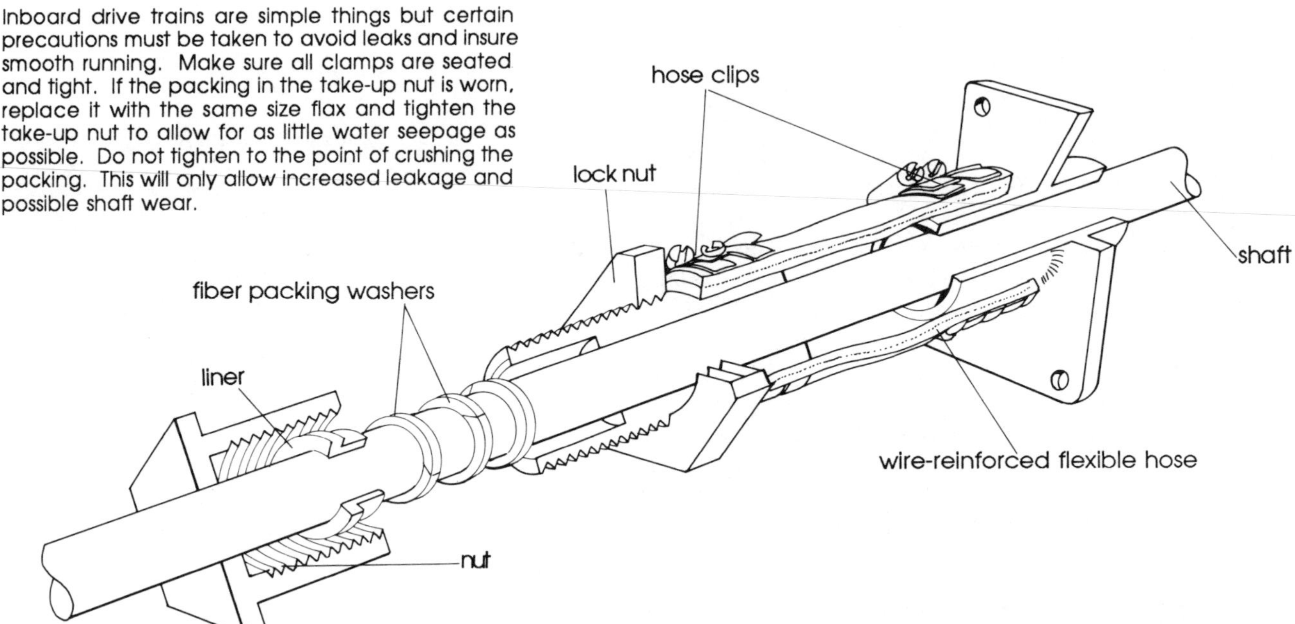

that are bolted, glassed or welded to the hull, depending on hull material. These bearers, particularly in production yachts, are often too short, the result being high-stress areas under the engine and at the ends of the bearers. If this is the case with your auxiliary, some consideration should be given to replacing or extending the bearers to help spread the loads, particularly the twisting torque, of the engine in operation.

Coupled with this is the sometimes severe vibration caused by misalignment and loose mounting bolts. The loads placed upon the bearers and the bearer cappings–metal bars bolted atop the bearers–are severe when everything is tight and functioning properly. When mounting bolts are loose, things get even worse. There have been cases where engines have torn themselves loose from their mounts. The results are worse than could be caused by a raging bull. Check the mounts at the beginning of each season and tighten all bolts.

Most modern auxiliaries are fitted with flexible mounts–synthetic rubber inserts between the engine and bearers–which help dampen vibrations, particularly in lighter hulls. Since few yachts are built to commercial standards, direct mountings are generally avoided by builders. However, flex mounts must be carefully sized to the engine and all other aspects of the installation should likewise be flexible: hoses in particular, as solid copper piping will be ruptured or yield to fatigue if fitted to a flexibly-mounted engine.

Stuffing boxes can be a source of annoying leaks. Generally, they need repacking every few years. All packing materials will compact and wear and, since one can only tighten up so much on the bolts of the box, eventually the packing must be renewed. Let the yard do the work.

OUTBOARDS AND STERN DRIVES

Outboard motors have come a long way since the first rude constructions of Ole Evinrude. They can be had in 4-cycle versions, in 2-cycle (the most prevalent) with auto-oil-injection

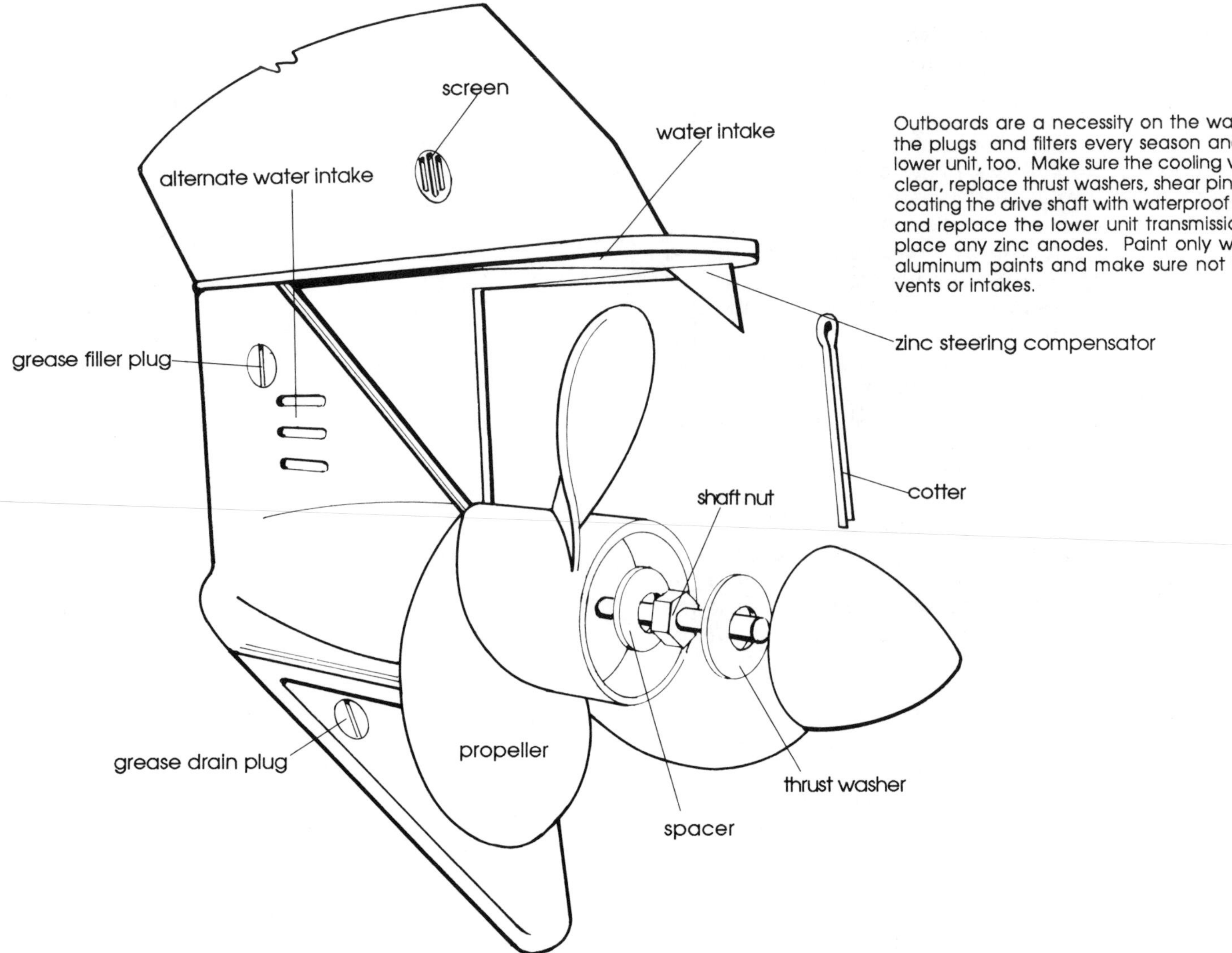

Outboards are a necessity on the water. Replace the plugs and filters every season and service the lower unit, too. Make sure the cooling water intake is clear, replace thrust washers, shear pins and cotters, coating the drive shaft with waterproof grease. Drain and replace the lower unit transmission oil and replace any zinc anodes. Paint only with approved aluminum paints and make sure not to cover any vents or intakes.

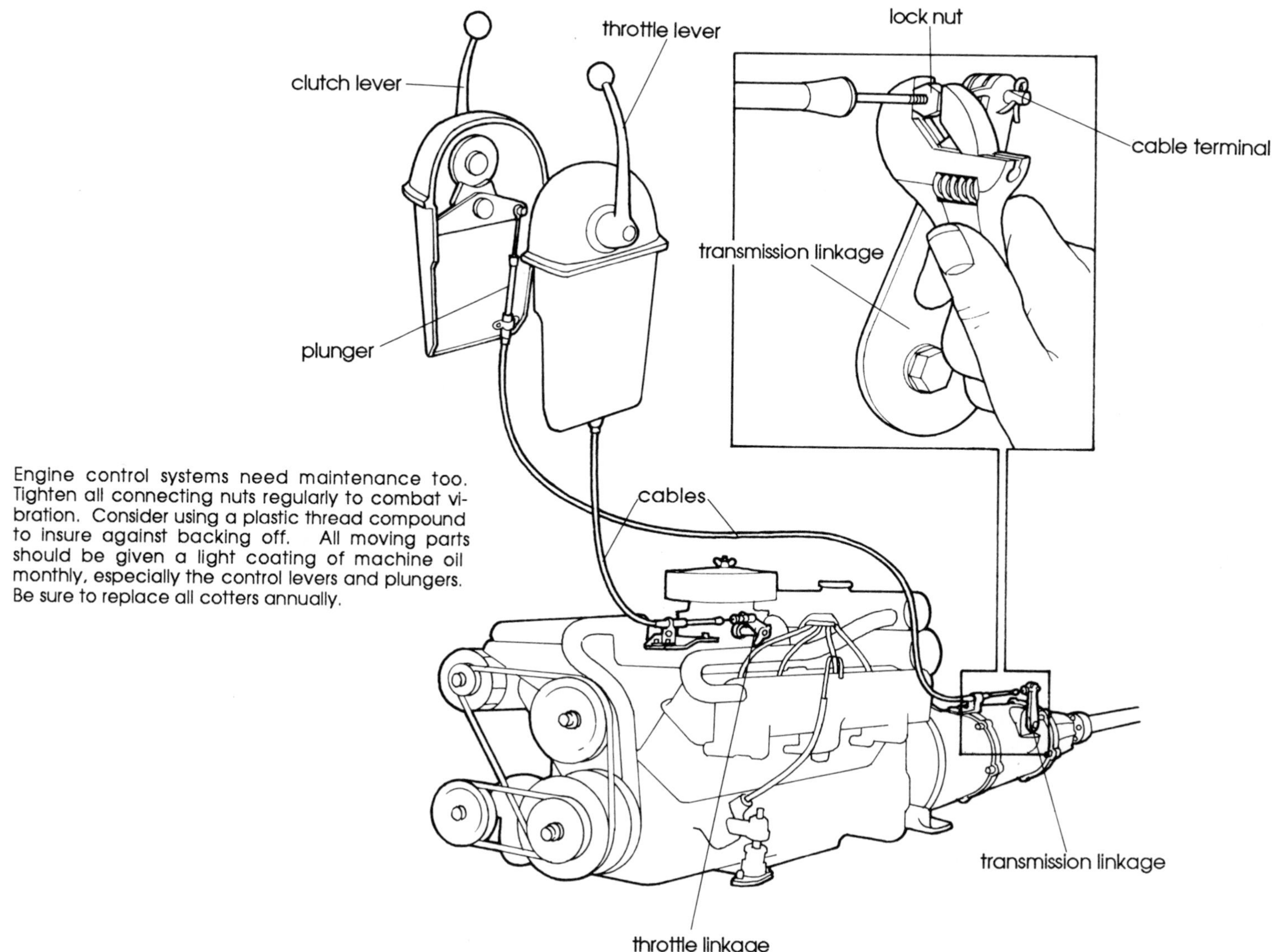

Engine control systems need maintenance too. Tighten all connecting nuts regularly to combat vibration. Consider using a plastic thread compound to insure against backing off. All moving parts should be given a light coating of machine oil monthly, especially the control levers and plungers. Be sure to replace all cotters annually.

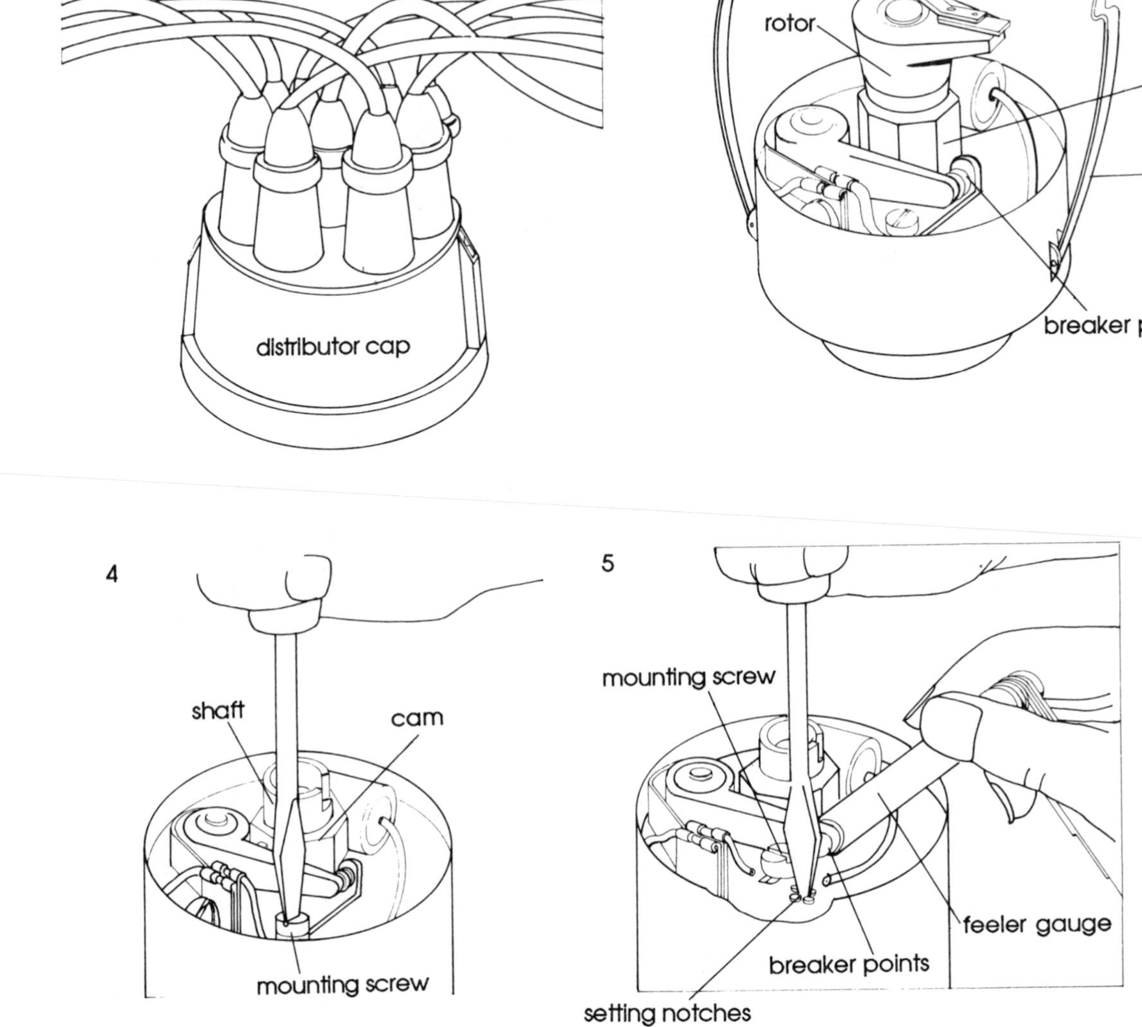
1
distributor cap
2
rotor
cam
clip
breaker points
4
shaft
cam
mounting screw
5
mounting screw
feeler gauge
breaker points
setting notches

3

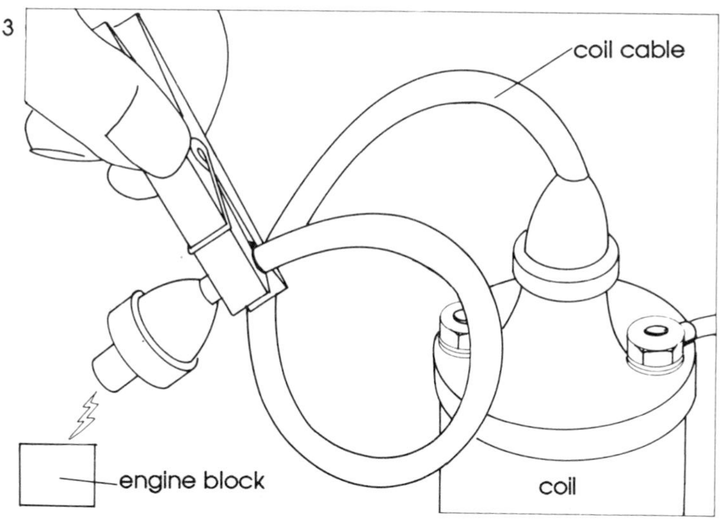

6

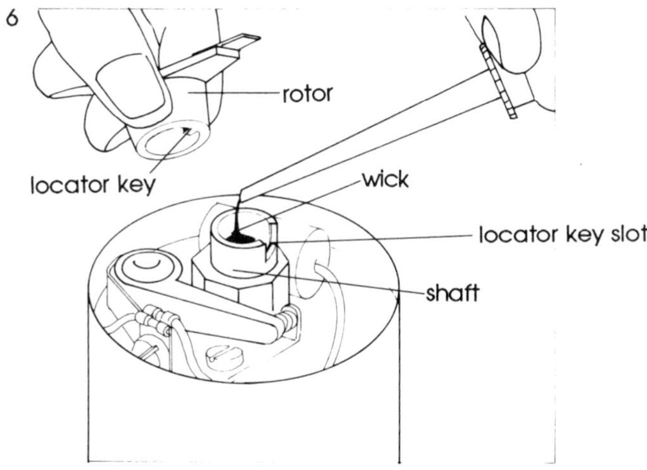

Distributor care is vital for the effective running of a gasoline engine. 1. After every 250 hours of use, the distributor should be cleaned, the cap replaced if there are any signs of cracking. 2. Check the gaps between breaker points and buff them lightly with an ignition file (from auto supply store). 3. Holding the cable safely, have someone turn on the ignition and crank the engine. A bright spark should leap from cable to engine. 4. If weak or yellow, reset gap. Remove rotor and crank engine until cam has opened gap to its greatest extent. Loosen the mounting screw. Then insert the proper feeler gauge and turn the set screw until the points just touch the blade on both sides. 5. Lubricate wick with a few drops of engine oil, align the locator key with the shaft slot, replace the rotor and install cap.

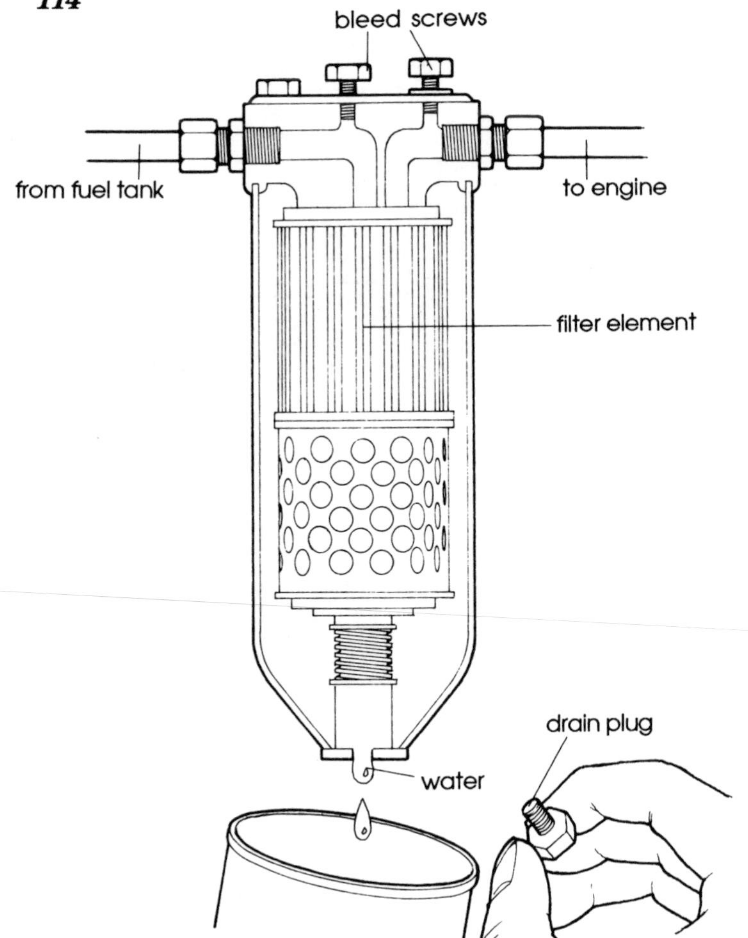

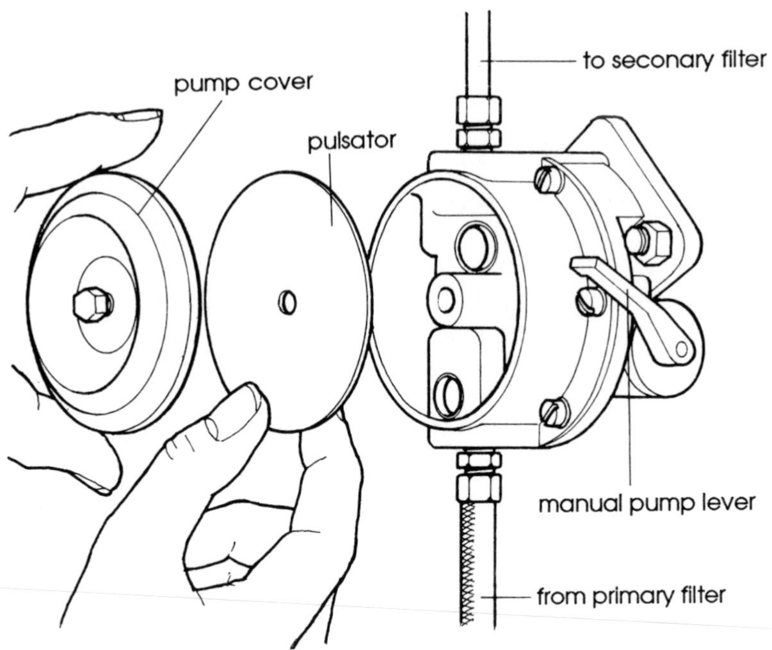

Fuel filters and pumps are vital elements in a diesel propulsion system. Drain the primary filter of water each time a tankful of fuel is used. Every 200 hours, replace the filter element. The fuel pump should be cleaned regularly. Small amounts of sediment should be scraped out, the pulsator replaced if it is deformed or torn, and the unit reassembled. Both filter and pump maintenance admit air to the fuel delivery system and it will have to be bled following manufacturer's instructions. A second filter, installed in-line between the primary filter and the pump, can lessen maintenance and help insure against injector damage.

and even in diesel (workboat) workups. The basic premise is simple. Make the engine and drive train one unit and do away with installation, alignment and insulation problems in one stroke. Four-stroke engines are cared for in much the same way as any 4-stroke auxiliary.

Two-stroke outboards all work on the principle of adding oil directly to the fuel mixture. In the evil, smelly old units, this was a 25:1 mixture and produced fouled plugs, dirty exhausts and rotten fuel economy. Today's versions run on 50:1 to 100:1 mixtures and are as reliable and clean as many inboards.

The major problems are encountered when using an outboard for slow-going and heavy-hauling tasks. Since most outboards are designed for fast-planing power boats, their appropriateness for other chores is often compromised. Major problems are fouled plugs, overheating and cavitation.

Fouled plugs occur when the oil is too heavy in the mixture or when the plug is not hot enough to burn the oil/gas mixture as fully as possible. The solution in the first case is to dilute the mixture in accordance with manufacturer's instructions. In the second situation, simply replace the plugs with a recommended "hot" plug, specifically designed to use in these circumstances.

Overheating in outboards usually is caused by a blockage to the raw water intake at the base of the leg. Another possible cause of overheating is buildup of deposits in the cooling piping. This can be caused by running in very dirty water and/or by neglecting to replace sacrificial anodes, especially in salt water.

In general, maintenance of outboard engines is an easy and quick matter. Change the gear oil, replace plugs and filters every spring. Give the entire engine, under the cowl, a light spray of penetrating oil. Make sure fuel is fresh and filtered. Check that the engine wiring is sound and secure. Check the carburetor for obstructions and the valves for freedom of movement. Replace shear pins and cotters and coat the

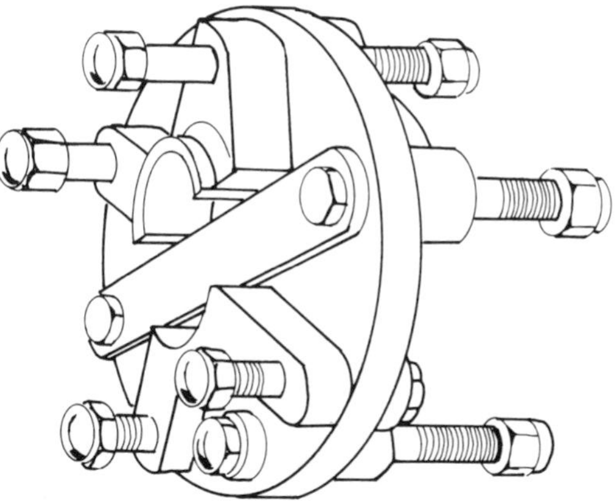

Flexible couplings are used only when shaft angles are greater than 15 degrees from horizontal. Professional help should probably be sought as extra thrust bearings may be required in the installation.

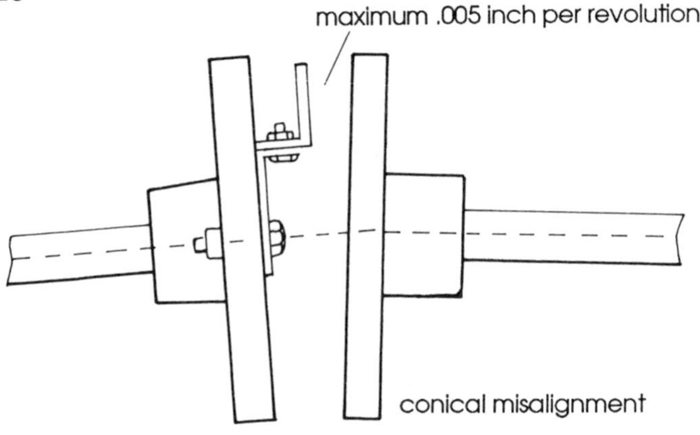

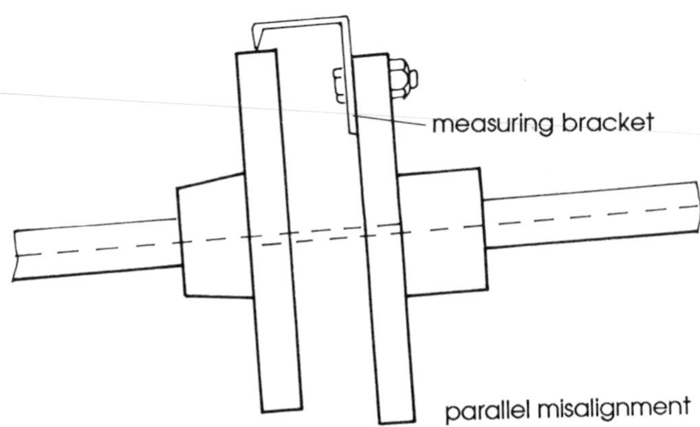

For a propeller to turn without vibration and use the full power delivered from the transmission, the shaft coupling must be aligned. This is true even of flexible couplings. Use a feeler gauge or dial gauge to check both conical and parallel misalignment and adjust accordingly. Parallel misalignment may be a job for the yard, as the engine bed may need adjusting for height.

propeller shaft liberally with heavy-duty waterproof grease before replacing the prop. If the propeller is nicked or bent, have it repaired or replace it. That's it!

Of course, catastrophes can occur, the most likely being dropping the entire unit overboard. If this should happen in fresh water, dry the engine off as well as possible and get it to your OB repair man. In salt water, things deteriorate rather quickly. Wash it off immediately with fresh water and go directly to the same repair expert. Any delays will likely ruin the engine for good.

At the end of the season, the engine should be flushed out with fresh water, oiled–remembering to remove the plugs and spray some penetrating oil in each combustion chamber–drained and brought inside.

During the season, please try to keep the engine leg and prop out of the water if possible. If not, treat the leg with antifouling paint specifically formulated for OB lower units. Most legs are aluminum and corrosion will occur if incompatible paints are used.

Stern drives are nothing more than inboard engines with outboard, pivoting propellers. Instead of going through the hull, the shafts are modifications of outboard lower units and exit the boat through the stern above the waterlines. The advantages are obvious, the disadvantages less so, especially in light of developments in all outboard propulsion units. The biggest problem with stern drives is their complex gearing and vulnerability. They are as subject to corrosion as outboards, but repair usually involves hauling the boat and their complexity makes them a poor choice for owner repair.

Secondary filters need element replacement too, usually every 100 hours. Make sure to replace gaskets at the same time. Tighten retaining bolts or clamps so no leakage appears. Bleed the system.

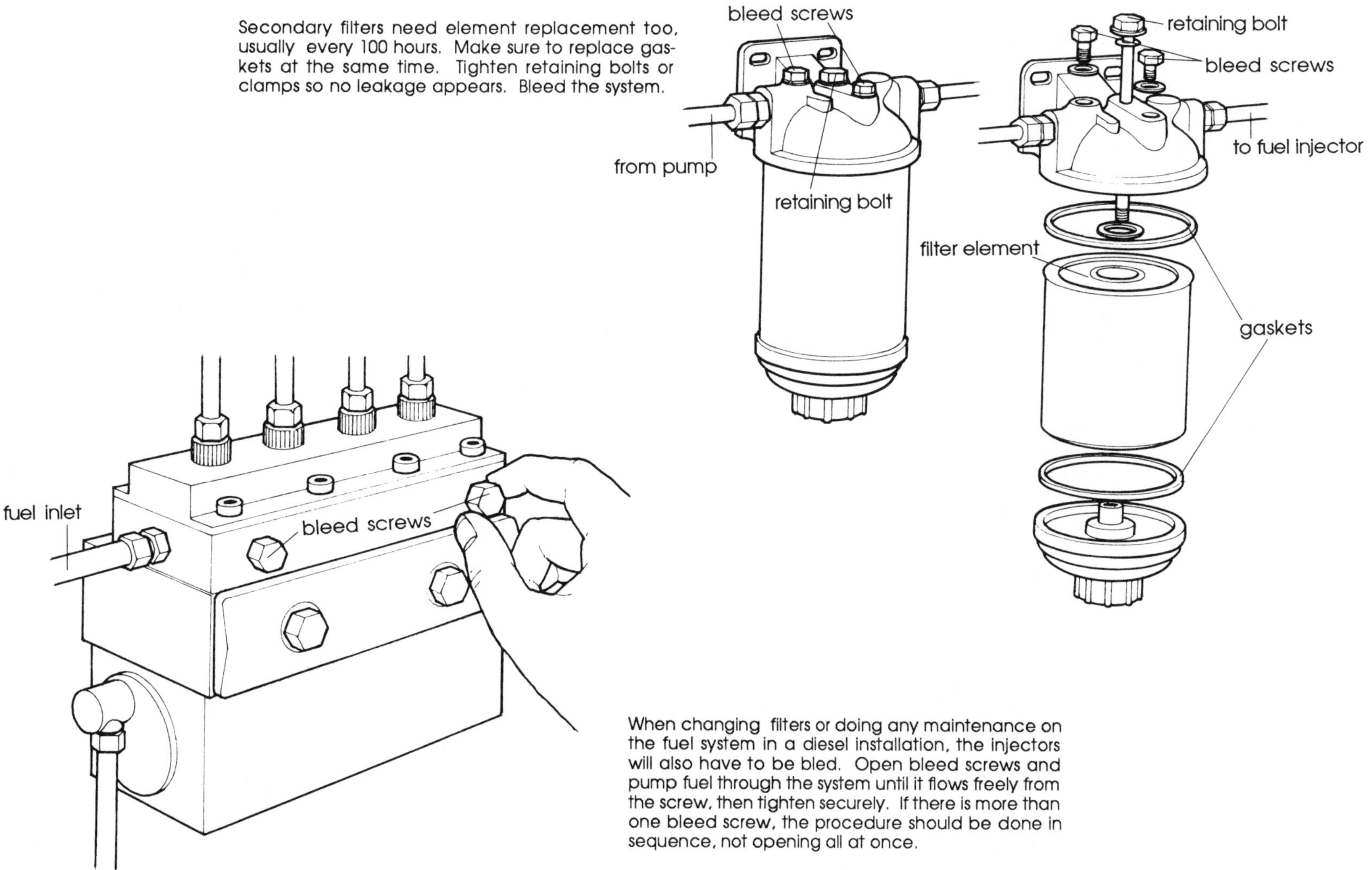

When changing filters or doing any maintenance on the fuel system in a diesel installation, the injectors will also have to be bled. Open bleed screws and pump fuel through the system until it flows freely from the screw, then tighten securely. If there is more than one bleed screw, the procedure should be done in sequence, not opening all at once.

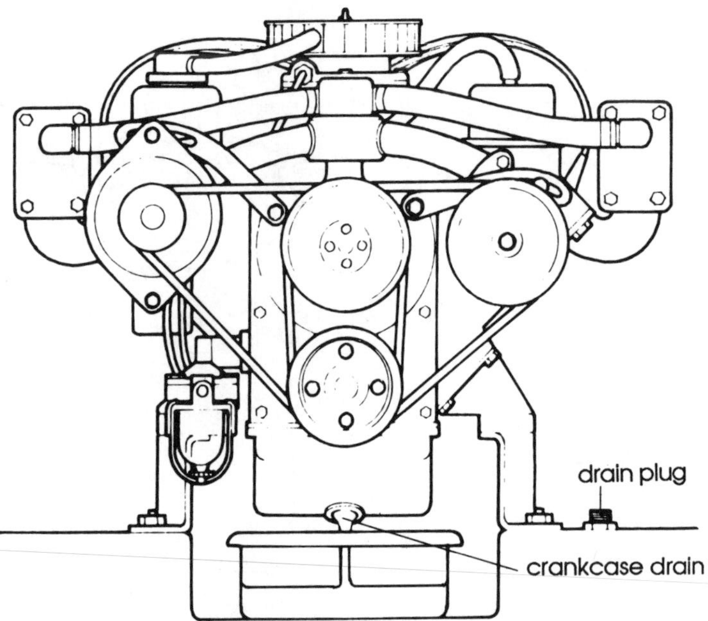

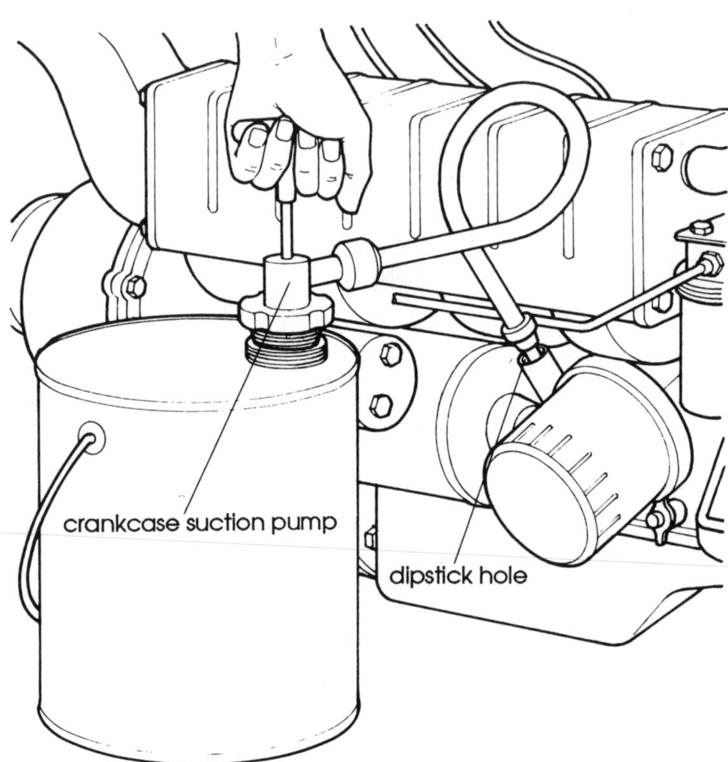

As in an automobile, oil changes keep things running. Change crankcase oil in a gasoline engine after every 50 hours running. Run the engine to warm the oil, then either use a crankcase pump and reservoir to pump out the old oil from the dipstick hole or, if the engine is so fitted, drain the oil into the fitted drain pan beneath the engine. The first method is preferable as you may then simply carry the old oil off the boat with no spills or mess. Once a year, however, use the plug to allow any sediment to be drawn from the crankcase.

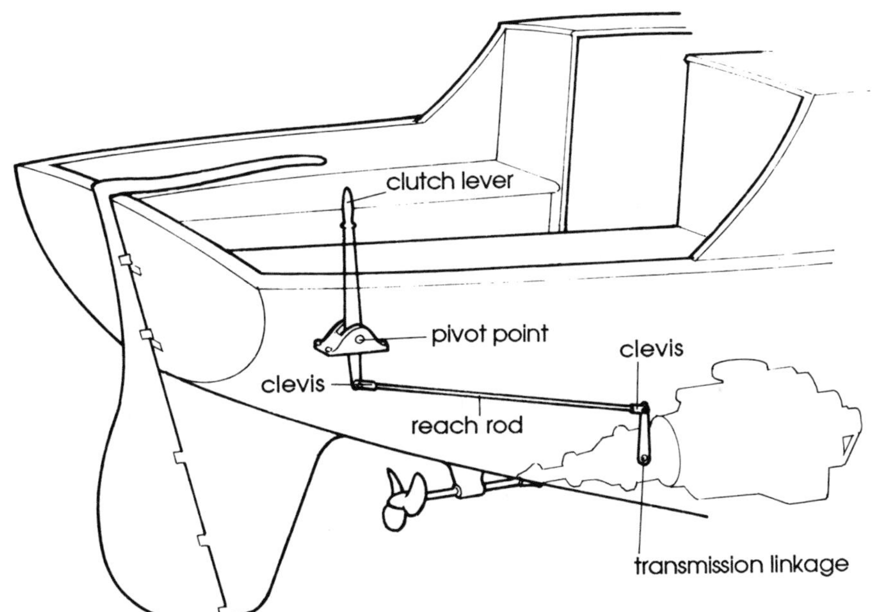

In older engine installations, the clutch is controlled by a lever connected to the transmission by a reach rod and clevises. The pivot and clevises as well as all linkages should be coated every couple of months with penetrating oil. To avoid galvanic action between engine and rod, plastic sleeves and washers are fitted to the clevis. These, as well as all cotters, should be replaced yearly.

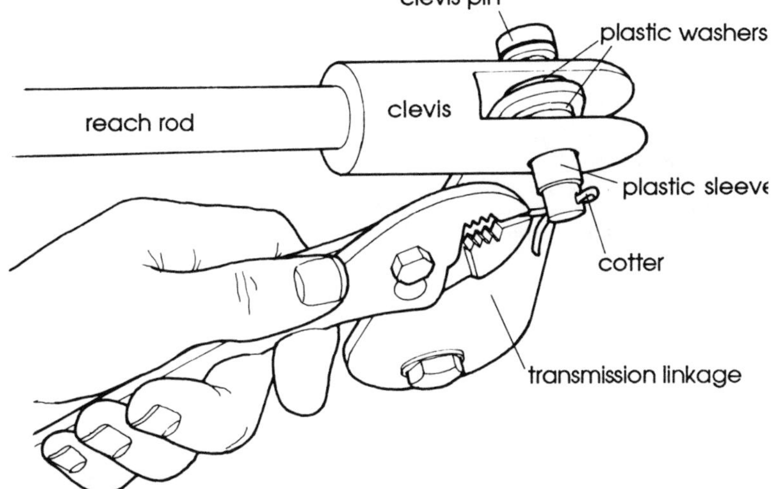

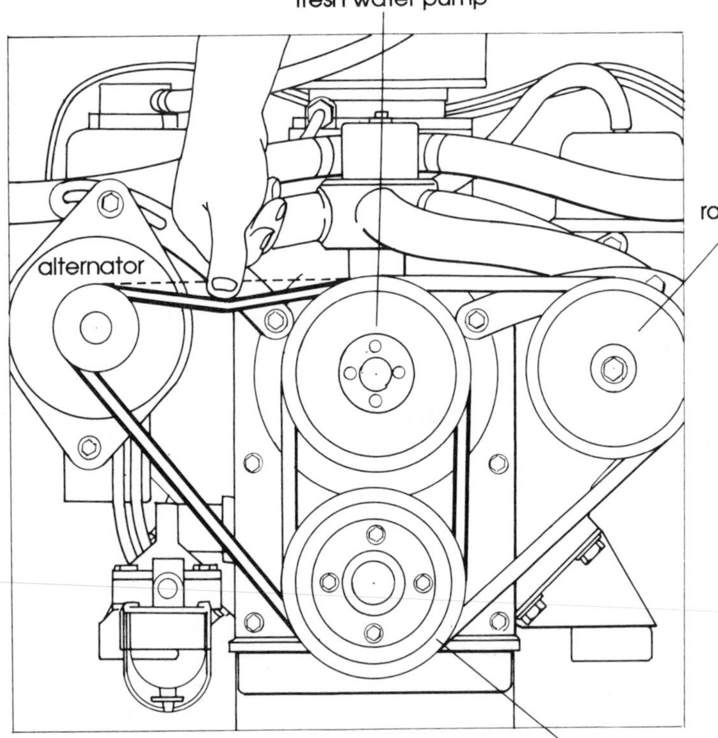

Engine-driven belts power cooling and electrical systems. If too tight they will wear quickly, if too loose the system will not function efficiently. There should be about one quarter inch play when the belt is depressed with a finger.

Belts are tightened by loosening the mounting nut on either the alternator or pump and moving it along the mounting bracket. Use a small pry bar, wrench or big screwdriver to hold the component off and the belt at tension while you tighten it. Check belts every 50 hours of running time.

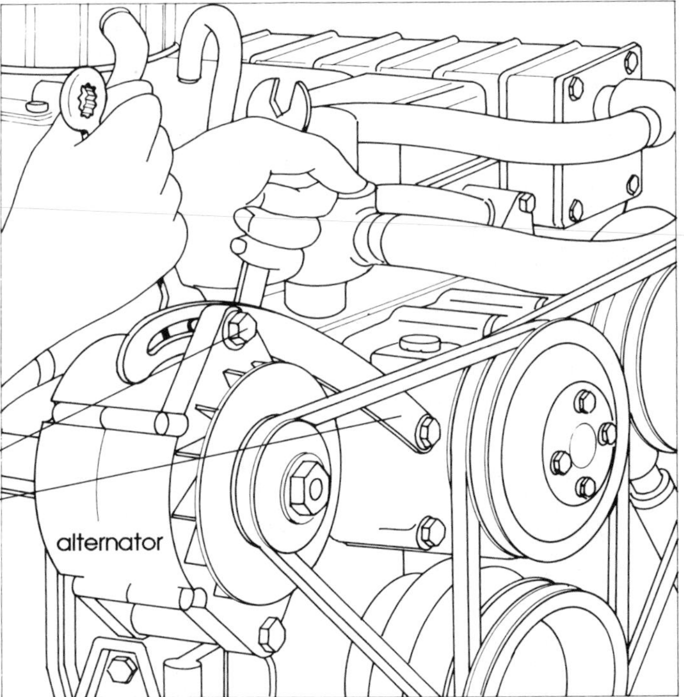

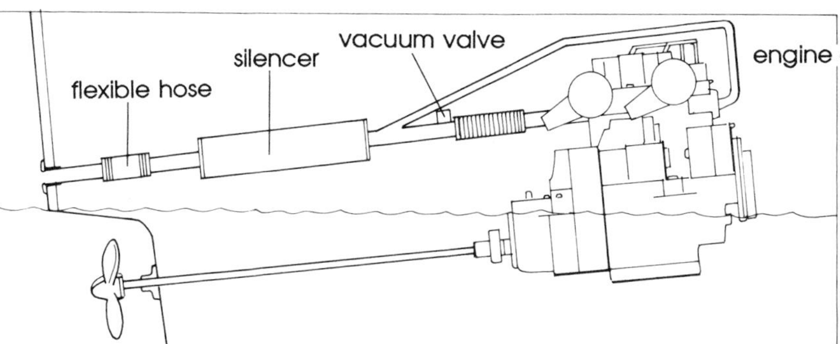

Wet exhausts are most common on small yachts. Two installations, one above the waterline, the other below. Note the vacuum valve (top) used to prevent water from being sucked into the engine. Watertrap (below) is used to prevent backflow. Manifold has condensation trap and drain to help prevent rust-out. In both, check valves, clamps and all piping at least twice per season.

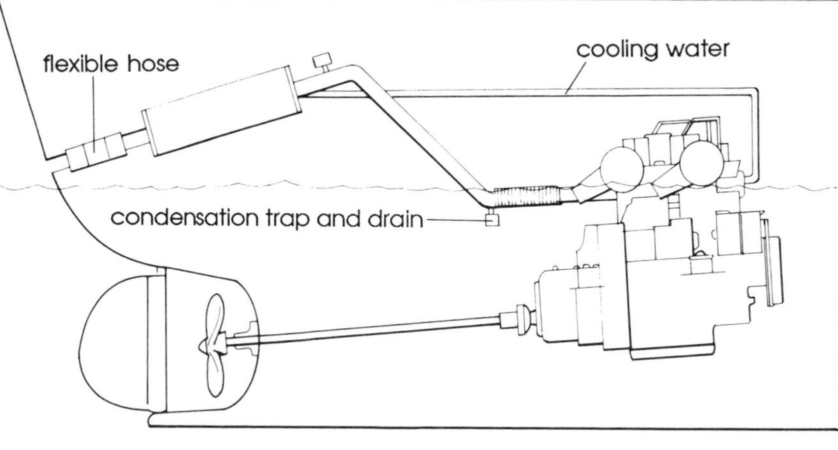

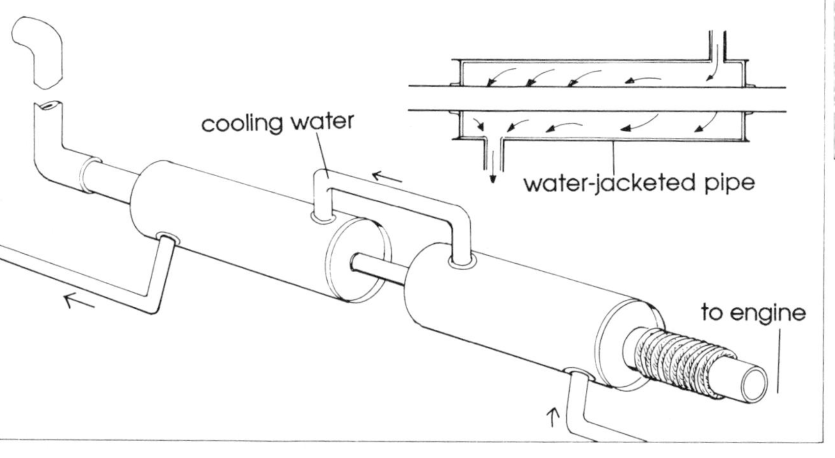

Dry exhaust vents to the air, much like an automobile. Pipes are water-jacketed to keep exhaust gases from becoming so hot as to cause a fire or explosion hazard. Some sort of rain cap is needed where through-deck pipe terminates.

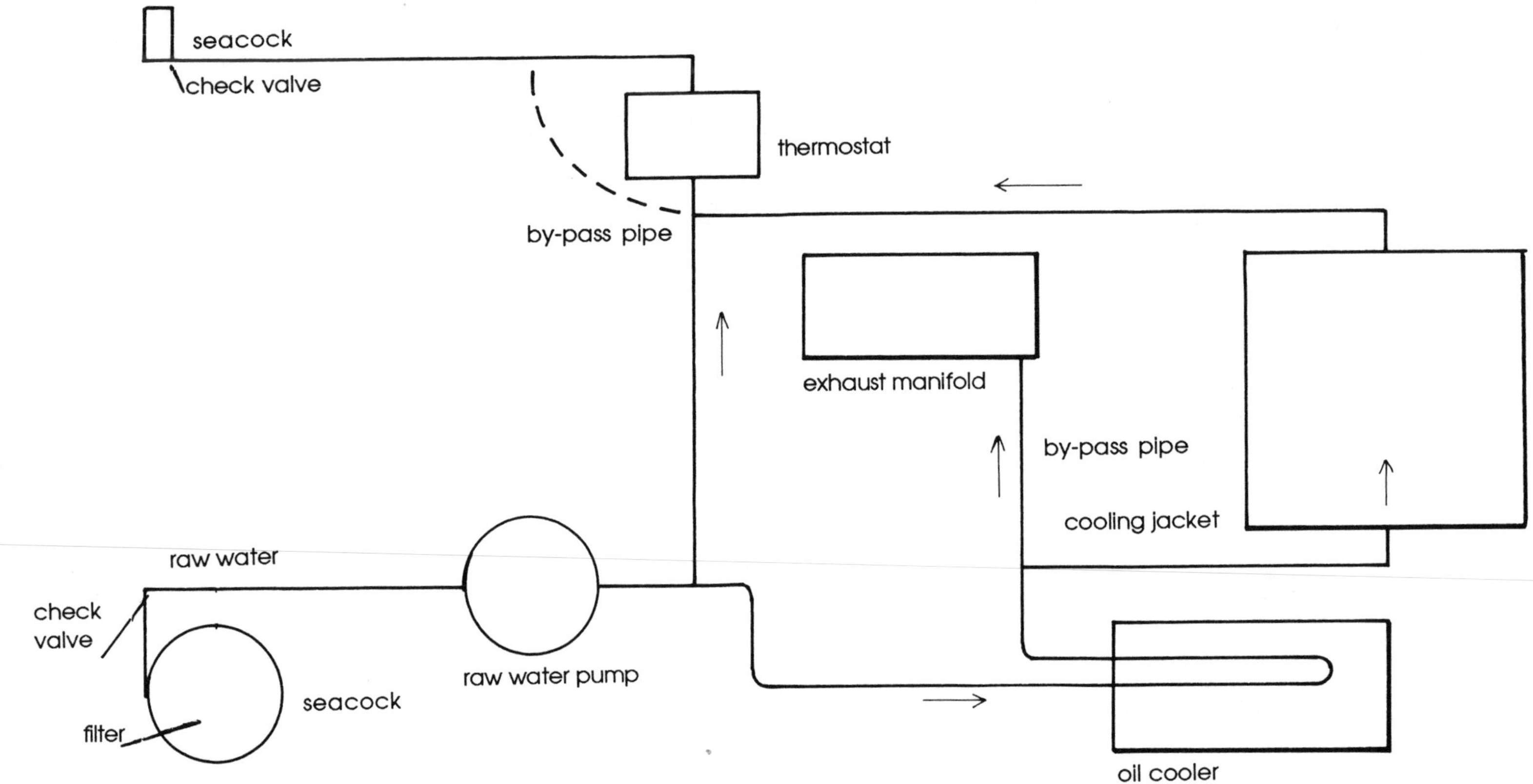

Schematic of typical raw-water cooling system. Make sure all waterways are kept clear and unclogged, flush twice a year with fresh water, replace impellers annually and make sure seals are tight. All piping and clamps must be checked before the start of the season to avoid damage to the engine.

6
SPARS AND RIGGING

Most of us think of spars as masts, and rigging as stays, but this is not exactly the case. A spar is any solid member that supports a sail–in any manner–or other equipment (a radar mast, for example). Rigging is any wire, rod or rope that tethers or controls spars, sails or ancillary equipment. Thus, almost anything from the gunnel up, on both sail and power boats, can be considered one or the other.

MASTS

On a sailing yacht, with the exception of one propelled by a kite, all sails and rigging are somehow connected to the mast–or masts–which stands vertical on or through the deck. This can be constructed of aluminum, wood–either solid or hollow–or steel or, more recently, of GRP and carbon fiber composites. No matter what the material, this column exists to allow a topmost point from which to attach sails and, in modern yachts, an after edge to support the luff of the mainsail. If the rig is not freestanding, it will be a column in compression, the forces exerted by the stays and shrouds acting to push the mast downward through the bottom of the hull if given the chance.

Most problems with masts come about from a combination of tension and fatigue. The tensions are not a constant. They vary from at rest to beating, to reaching or running; they vary with the sea state and the strength of the wind. They vary with the tune of the rig and the pressures applied by the sails and the running rigging. In other words, you cannot calculate all the variables and say with any assurance if and when something will fail.

Fatigue is a bit different. Tension can be visually demonstrated easily enough. Fatigue is due to the inherent properties of different metals, and the changes brought about to the structure of the metal by movement and oscillation, particularly by

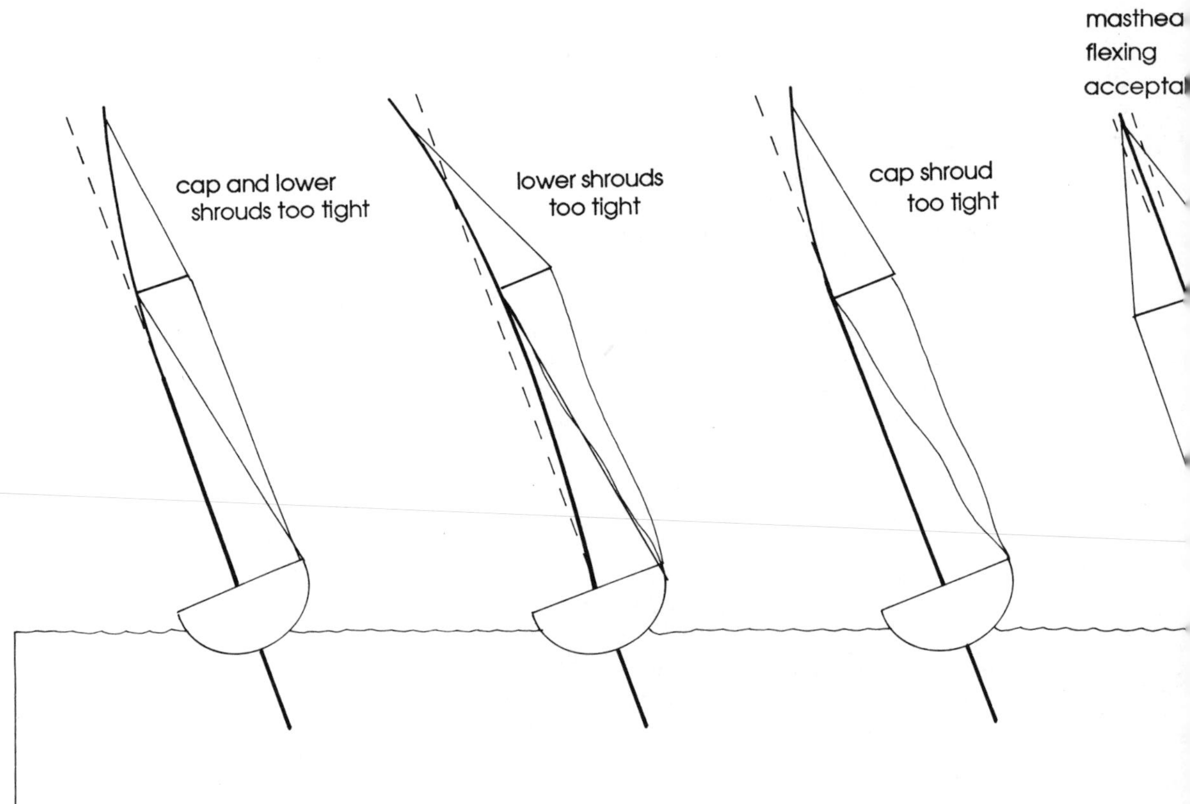
cap and lower
shrouds too tight
lower shrouds
too tight
cap shroud
too tight
masthea
flexing
acceptal

Tuning the rig is vital to good performance and safety. These drawings show faults in tuning and how to correct them.

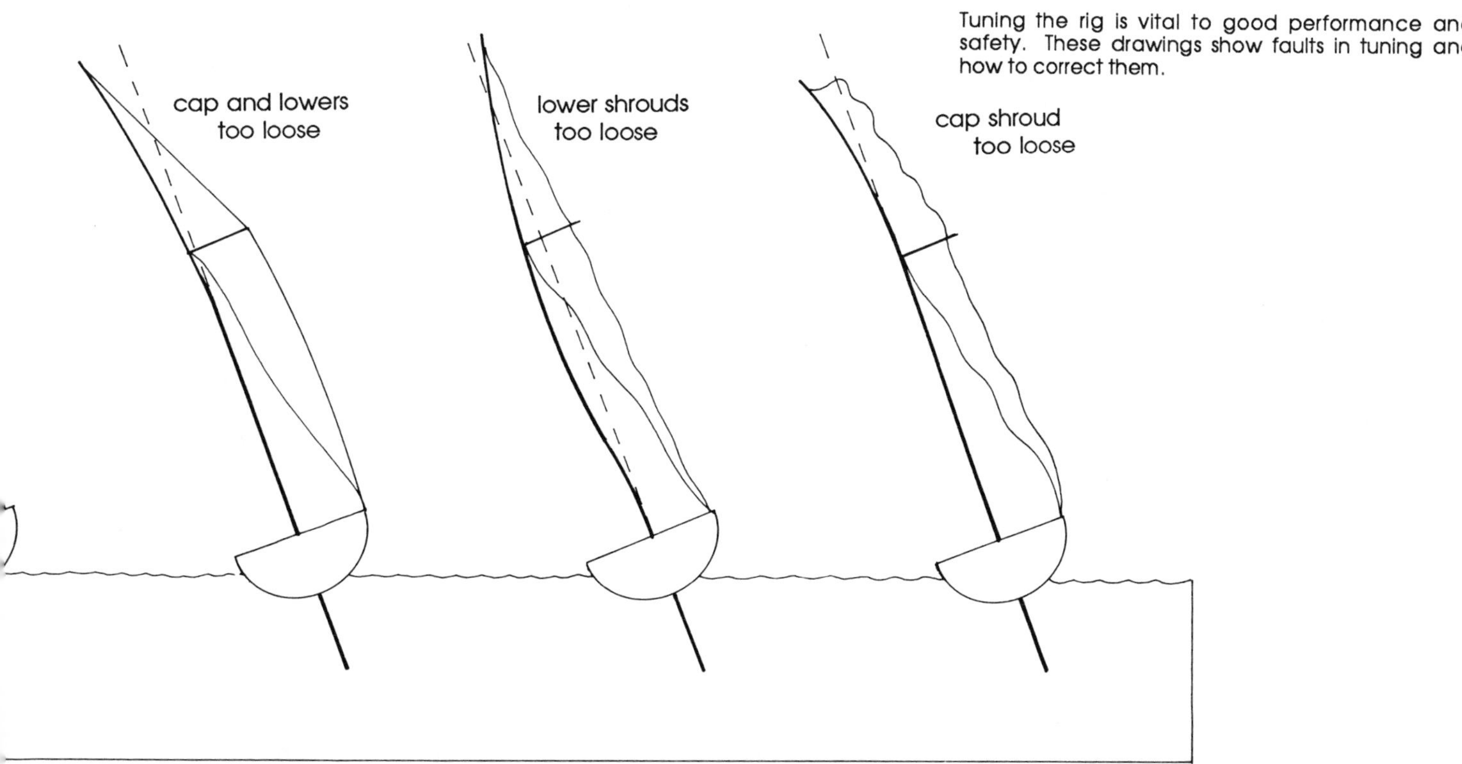

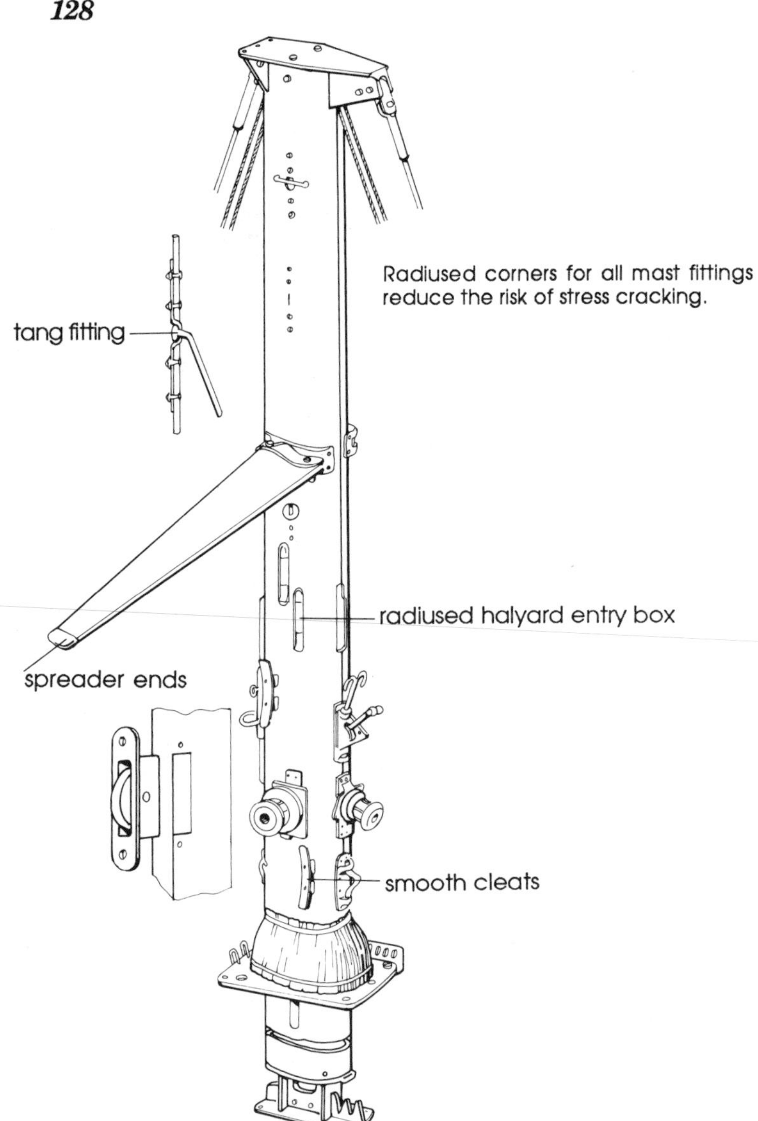

rhythmic motions. The only way to avoid a fatigue failure is constant inspection and knowing what to look for. Masts are prone to fatigue and fail at the two points of greatest stress: the partners–where the spreaders meet the mast–and at the point the mast passes through the deck.

At the spreaders, all the forces transmitted to the shrouds are transferred to the column. This is also the point at which the mast undergoes the greatest flexing. The combination of constantly varying tensions and the oscillation from flexing is astounding. In an average 24-hour passage, it can be measured in thousands of movements. Over a period of time, the mast metal can weaken and suddenly let go. You have little or no warning, and the results are not pretty.

To repair this at sea is more a case of rigging a jury mast than effecting permanent repairs. That is not the purview of this volume, though some will be shown in illustrations. To repair a mast on land is another matter altogether. Since only two types of mast are in common usage–metal and wood–we will limit ourselves to those. Carbon fiber, GRP and exotics are best left to a specialist, since the makeup of these structures and their eventual integrity is not a matter to be dealt with lightly.

Since aluminum masts, when they fracture, usually break, and since the break is not ever clean–a certain amount of distortion and bending occurring in most cases–the only way to salvage the structure is to create a sleeve to join the two parts. Such a sleeve can best be made of an extrusion of compatible material slightly, but only slightly, smaller than the original. This can then be fitted inside the two pieces of the original extrusion, after the distorted segments are cut away and deburred. The internal tube should extend at least 18 inches to either side of the join and two feet or more with larger extrusions. The most effective way to make this whole setup permanent is to epoxy the insert, first to one piece of the extrusion, then to the next. The reason for this procedure is that you want to avoid slippage or displacement of the insert.

Until several years ago, the insert would be riveted to the mast parts. This, however, weakens the entire structure and is not to be recommended. Do not use hardware store epoxy for this! Special metal-compatible epoxies are made, and you will have to track them down through mail order sources or specialty chandlers.

In undertaking this repair, remember that the mast will be shortened, unless you add a section equal to that removed originally. This can usually be obtained from the original sparmaker and is of very modest cost for the foot or two one needs. This center section then becomes the first to be fastened in place, followed by first one end, then the other. If the original was fitted with external track, no problems exist, except for alignment in reinstalling the track. If, however, the original contained an extruded track, the replacement section will have to match and the interior tube will have to be cut away prior to installation. This is not a tricky job, but it must be done with care and a steady hand. You want any cutouts to be parallel and to fit around the internal luff groove as closely as possible. Also, be sure that the edges of the cut are carefully epoxied to the mating surfaces of the luff groove.

Wood masts, though not often seen on most modern production boats, do exist on thousands of older boats, and the current revival of wooden boat building has certainly done much to increase their production. Solid masts are usually too heavy to be considered for any except square riggers or true character boats. Hollow spars are lighter and generally stronger, especially with modern adhesives, not only epoxies, but also Resorcinol and some of the aircraft glues. Most breaks in a wooden spar are easier to repair than in the equivalent metal mast. The problem arises in finding suitable stock, properly sawn and cured. It should be quarter sawn and air dried. Spruce or fir make the best spars, but any long pieces must be free of knots,

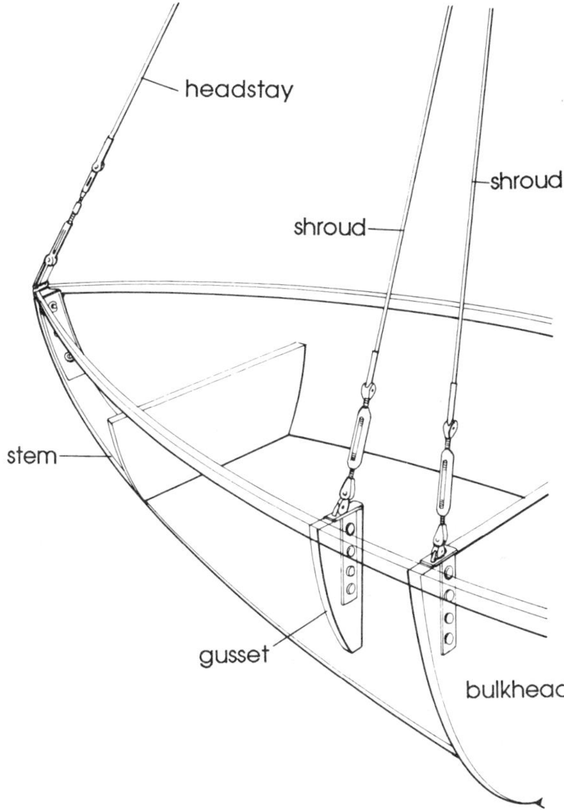

Chain plates are often bolted to molded-in or bolted-on structural members. Make sure all chainplate bolts are secure and tight. Remember that the plates keep the rigging in tension, while their attachment points help spread the very great loads in shock situations–coming off a large wave–and strengthen the hull in general.

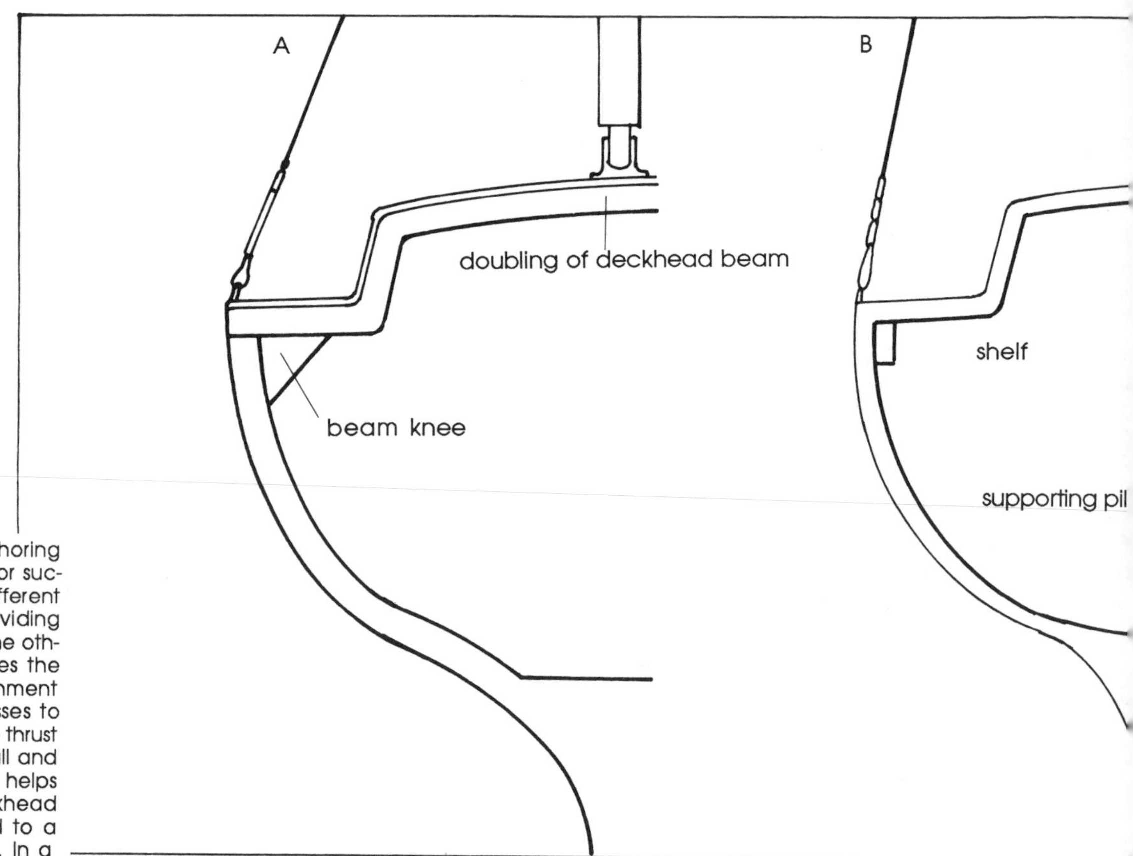

Counteracting the pull of the shrouds. Anchoring chain plates with fail-safe security is a must for successful tuning of the rig and safety at sea. Different methods may be used, but all will work–providing every link in the connecting parts is equal to the others and to the job. A. A molded-in knee ties the deck and hull together and acts as an attachment point for the chainplate, spreading the stresses to the hull, while reinforced deck beams carry the thrust of the mast. B. An encapsulated shelf ties hull and deck together and a steel support stanchion helps counteract the thrust of the mast. C. A bulkhead supports the mast while a tie bar attached to a molded-in stringer takes the chain plate. D. In a metal hull, the frame, beam knee and deck girder take the respective strains.

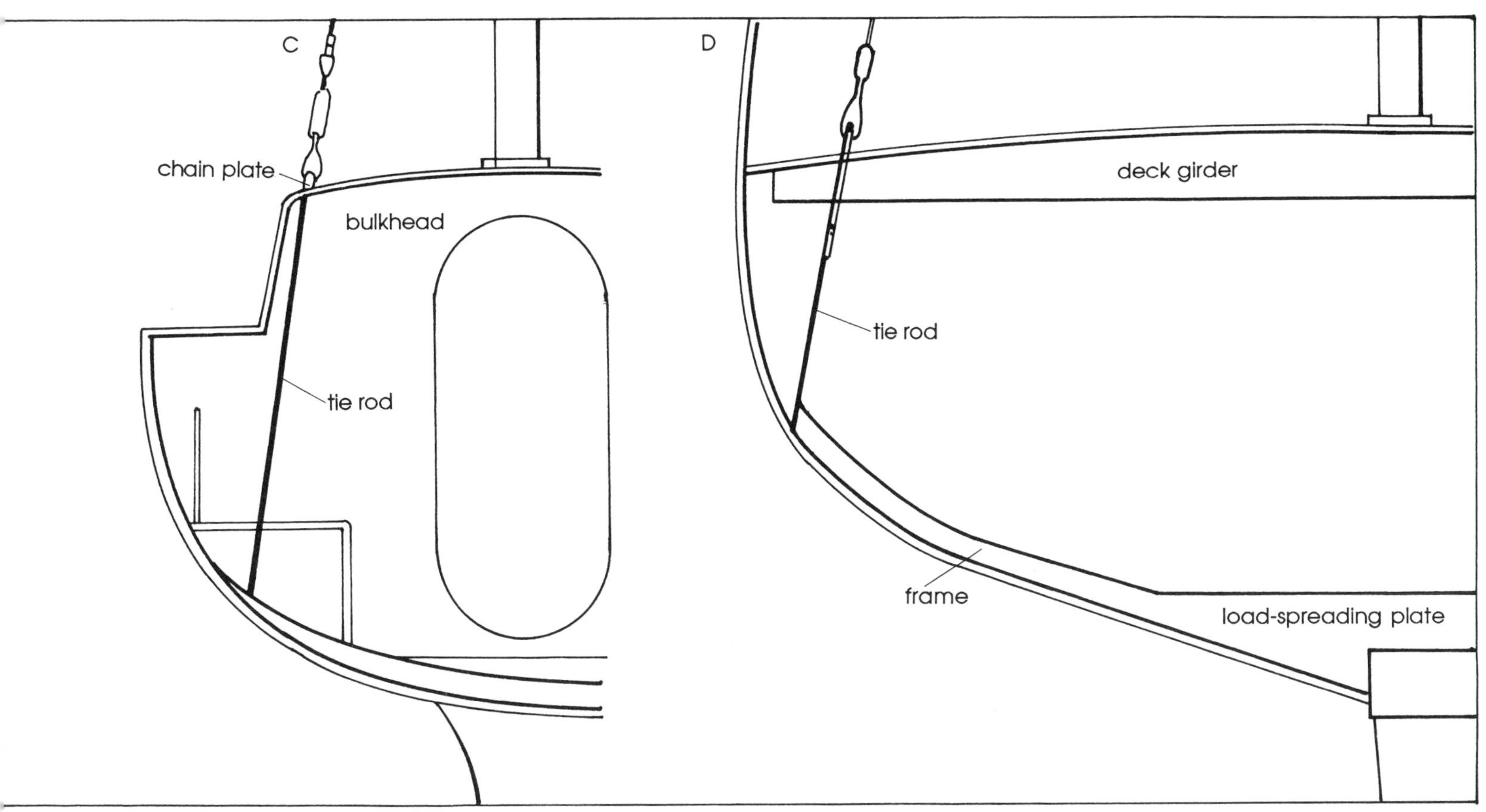
C
chain plate
bulkhead
tie rod
D
deck girder
tie rod
frame
load-spreading plate

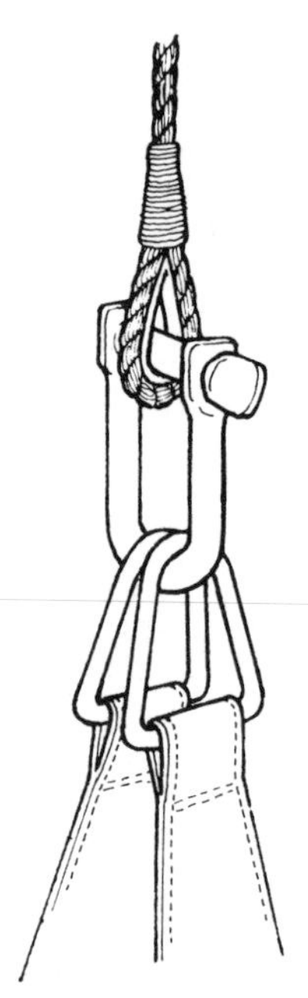

The bosun's chair should be attached to the halyard with a shackle. Do not use a snap shackle under any circumstances as the chance of accidental opening is always present. Even with a standard D-shackle, take the time to wire the pin closed.

clear and straight-grained. Joining lengths involves careful scarfing–at least 8:1, length to plank thickness–and very careful gluing and clamping.

MAST MAINTENANCE

Aluminum spars are comparatively easy to maintain. Most are either hard-anodized or else are painted with a two-part polyurethane. It goes without saying that every fall, spars should be removed from the yacht and thoroughly checked for damage, corrosion and abrasion. For winter storage, they must be supported no less than every six feet and have all shrouds and stays tied off to the spars at the same intervals. Prior to any laying down, coat the spar with a decent paste wax and do not buff. In the spring, this can be removed with cleanser, and the mast properly recoated with wax.

Both anodized and painted spars can be scratched, chipped or roughed-up.Small marks can be protected with wax. Larger scratches and scrapes may need more drastic treatment. Sooner or later, all coatings will weather and wear. A mast can be reanodized, though this is a time-consuming and expensive process. Far better is to paint it.The following also applies to repainting bare aluminum or previously painted spars.

First, the spar must be washed down with solvent to remove all traces of wax and grime. Second, any gouges or dents should be filled with epoxy putty, sanded flush after curing. Third, apply an etching primer! For some reason, many yachtsmen think they can simply paint over a surface which is inherently smooth without first using a primer. Don't! You will be courting disaster, especially with aluminum. Use paints specifically designed for the job. Aluminum primers etch the surface to create a tooth-laden surface to hold the finish coats of paint. Without this step, chances are you will end up with peeling and flaking paint.

Of course, you have removed all fittings from the mast prior to any of this. Painting with two-part polyurethane can be tricky

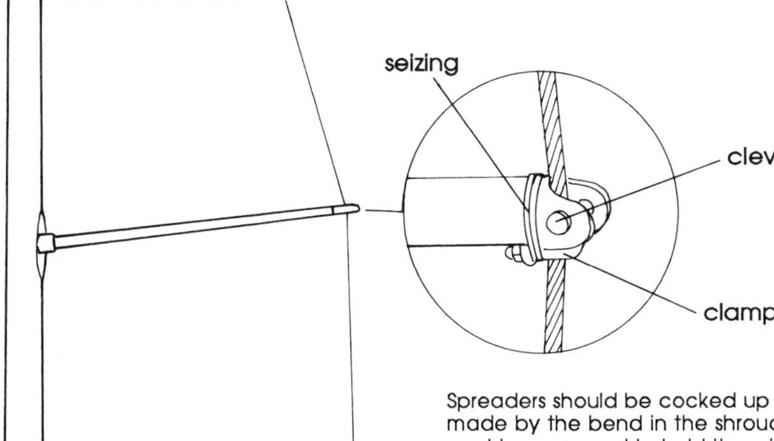

Spreaders should be cocked up to bisect the angle made by the bend in the shroud. The spreader tip must be arranged to hold the wire captive while allowing it movement due to tightening and slacking of the rigging on different tacks. One possibility is a clevis pin used in conjunction with a wire rope clamp as shown.

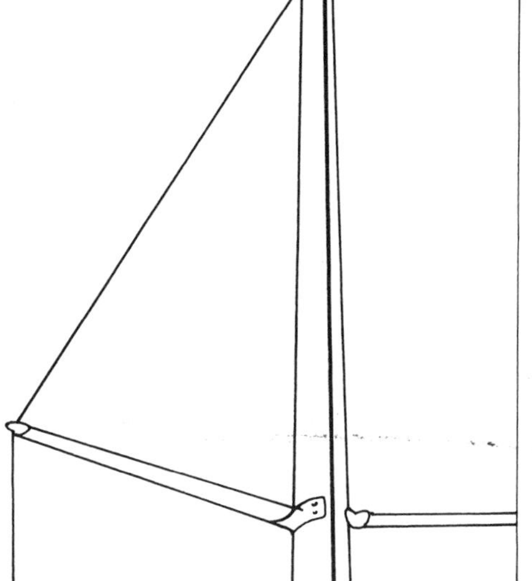

When someone must go up the mast for repair work, make sure that at least two people–and strong ones–are on deck, one to winch the bosun's chair heavenward, the other to tail the halyard, preferably around a strong cleat. Additionally, the person in the chair should be secured to the mast column with a lanyard attached to the chair, going around the mast and coming around to another attachment point on the chair. This will keep the person aloft from swinging away from the mast and possibly coming to harm.

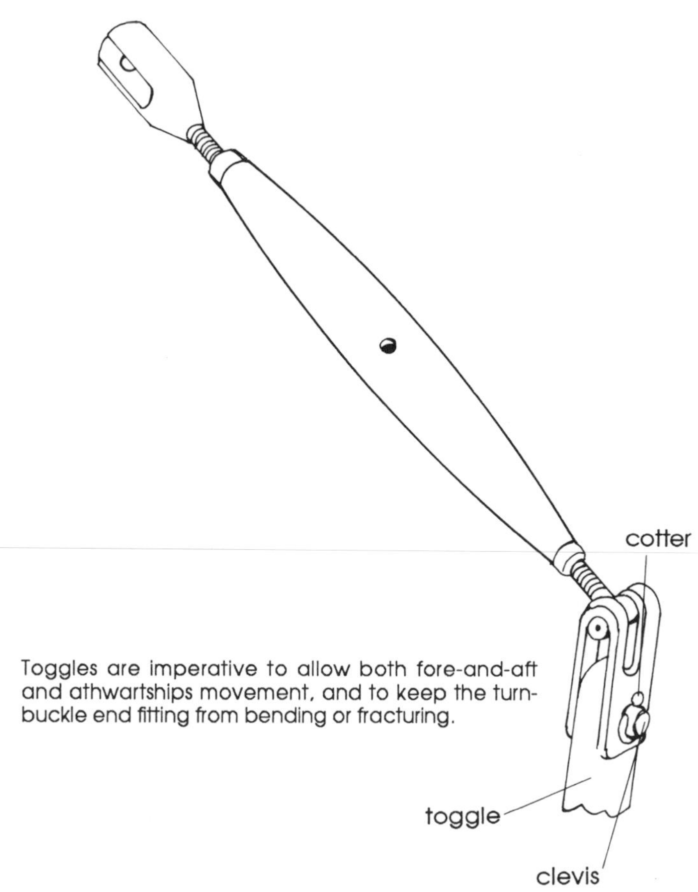

Toggles are imperative to allow both fore-and-aft and athwartships movement, and to keep the turnbuckle end fitting from bending or fracturing.

as it dries very fast and the pot life is fairly short. Follow the manufacturer's instructions to the letter. Paint on a dry, still day, out of the sun, in as dustfree an environment as possible. It's a good idea to make this a two-person job, one applying the paint, the other smoothing it out, following directly behind. Two-part polyurethanes can sag and spot if this procedure is not followed. And removing it to start over will sorely try your patience.

Inspect the heel of the mast. This is an area highly susceptible to galvanic action and corrosion. The mast step should be of epoxy-coated aluminum or if not, carefully insulated from the mast with neoprene gasketing. However, even with gaskets in place, if the mast goes through the deck and the step is in the bilge, beware. Too often, steel mast steps will be installed. The combination of steel and aluminum in a salt water electrolyte will eventually spell disaster. If the steel is totally glassed in place, you are better off, but make sure there are no fractures in the GRP covering of the step.

Inspect the masthead. All fittings should be tight fitting and aligned. Spinnaker broaches and sudden gybes can sometimes knock a masthead fitting out of alignment and this will cause chafe and eventual breakage. Check all masthead sheaves for free motion and lubricate with silicon or Teflon spray. Make sure all electrical connections are tight and secure.

All mast fittings, whether riveted or bolted to mast pads, must be securely attached. Tangs should show no signs of stress or bending and the mast area around them should be free of hairline cracks. If you doubt their integrity, use a special dye to check for cracks and fatigue. Spreaders must be aligned slightly upward, ideally to bisect the angle made by the shrouds passing over them. Many spreader attachment schemes have been used over the years, but anything hinged is suspect and should be replaced with a socket arrangement or some device to hold the spreader securely at the proper angle to the mast.

All moving parts should be lubricated. The oldtime tallow

and lanolin still work, though I prefer silicone or Teflon sprays. They don't gum up, they don't collect grit and dirt, and they stand up to extremes of cold and heat far better than oils or animal fats. All nonmoving metal parts should be cleaned with a mild detergent, dried and coated with a good carnuba paste wax, either a proprietary marine wax or any good automobile wax. Rubbing compounds are generally to be avoided on masts as they will wear away coatings if too much elbow grease is applied.

Occasionally, one will find stainless fittings attached directly to an aluminum mast. Remove the fitting at the soonest possible moment and install a neoprene gasket between the two, for the same reasons–though not as severe–as mentioned above about mast heels. This applies especially to mast-mounted winches made of bronze or stainless steel. Make sure the mounting pad is insulated from the mast and the winch from the pad.

BOOMS

Most of what has been said about masts can be applied to booms, except that the abrasions and chafe a boom undergoes will usually be far greater than anything a mast will suffer. Of particular importance is the gooseneck fitting. Whether it is sliding or fixed, this must be checked as a matter of course. If the boom is fitted with roller reefing, this is even more important. Goosenecks are made of bronze and stainless steel. The same isolation from the metal of the boom is necessary as with any two dissimilar metals. Though the tendency is to use stainless as being stronger than bronze, the fact is that stainless is subject to fatigue fractures and should thus be constantly inspected for any sign of potential failure. Hairline cracks are the most common sign, but stainless fittings have been known to let go with no warning whatsoever. Bronze–in reality, an entire range of alloys–will not sparkle as much but, if the proper aluminum-silicon-bronze is chosen, may offer better service.

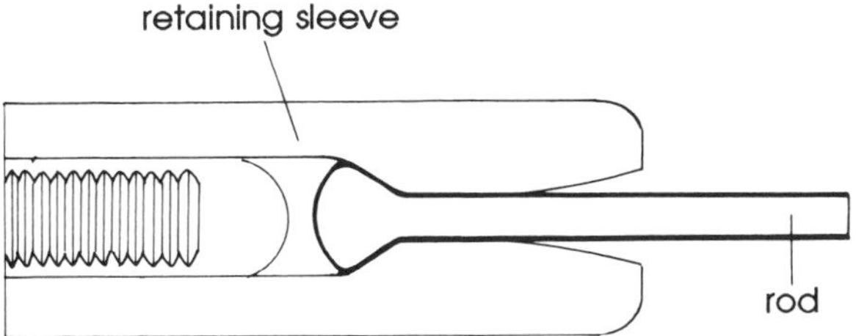

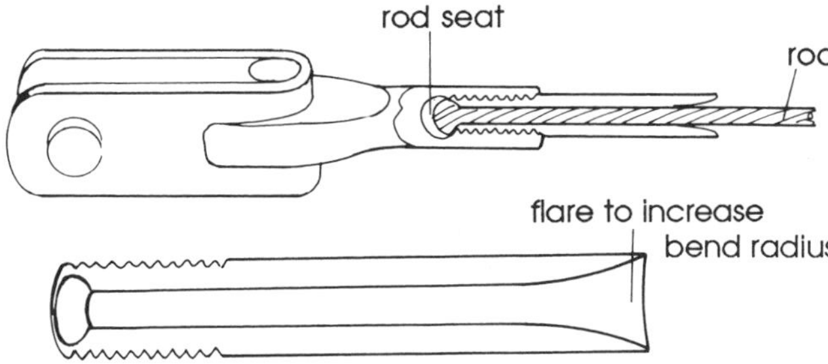

Rod rigging. Make sure no kinks have appeared during storage and that all sockets are uncracked and fair. Rod should be washed regularly and stored in very large coils. Any damaged rod or sockets should be replaced immediately.

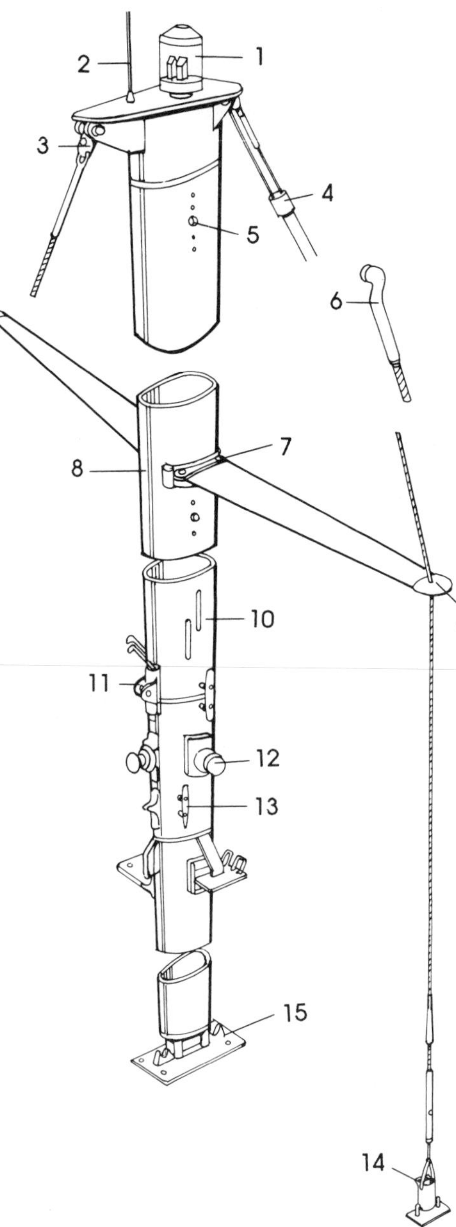

All parts of the mast should be checked out at the beginning of each season. 1. Masthead light working. 2. Aerials and sensors secure and connected. 3. Upper terminals secure and sheaves lubricated. 4. Halyard swivel for roller reefing free. 5. Shroud terminals aligned. 6. Tangs undamaged. 7. Spreaders secure and undamaged. 8. Mast track smooth and secure. 9. Spreader tips chafe-free. 10. Mast column free from corrosion and chafe. 11. Lubricate gooseneck. 12. Make sure all mast hardware is smooth running. 13. Make sure all cleats are securely attached. 14. Check chain plates and turnbuckles; make sure turnbuckles are right-turning. 15. Make sure mast base is secure and aligned and that, if stepped through the deck, mast boot is undamaged.

Booms will often have padeyes, blocks, internal lines, sheaves and more within and without. All these must be inspected for secure attachment and free motion where applicable. The attachment point(s) for the main sheet needs especial attention as great strains will be generated with any pressure of wind. Through-bolting is preferable to riveting if practicable, as the strains are more evenly spread and a pinned or locked nut is less likely to back off than a rivet is to distort and pop. Too often, commercial aluminum rivets are used to hold strain-taking fittings. Either monel or stainless should be used to fasten these in place.

STANDING RIGGING

All standing rigging is either galvanized wire, stainless steel wire or stainless rod. I suspect some will suggest rope rigging and chain, but these are only seen in either ancient or odd boats and need not concern us here. In fact, except amongst stern traditionalists, you will rarely find galvanized wire, despite the fact that it costs far less than stainless and, for a given diameter, is stronger. It needs coating with linseed oil mixed with mineral spirits (the oil to keep rust at bay, the spirits to act as a medium to allow the oil to penetrate) on a regular basis, once a month in the tropics, less often in more northerly locales. For some reason, galvanized wire is more prone to developing hooks or broken strands than stainless. This must be watched for–at least at fitting-out time–as it is a good sign that a particular length of stay or shroud will soon need replacing.

Most yachts today use stainless steel wire fitted with swaged terminals, or else with Sta-Lock or Norseman type terminals. Swaging, the process by which a tubular fitting is compressed around the strands of a wire by enormous pressure, has been around for years. It is reliable and strong when properly done. However, the same pressure that holds things together can occasionally be applied with slight unevenness. When this happens, the fitting can be weakened and can eventually fail.

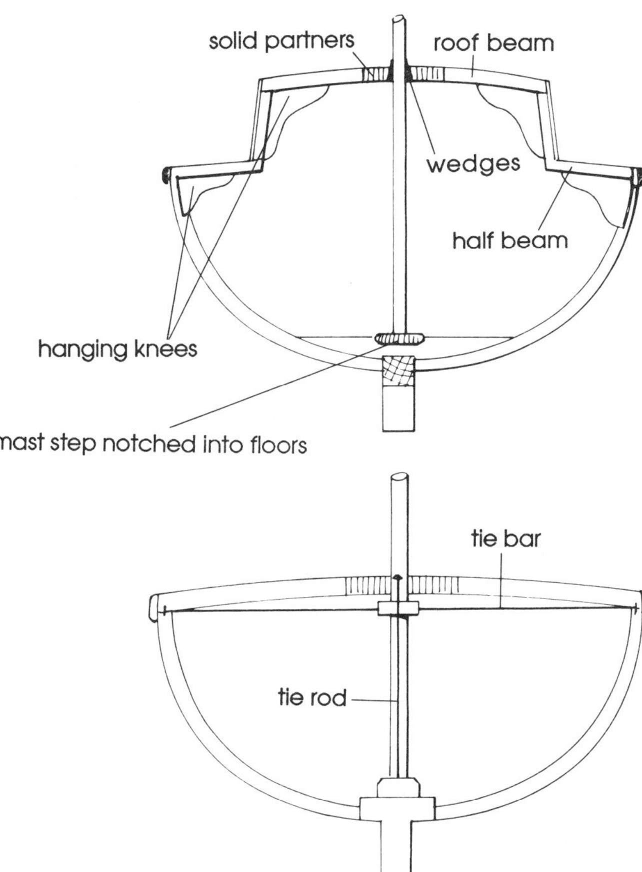

Top picture shows a conventional mast-stepping arrangement. Bottom picture shows tie bars used to transfer the loads to the keel and structural members of the hull.

Sails and ropes must be protected from snagging. Tape all cotters or, less recommended, use plastic turnbuckle boots (this makes regular inspection less likely). Spreader boots can be fitted to spreader tips and create less windage than other protection methods. These can be taped, but be warned the tape will probably unravel in midseason. Better is to bind them in place with marline or use plastic clamps.

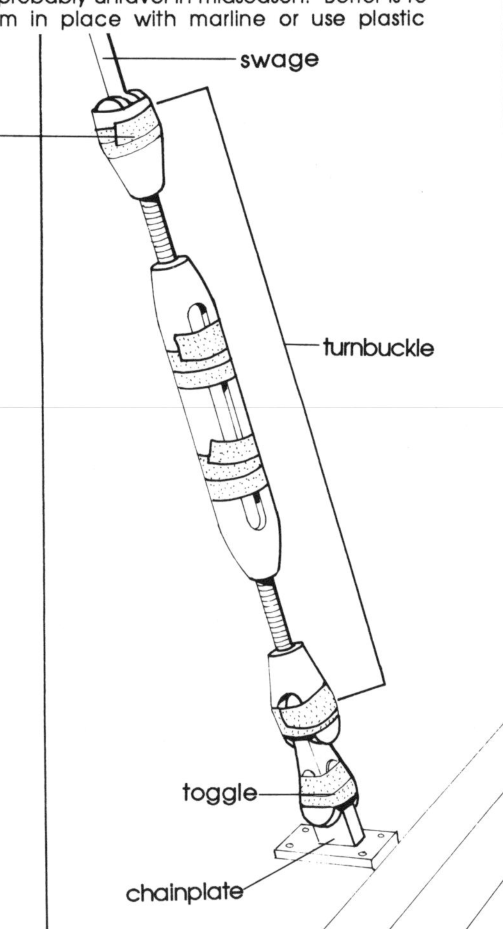

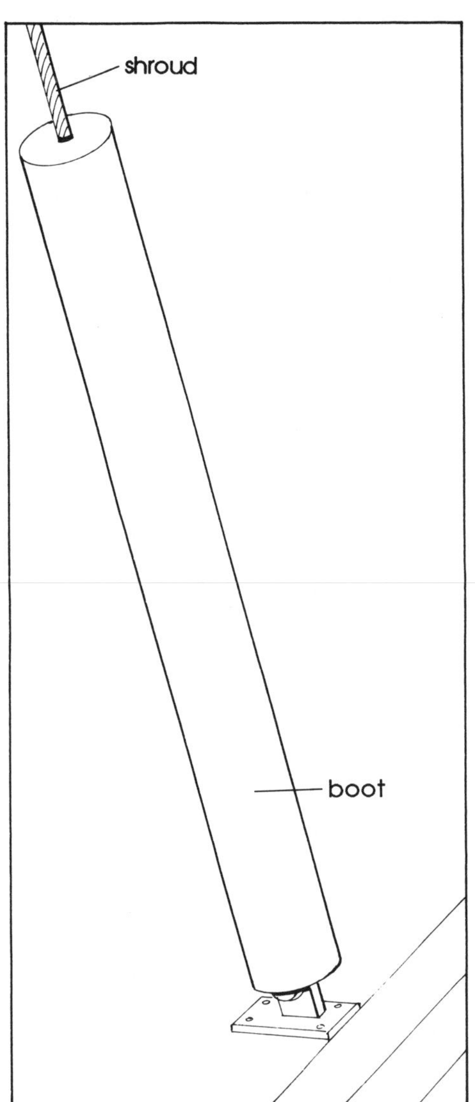

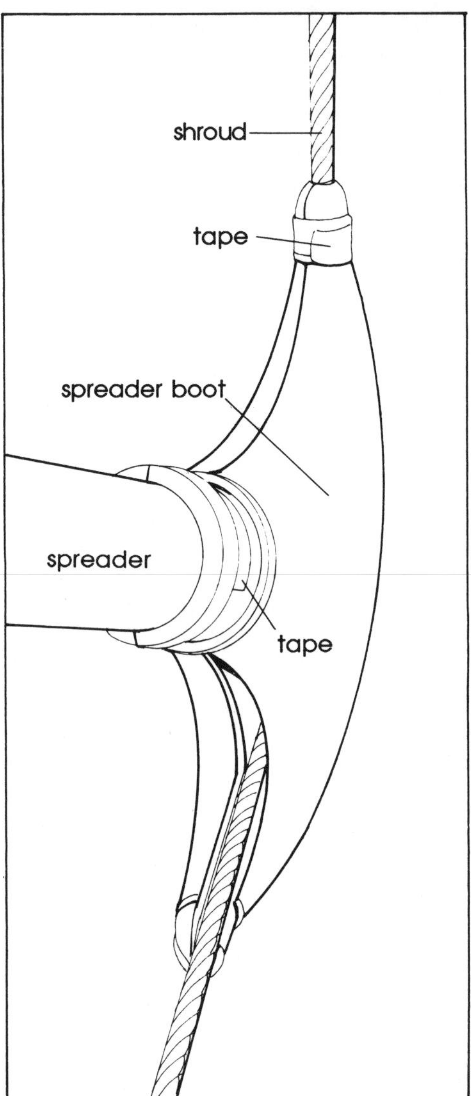

An inbent edge to the terminal or slight cracks near the edge of the swage adjacent to the wire are signs to junk the fitting as soon as possible and refit the entire end.

Sta-Lock type terminals have two advantages: they can be applied on board by anyone with basic hand tools; they can be easily inspected for cracks and stress, and when repair time comes, the only nonreusable part is the internal cone.

Another alternative is Nicro or Talurit press-type fittings. These can be very useful on smaller boats and can be a godsend for emergency repairs. In this method, a sleeve is compressed around a wire loop or thimble, thus creating an eye for the attachment of rigging screws. These work quite well, though there is some chance of distortion if the thimble is not chosen with care or if it is galvanized and the rigging wire is stainless. Also, the wires must be kept as tight as possible around the thimble. Otherwise slippage and bending will undoubtedly occur, leading to failure.

The replacement of any standing rigging is, unless circumstances dictate otherwise, something to be done in the calm of a slip or on the hard, with the yacht hauled. If the replacement is to be undertaken with the mast in place, then halyards can double as jury rigging until the offending stay is replaced. The uppermost end of the stay must be detached, and this is a chore to be carried out from the bosun's chair. In its simplest form, this is a board attached to a bridle which can be hoisted aloft. To be both safe and comfortable, newer types are highly recommended. Those which totally support the user with safety straps in front and soft sides and back are best. In addition, some sort of pouch or tool holders should be provided for.

When using a bosun's chair, it is imperative that some sort of redundant safety factor be built into both method and system. Someone stationed at the winch below, with at least four turns on the winch, should be considered a minimum. An additional backup on deck is a good idea. A bridle should be made up beforehand to allow the person in the chair to tether himself to the

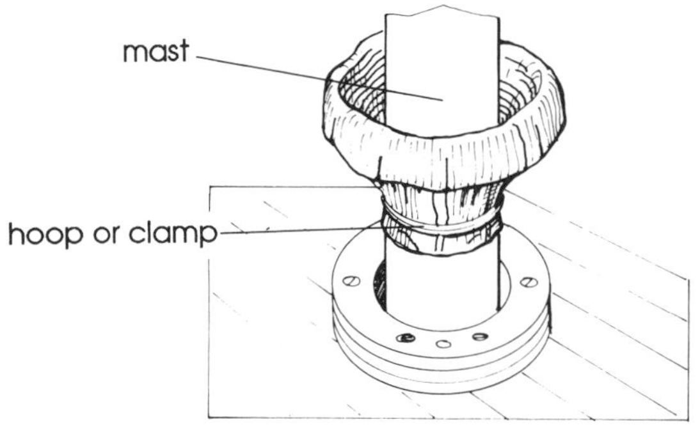

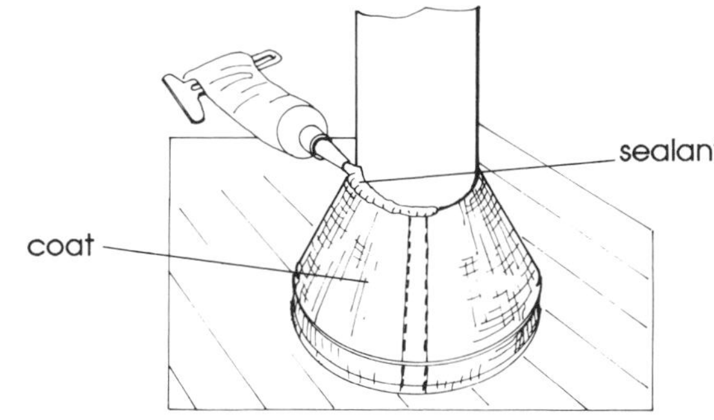

A proper mast coat is necessary with any through-deck mast to keep the cabin dry. Neoprene held in place with a large stainless screw clamp is best, with a second clamp to keep the boot in place at deck level.

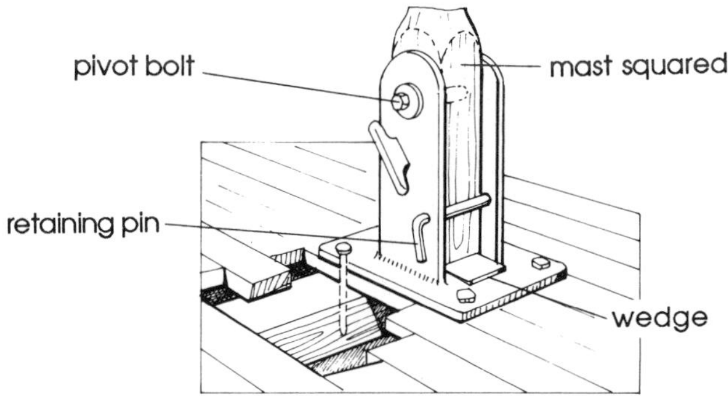

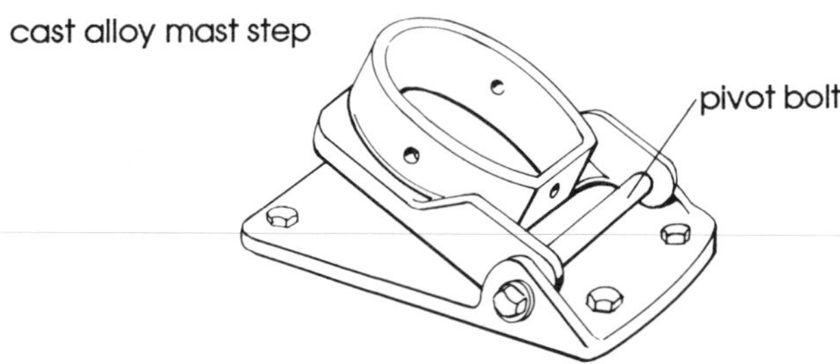

Tabernacles or pivoting mast steps can be most useful in any situation when lowering the mast is likely to be necessary. Supports for the lowered mast can be built into the pulpit or gallows frame.

mast as an added safety feature, especially if there is any movement to the vessel. Swinging into a mast from even a few feet will damage the sailor more than the mast.

FITTINGS

All the various fitments that go into rigging–turnbuckles, blocks, chainplates, tangs, exit boxes, masthead instruments, wiring, reefing arrangements, etc.–are actually the most likely sources of problems. Since each is an individual link in the rigging system, the failure of any one may well spell the demise of the entire rig. From a safety point-of-view, those parts which keep the mast up are the most vital: chainplates, turnbuckles (rigging screws), tangs and spreaders with their attendant clevis pins, split pins and shackles. Each and every part must be mated in strength to the others or havoc will result.

It should go without saying that split pins are replaced every year. Do not use brass. All should be marine stainless and sized to the job. A split pin should only project by a maximum of 3/8 inch from the clevis. The clevis, in turn, should fit snugly through its boring, and project just enough to allow the split pin to be inserted. Any greater extension will allow excess movement, chafe and metal fatigue. This goes for all fittings held together in this manner.

Turnbuckles need to be disassembled and cleaned every year and should be installed so that they are all right-turning. There will never be a question as to how to adjust them on a dark and stormy night. Threads must be greased, either with lanolin, rapeseed oil or Teflon. This last is the cleanest and most effective as a penetrating lubricant. Bent forks or screw shafts ought to be replaced as these are potential danger points. Likewise, closed-bodied turnbuckles, though they may look sleeker, have no place on a yacht. You can never tell how much screw is imbedded and I have seen masts go overboard when one popped apart. Finally, make sure that all clevis pins are secure and pinned. Split pins should not be spread open more than about 15 degrees. Too-long pins that are bent back will hamper quick removal in emergencies. Tape the pins. Turnbuckle boots are to be avoided as they trap moisture and prevent ready inspection.

WIRE

With a few exceptions, masts are held aloft by wire rope or rods in tension. Wire can be of several types, though for pleasure craft use, galvanized steel wire rope is rarely seen except for character craft. Most is stainless steel in various configurations, the pattern dictating its relative flexibility and use: 1x19 wire is usual for standing rigging; 7x19 for running rigging.

All wire is subject to great fatigue through bending and oscillation. Bending or running around sheaves will obviously cause friction wear. Repeated bending will cause stress fatigue. Oscillation fatigue is caused by the harmonic vibrations set up in all taut rigging wire by the combined action of wind and wave. Since the hourly rate can be in the thousands, there is no reliable method to gauge when the wire may be near the point of collapse. For most of us this is fairly academic. For anyone undertaking an ocean passage, however, with days at sea nonstop, oscillation fatigue can be a major concern. Wire rope should be thoroughly checked before setting out on any major voyage and any suspect lengths replaced.

Corrosion is another problem often ignored on the supposition that stainless steel cannot corrode. All ferrous metals can and will break down with time and exposure. Corrosion is most often found at terminal fittings and in the inner core of wire rope. Careful inspection and thorough biseasonal washing can keep it at bay, but once the core is corroded or a terminal fitting is highly stained, best replace the offending part of the stay.

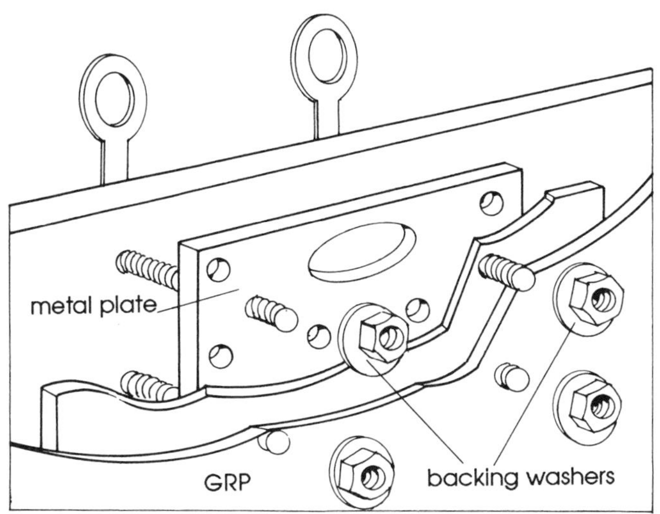

A sound mechanical reinforcement for chain plates, bolting through hull and a GRP backing plate with a metal plate in between assures that the bolts will not pull through the softer material.

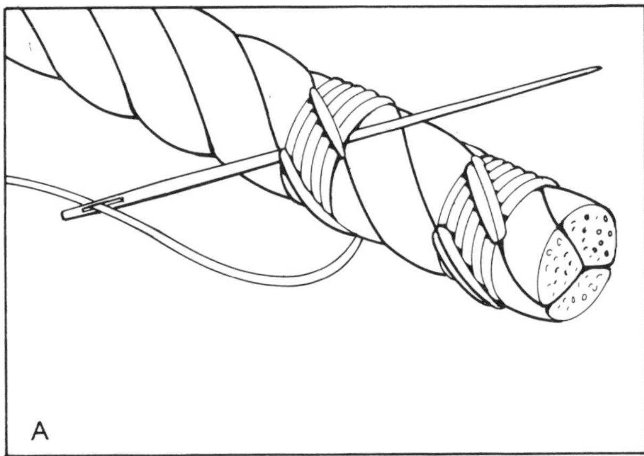

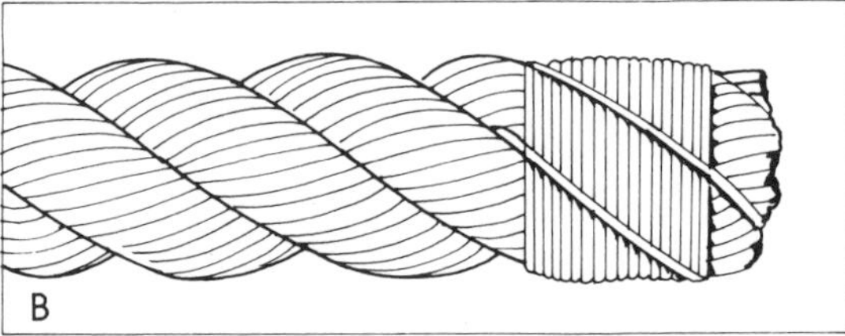

A. A needle whipping is the best way to finish off the ends of halyards and sheets.
B. When whipping ends, make sure the lock stitches go with the lay of the rope.

ROPE

Whether power or sail, you cannot go to sea without endless coils of rope. This has always been so, and there is not likely to be any change in the near future. All ropes today are relatively carefree and long-lasting compared to the hemp, manila and cotton of yesteryear. However, they still need care to function at full strength.

Dacron/terylene is the standard for sheets and halyards; on larger yachts, halyards may be of stainless steel wire with dacron tails. Dacron is highly durable and comes in any number of variants: cored, twisted, braided, reinforced with kevlar and other synthetics. All will stretch to some degree, but the reinforced types much less than everyday, twisted 3-strand line.

Nylon, used for anchor rodes and dock lines, should stretch and although great claims have been made for braided types, these will usually have less stretch than twisted lines. They are also easier on the hands, but cost close to double.

And then there's wire rope, which is rope, after all. Most is made of stainless steel, though you can still obtain plough steel wire rope. This must be treated with a mixture of linseed oil and mineral spirits to preserve it and keep it from rusting.

Dacron and nylon and, for that matter, stainless steel should be kept clean, as salt-free as possible and coiled when not being used. All lines have natural coil depending on how they were woven–either right- or left-handed. A rope will naturally coil one way or the other. Do not coil a line around your hand and elbow in the hope of getting a neater coil. This will invariably kink the coil. Let the coil fall naturally from one hand.

Synthetic ropes should be washed prior to winter storage in lukewarm water and a mild detergent–dishwashing liquid is perfect–then rinsed throughly and hung in loose coils to dry.

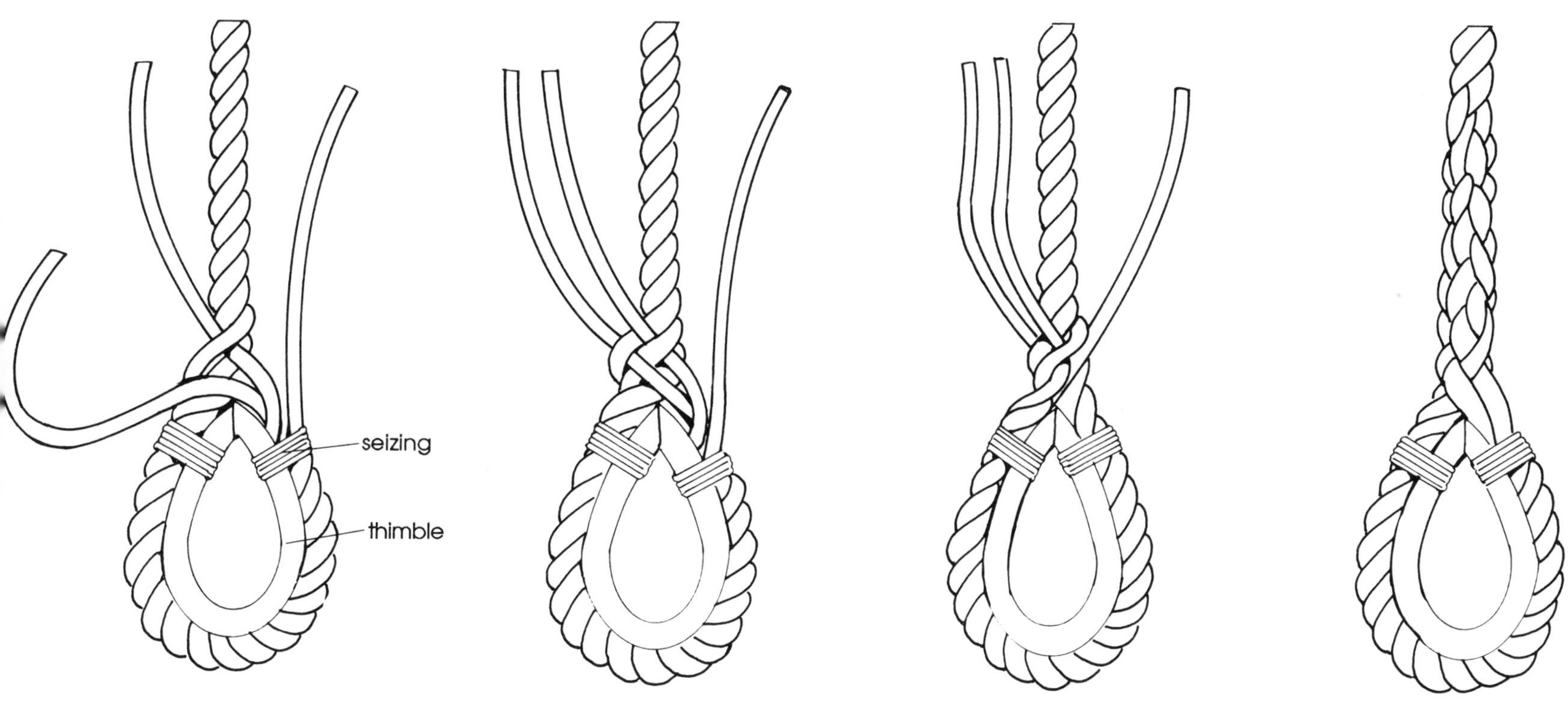

The best way to end rope halyards is to splice in a hard eye–plastic or metal–as this sequence shows.

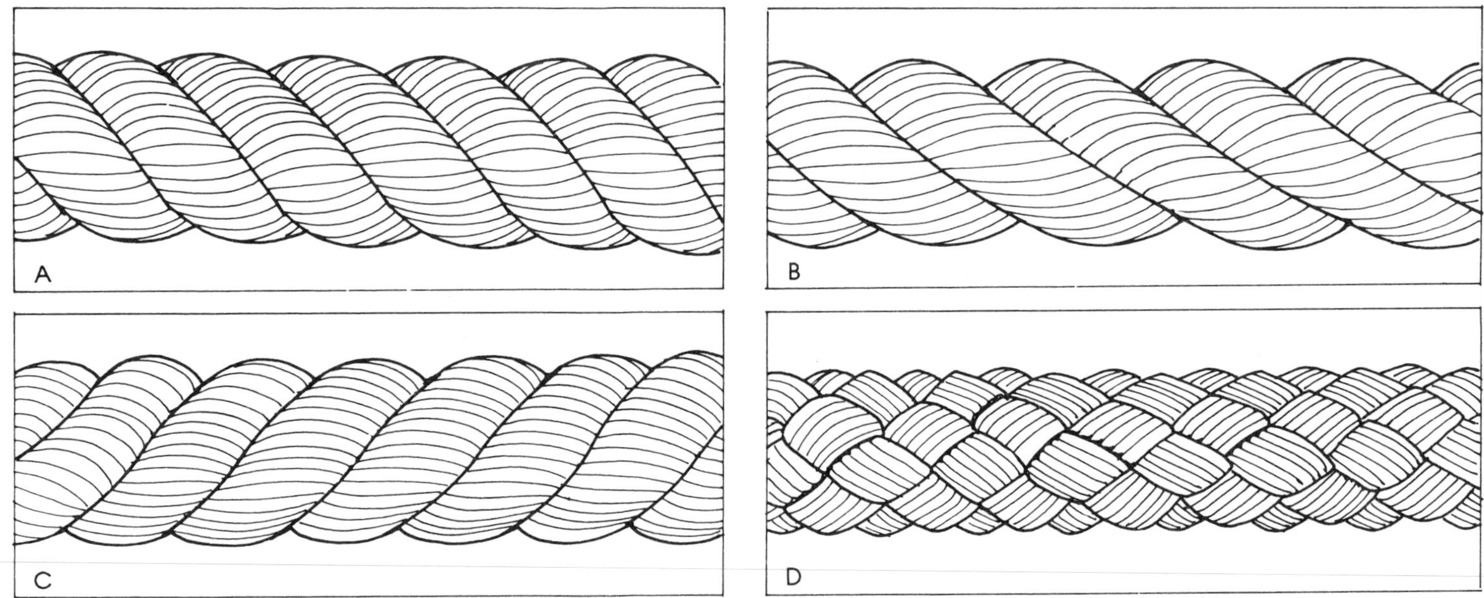

Four common rope types: A. Hard lay, right-hand rope. B. Soft lay, right-hand rope. C. Left-hand lay. D. Braided.

Before attempting splicing, tape the rope at a length back from the end so that only the amount needed for the splice will unlay.

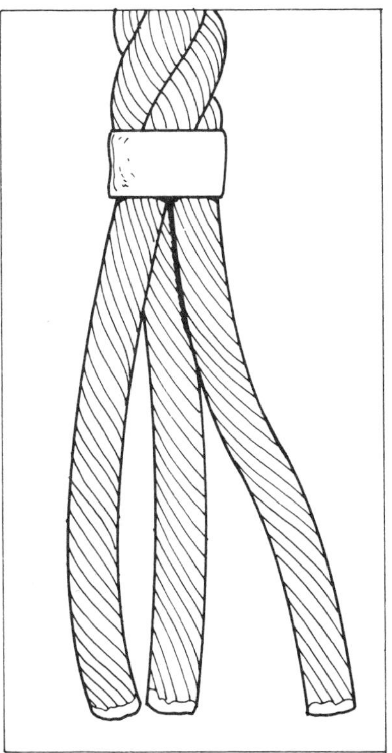

Different types of braid and plaited line as compared to three-strand.

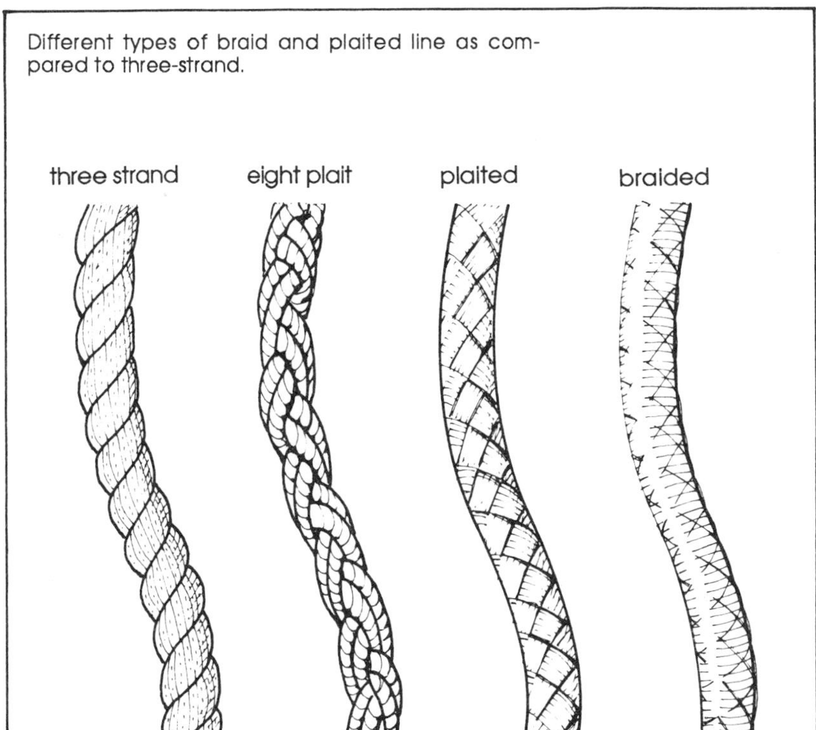

7
PLUMBING

Surrounded by water, a yacht must be able to both keep unwanted water out and remove any water or other liquids which may collect within. To do this effectively, plumbing systems must be installed and maintained with care. Too often, a new yacht will be delivered with lots of shiny fixtures and little or no safety margin. Some of the *don'ts* aboard:

1. single-clamped hoses
2. gate valves below the waterline
3. hoses not properly clamped along their length
4. pumps not readily accessible
5. pumps of inadequate capacity
6. no strum boxes on bilge pump hose ends
7. head hoses not looped above waterline
8. engine water coolant entry not equipped with strainers
9. tanks without access plates
10. tanks without baffles
11. tanks not properly cleated or strapped down
12. hoses of unsuitable materials
13. seacocks not lubricated or tight-fitting
14. cockpit drains too small or incorrectly led

This is by no means a complete list, but it does cover some of the major points to look over when running an inspection. Each and every one of these conditions can cause major problems and many can cause foundering. The brave little Dutch boy may have closed a dike with his finger, but you must have more effective means to keep your vessel watertight.

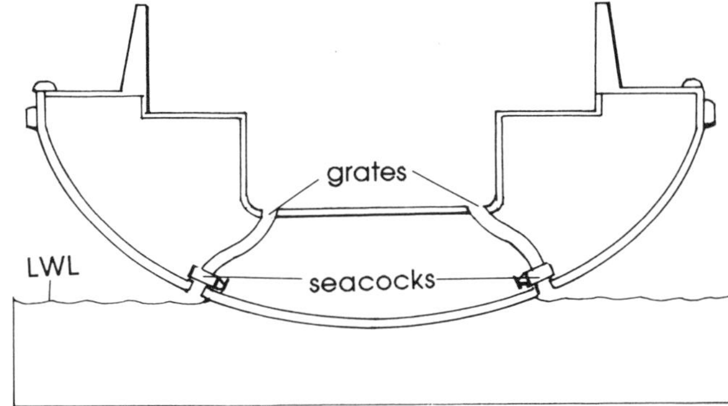

Cockpit drains should be fitted with seacocks and be arranged to drain the well at all angles of heel. Most are too small: 2-inch diameter each should be considered the bare minimum for any boat over 25 feet.

BILGE PUMPS: MANUAL

The first and foremost pump on board should be the bilge

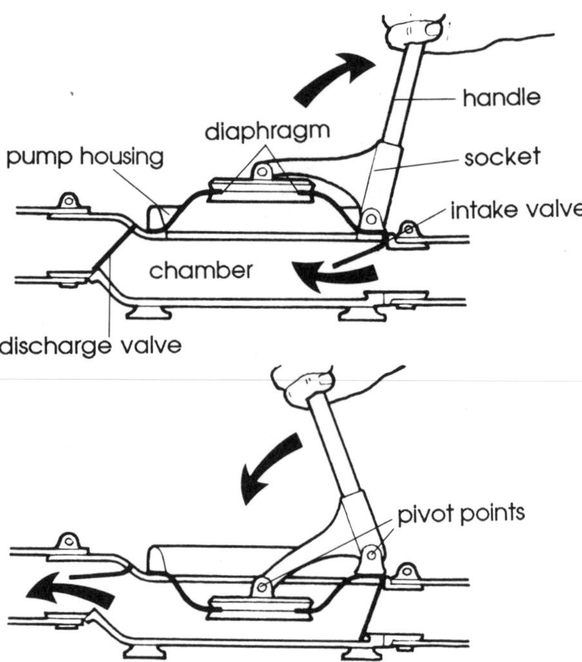

Diaphragm bilge pump works by creating a vacuum, sucking water in through a check valve. Compression stroke forces it out through another check valve. Any leaks in the diaphragm membrane indicate immediate replacement.

pump. After all, this is your first line of defense against the ingress of water. On far too many yachts the bilge pump is installed *inside* a cockpit locker. Take it out! Assuming you are in a seaway, with green water coming over the rail, the last thing you want is to add to the bilge water through the top of a locker. Either mount it in the cockpit with the intake hose running through the cockpit side in a watertight gland, or mount it with a through-deck accessory kit.The handle–removable in this case–should be drilled and tied off to a deck fitting with stout cord. To keep it from banging about, fit a plastic or stainless clip to the cockpit adjacent to the pump fitting.

Most modern bilge pumps–manual ones, that is–are of the diaphragm type. About the only problem you are likely to have is that the diaphragm or the flap valves will wear out or become brittle. These can usually be replaced with a screwdriver and fifteen minutes of your time. It is a good idea to check these regularly. Should there be any sign of wear, splitting or cracking, replace them immediately. Most are made of a fairly resilient and strong synthetic rubber compound. Still, everything wears out, and when you need a bilge pump, you really need it!

Older pumps, of the Navy or plunger type, usually have a leather sealing flap which will need seasonal replacement. Leather, no matter how heavily you lubricate it with lanolin or grease, will shrink, crack and lose its shape. Another old standby is the rotary or semi-rotary pump. If you have ever had to work one for more than five minutes, you will know that it ought to be junked at the first possible moment.

Assuming you have installed the proper pump–and a double-action, large capacity job should be considered the minimum–hoses have to be connected and an outlet provided. Under no circumstances should you be tempted to use rigid hoses for water supplies. The old days of iron and copper pipe are well behind us. Metal piping is prone to fatigue, cracking, split fittings and chemical and electrolytic deterioration. Plastic, of an approved type for drinking water, or neoprene for waste lines, are the longest lasting, easiest to install and least prone to failure. Hose for bilge pump applications should be re-inforced and with a smooth *interior*. The outside can look like a moonscape, but bumps and ridges inside will lead to built-up dirt, clogging and a permanent home for algae and bacteria.

All bilge pumps must be regularly inspected. Make sure glands are tight, clamps snug and diaphragms without pin-holes or splits. Flapper valves should be pliant and free moving. Make sure the handle is secured–if it is removable–where it will not be lost when needed.

BILGE PUMPS: ELECTRIC

Any boat that hangs on a mooring, or is left unattended for any length of time, should be equipped with one or more electric bilge pumps with automatic water-level switches. In installing one or more, make sure sufficient limber holes exist for water to pass from any area of the bilge to the sump in which the pump is located. Also, the discharge line should be looped and should exit as high up as practicable, especially in sailing vessels where heeling is likely to cause backflow.

Switches should be of the simple float type and all wiring must be as heavily insulated as possible, with each pump grounded. Failure to do so can result in electrolysis as well as current leaks and shorts. Remember, these pumps are going to spend most of their time in the wet, and nothing will do in electrics faster than seawater.

Backflow is usually caused when the inlet hose is not looped high enough above the waterline. The elbow must be at least a foot above the waterline *when the boat is heeled.* Make sure the elbow is vented, otherwise the pump may end up sucking air. Until recently, most elbows were made of rough bronze castings and weed, muck and other impedimenta were liable to build up. Newer models are plastic and don't usually suffer from this problem. At the beginning of the season, check to see

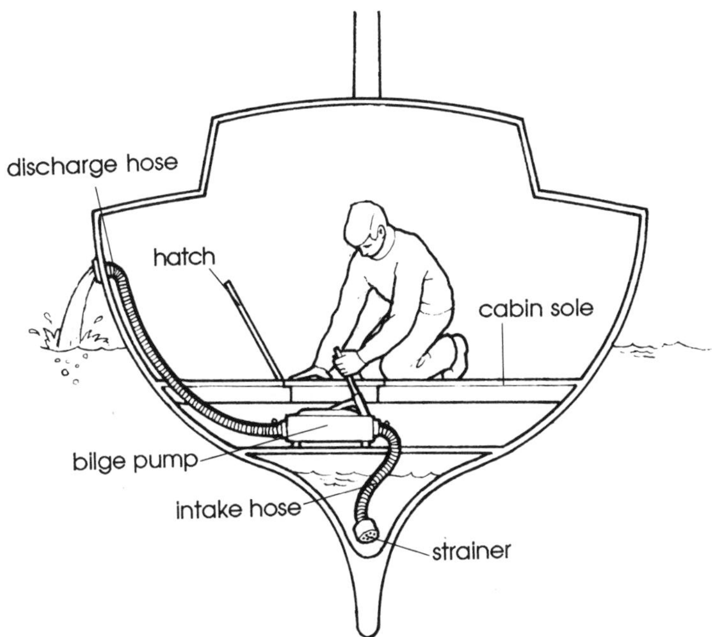

Mount the bilge pump above the bilges, but in a position that makes working it as easy and untiring as possible. Intake hose should be as low as possible, discharge hose must be mounted above the waterline, taking heeling into account.

all hoses run clear. If a hose is wire-reinforced but ridged inside, replace with a smooth-bore length.

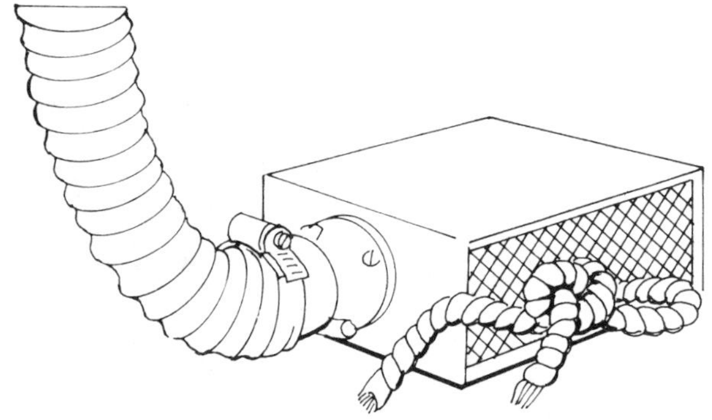

All bilge pump intake hoses must be fitted with strainers called strum boxes. These can be made of bronze or plastic and should be bolted in place in a part of the bilge that can be reached for clearing debris that might clog the box.

HOSES

Speaking of hoses, so many types exist and so many are unsuited for marine applications, that some care is needed in selecting the proper one for installation or replacement of plumbing. As mentioned above, all hoses aboard should be smooth-bore types. Wire-reinforced hoses are often made with the interior following the contours of the wire. These are an absolute no-no! They will collect debris in a bilge pump installation, house bacteria in any installation and are subject to cracks at the wire to plastic bond, especially in bends.

For water passage, clear plastic vinyl hoses are usually adequate, though not for discharge lines. These should be reinforced neoprene, that is, neoprene inside and outside with a wire mesh surround between them. Waste lines can be large-diameter, smooth-bore reinforced neoprene. The one hose type to be avoided, despite Lloyd's rules, is copper tubing. This was standard aboard most all good boats of 20 or more years ago. However, copper is subject to stress fatigue, and can develop cracks. This can mean a tainted water supply or loss of potables. In a gas or oil line, it can mean fire and/or explosion. Vibration is the enemy of rigid metal lines and vibration–from machinery, sea motion and rigging oscillation–is unavoidable at sea.

All hoses need to be clamped securely. This means stainless steel screw clamps, with stainless screws. Make sure the screw is not steel by using a magnet. If a steel screw corrodes (and it surely will) the clamp will sooner or later let go and the hose will slip off its pipe end. Use double clamps at *all* hose junctures. If the pipe end or fitting is too short, replace it rather than rely on a single clamp. This all sounds like an awfully complex procedure for a simple hose, but redundancy is the only thing to prevent disaster in anything which carries liquids, volatile or not.

All hoses should be inspected annually and any that show signs of hardening or cracking replaced immediately. Clamps should be tightened in the spring before launching and any suspect ones replaced. Be especially careful in inspecting fuel lines, making sure they are supported at frequent intervals. Also make sure that all hoses are isolated from potential chafe. Support clamps should be the padded type and all bends and turns should be padded and smoothed.

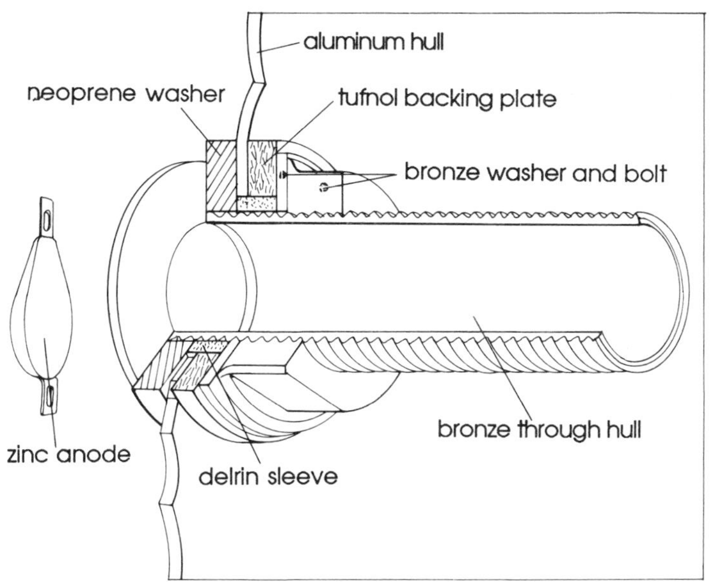

Through-hull fittings for aluminum hulls must be carefully installed to avoid galvanic and electrolytic actions. Make sure that all dissiimilar metals are isolated with neutral gasketing and heavy bedding. Fit an anode to the hull near each through hull. To avoid problems altogether, use plastic fittings, if possible.

THROUGH HULLS AND SEACOCKS

Wherever a hose exits the hull–drains, pump outlets, exhaust–a positive-action seacock needs to be fitted. Not gate valves, not stop-cocks, nothing but an approved-type seacock will suffice. Certainly, internal valves can be gate types. Tank to faucet lines and sink controls can be gate valves. That's it! The only positive, nonleaking valve to prevent the ingress of the sea is a seacock.

Traditionally made of bronze in several patterns, some are now made of modern thermoplastics, and these have so far proved to be reliable. They are especially recommended for metal-hulled vessels. They should not be used for hot water–exhaust cooling water, for example–since their coefficient of expansion is great compared to bronze and they might, just might, distort. However, there is no reason to avoid them for most applications, especially as they are cheaper and lighter than metal valves.

All seacocks must be inspected yearly, preferably with the vessel out of the water. The valve seat must be inspected for corrosion and scratches or gouges and, if any are found, it should be buffed with emery or crocus cloth until a smooth fit is obtained. All moving parts should be lubricated with waterproof grease and the whole tested for smooth movement and no binding. Make sure the handle is clearly marked for open and closed positions. Sometimes you will need to use penetrating oil to get a long-unused seacock to move. Spray on the penetrant

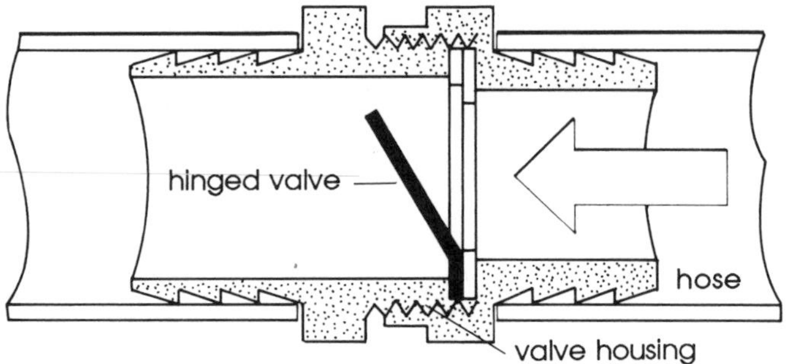

Check valves should be fitted to all water pumps. These not only keep water from backflowing, but also keep the pump always primed.

thoroughly and leave it for a couple of hours, then use a rubber mallet to gently dislodge the valve.

If you are installing new equipment, try to lead all outlet hoses to one common area of the bilge, all inlet hoses to another. In this way, the majority of through hulls and seacocks will be in one or two easily accessible areas and emergencies can be more quickly isolated and hopefully overcome.

Through hulls are made of bronze (gunmetal) or plastic. They should be both bedded and bolted to the hull. Those that lie flush with the surface of the hull are preferred, but this will involve routing in a wooden hull and some careful counter-cutting in GRP. All through hulls, since they are milled flat, will need some sort of shimming block made to follow the hull contours. Sealant alone will not be enough to make a leak-free bond. Through-bolting is to be preferred, but some through hulls have only a captive flange on the outside, not a full plate with bolt holes. These will have a screw pipe inside the hull and a large nut to hold them in place. A good idea is to install a second nut as a locking mechanism. Also, coat the threads with a light layer of Lock-Tight or silicone to keep the nuts from backing off.

Some of these through hulls will have barbs on the pipe to hold the hose in place. Do not rely on these alone. Still double clamp. Anything else is to court potential disaster.

Since the pump will activate whenever the float switch reaches a certain minimum level, be sure your batteries are kept charged and that there is a hefty capacity, at least 100 amp-hours, available for the pumps. A very intelligent solution, especially if the boat is on a mooring, is to invest in a solar charger. Although most automatic pumps will not use a vast amount of electricity, they are motors, and the drain over a period of time will be severe, even from slight ingress, like a leaking stuffing box.

HEADS

The toilet is one of those absolute necessities which invariably malfunction in a gale, heeled 35 degrees. As a rule, the larger the yacht, the more complex the head installation. Obviously, there are many different types installed in boats of all sorts, but there a few characteristics common to all.

All marine toilets need to be mounted securely, preferably with the lip of the bowl as far above the waterline as possible. All need inlet and outlet hoses, with accompanying seacocks and double-clamping. The inlet through hull must be located afore the outlet, this last to assure that clean water is pumped to flush out the bowl.

The problem with heads is when they leak or smell or suck back water when they shouldn't. Leaks can be squelched by renewing gaskets and making sure that leather valves in older heads are flexible. If they seem borderline, rubbing with copious dollops of lanolin may cause them to swell and seat securely. But most modern heads contain seals and pump diaphragms of neoprene or nitrile rubber, synthetic compounds that can withstand much, but when they go all you can do is replace them. It's a good idea to keep a spares kit for the head aboard in any case.

Smells, and not the natural smells of human excretions but the peculiar smells developed by marine toilets, are usually due to a bacterial buildup in the hoses or in the water passages built into the bowl. The regular addition of ordinary household bleach, say two or three ounces every week during the season, should prevent this. Also, if the fresh-water inlet hose is of clear plastic, the light that might strike it can cause the multiplication of bacteria. Use black or gray opaque hoses. Head compartments should be well-ventilated, of course, and an extractor fan, either electric-powered off the mains or solar-powered, is recommended. Finally, make sure all surfaces and compartments and lockers in the head are kept scrupulously clean and disinfected.

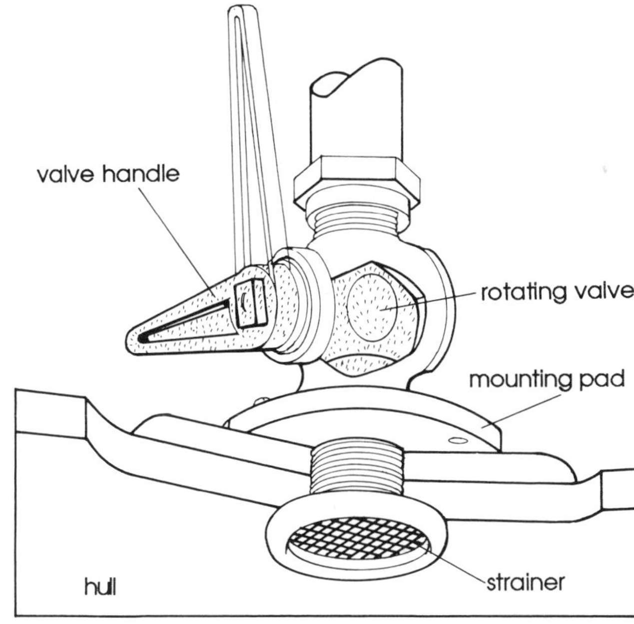

Seacocks are absolute necessities on all underwater through hulls. They must be through-bolted and bedded with backing blocks. Once a year they should be disassembled, lubricated, ground down if necessary and open and closed positions clearly marked with waterproof ink or paint.

The head, or marine toilet, is the bane of the yachtsman's existence. Pump forces water through into the bowl, flushing the waste through discharge line overboard or into a holding tank. Both intake and discharge lines should be fitted with seacocks and the intake located afore the discharge hull fitting. Also, make sure the line for overboard discharge is looped well above the waterline and fitted with an air release valve to prevent possible backflow. Service the entire system once a year, and add a small amount of bleach to the bowl once a week, pumping vigorously to avoid bacterial growth and algae.

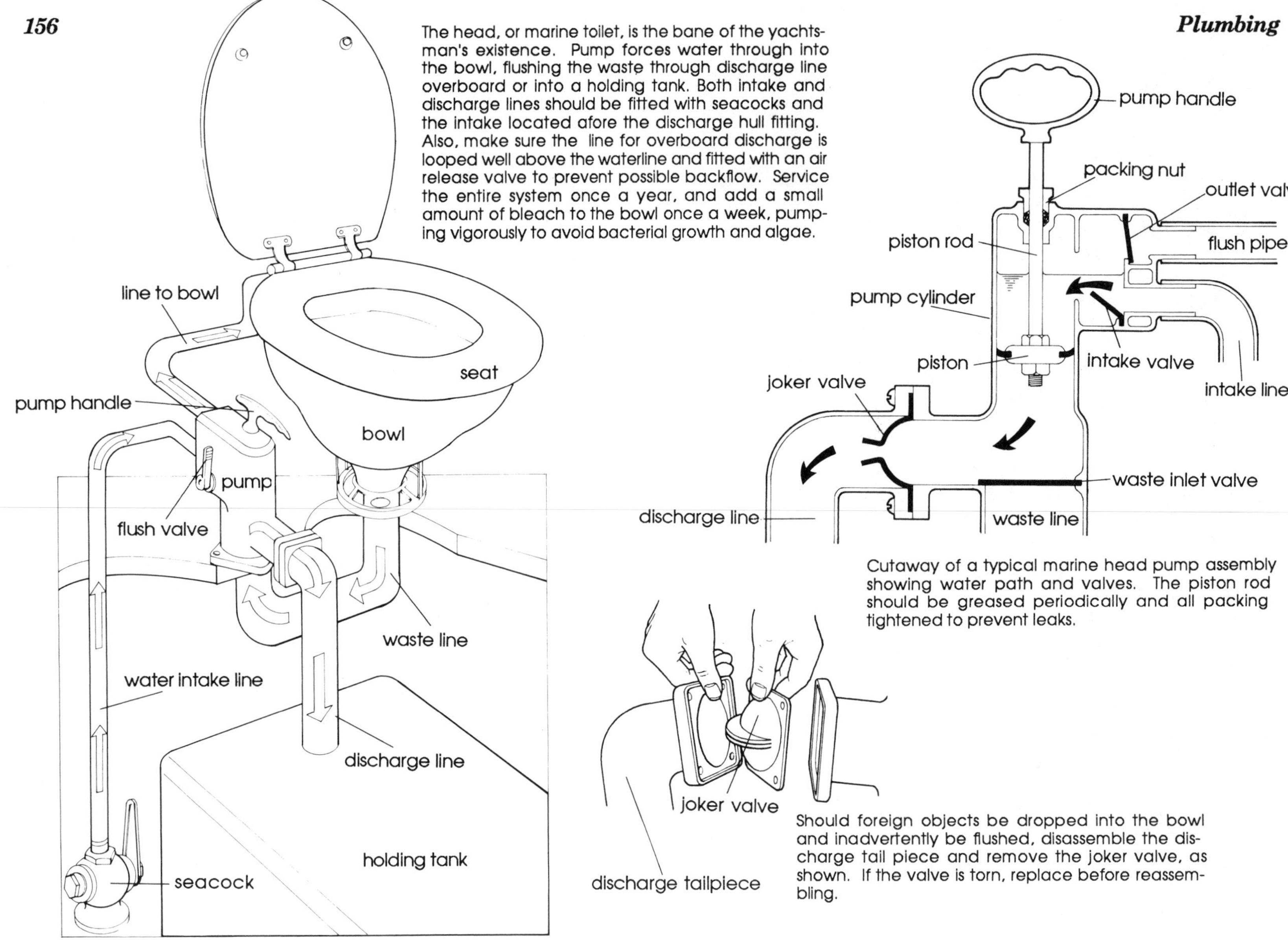

Cutaway of a typical marine head pump assembly showing water path and valves. The piston rod should be greased periodically and all packing tightened to prevent leaks.

Should foreign objects be dropped into the bowl and inadvertently be flushed, disassemble the discharge tail piece and remove the joker valve, as shown. If the valve is torn, replace before reassembling.

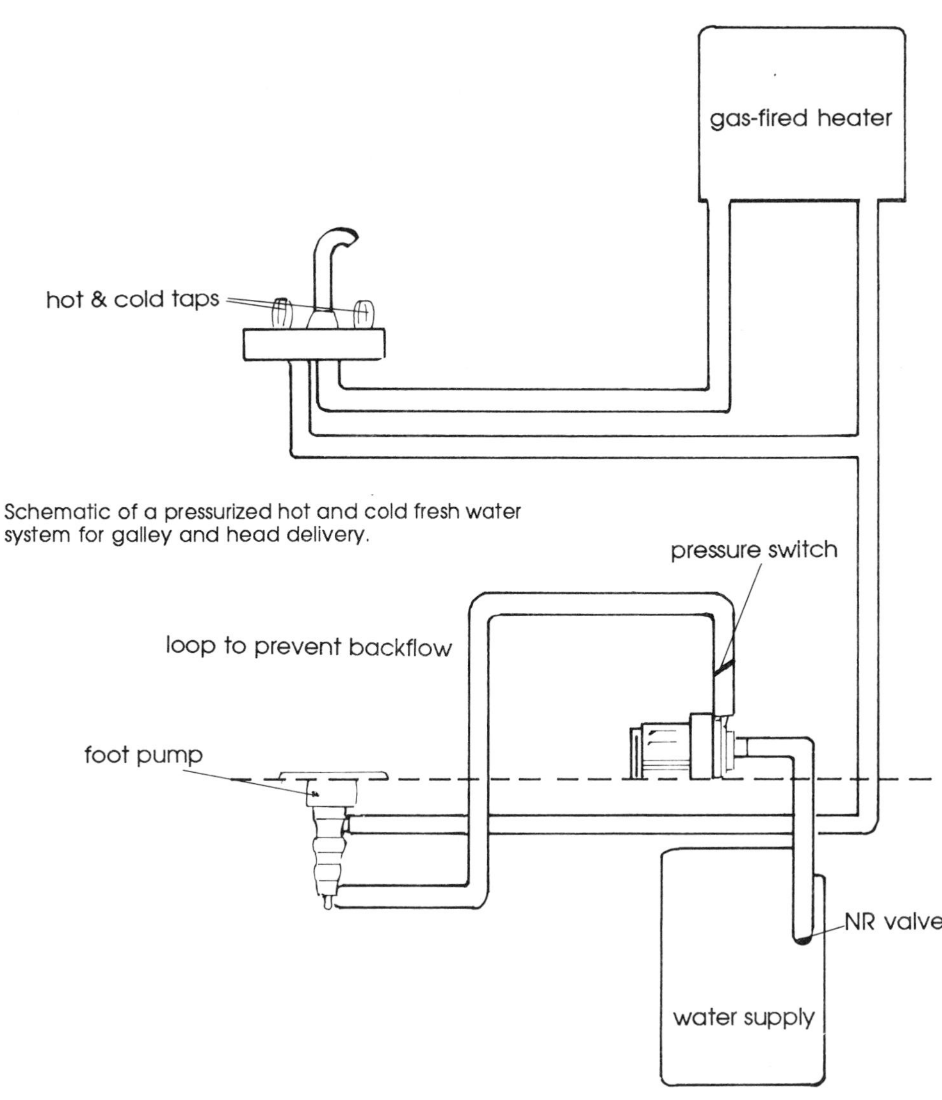

Schematic of a pressurized hot and cold fresh water system for galley and head delivery.

8
ELECTRICS AND ELECTRONICS

The modern yacht has become a collection of complex systems, no more so than in electrical apparatus and circuitry. In the old days, one battery for both engine starting and lighting, a small fuse board, and cabin and navigation lights made up the total electrical system. No more! What with refrigeration, electronic navigation aids, multiple batteries, fans, stoves, heaters and communications equipment, demands are getting greater and greater. Complexity is also becoming more of a headache, and with it the increased chances of failure somewhere in the very innards of the whole kit.

Despite the ever-increasing complexities, a yacht's electrical system is conceptually quite simple. The engine powers an alternator that charges the batteries. The batteries supply direct current to various electrical fixtures. Assuming the alternator is working, the batteries are kept topped up, and the distribution system of circuits and wires all work at optimum levels, all is well. Should one link in the chain weaken, you will be powerless. Generators, any heating or motorized appliances and such add untold complications, but we will cover those later.

BATTERIES

The first area of concern is the battery. If the time has come to replace one or more, use marine batteries. Automobile and utility batteries cannot hold the charge needed to start a marine diesel or to receive repeated deep charges. Cost should be a secondary consideration as a top-flight marine battery will last through five to seven years of heavy use. The batteries must be installed in a leakproof box, preferably above the waterline–

A hydrometer is used to check battery acid concentrations; a figure of 1.26 indicates a strong acid level and a full charge. When the lead electrolytes are not covered by acid, the solution must be topped-up, using distilled water. Do not overfill as corrosive acid will be spill out. Blot immediately and neutralize with baking soda in solution. In hot weather, check the battery solution level at least once a week.

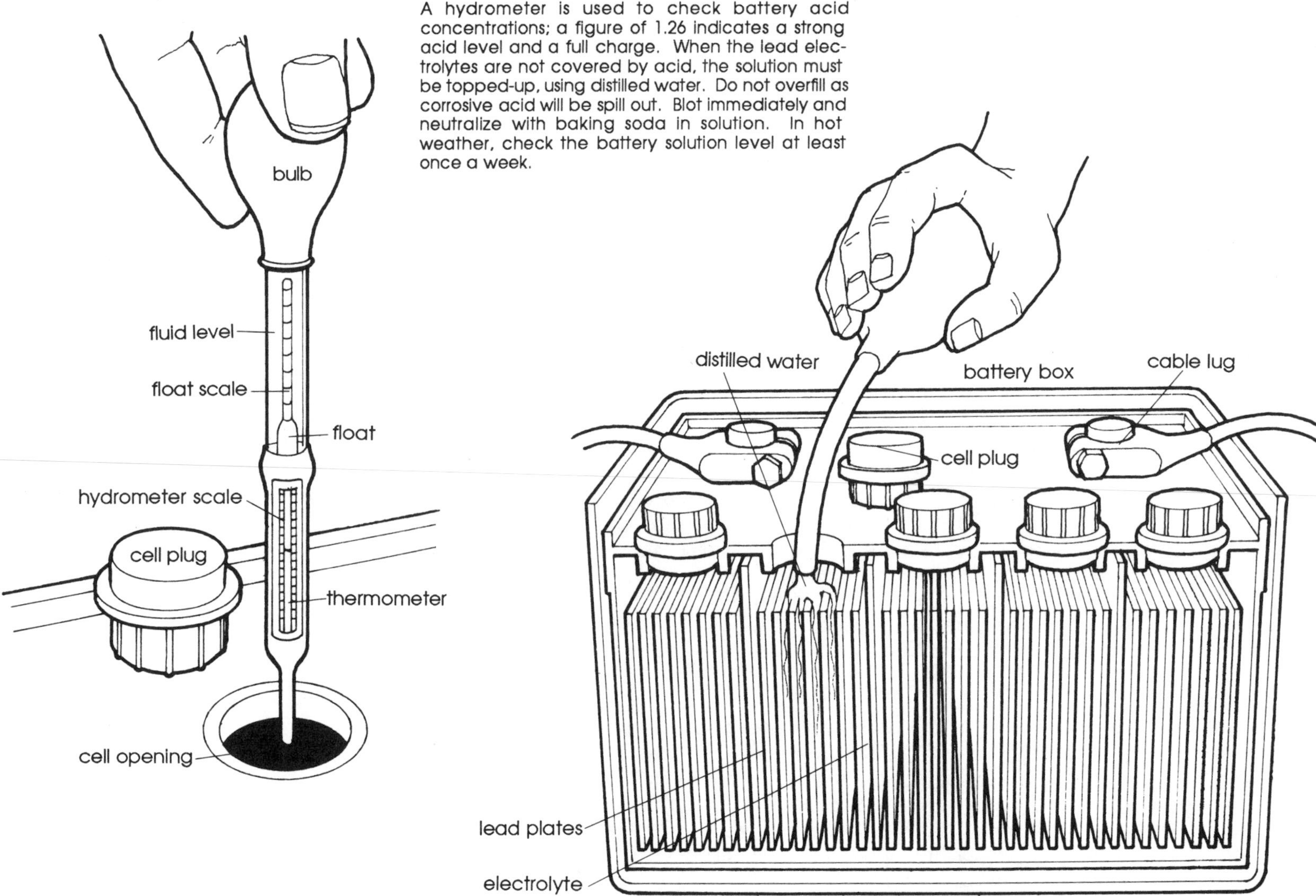

batteries can leak hydrogen gas and, in the bilges, this is an invitation to disaster. This box must be vented overboard from both high and low positions within the box. With the newer, sealed batteries, this is not quite as insistent a requirement, but some provision to keep the battery isolated from the engine and living compartments is absolutely necessary. In addition, the batteries must be securely strapped down to through-bolted strong points.

Electrolyte levels ought to be checked weekly, more often in very hot climates. Any wet-cell battery will lose its charge faster if the plates are exposed. Likewise, batteries should be charged weekly, preferably by running the engine for a couple of hours. If you keep the boat dockside, you can use an automatic trickle charger, but be forewarned that this can short out or, even worse, the trip switch that shuts it off can malfunction. The net result will be destroyed batteries.

In fact all single-and multiple-battery installations should be equipped with a selector/shut-off switch properly rated to the *total* ampere load of the batteries. These switches should be mounted near the companionway, protected from spray and used with regularity, as a matter of course. They will save you drained batteries and ease charging.

WIRING

Many a boat, especially purchased used, has been tinkered with. Everyone seems to think he can add whatever electrical bits and pieces he wants without any problems. What you get is a circuit board which no housing inspector would ever pass, accompanied by a jumble of mismatched, missized wires totally unidentified. My only advice is to rip out the entire mess and start over.

Boat wiring is subject to far more severe conditions than house wiring. First off, it is located in a hostile environment; humidity and water are anathema to any electrical circuit. Not only is there a constant threat of current leaks, but also the

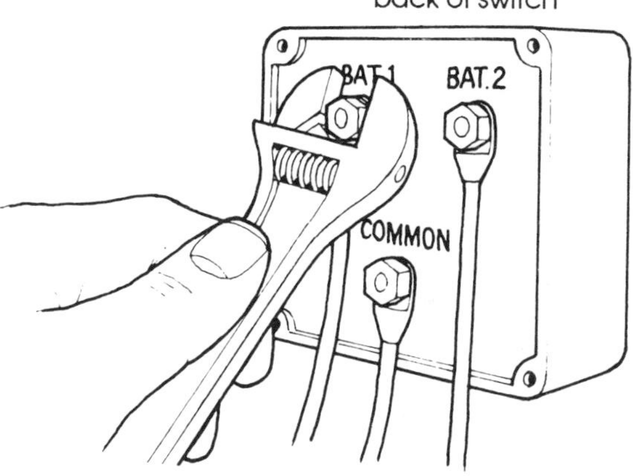

A dual battery switch is connected to the positive terminals of both batteries and a common cable leads to the engine starter. Make sure this switch is turned off when you are away from the boat or when you are making any electrical connections to avoid battery drain and damage.

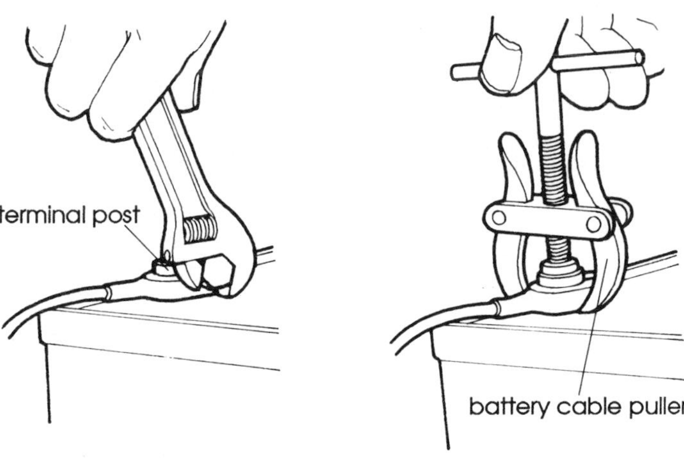

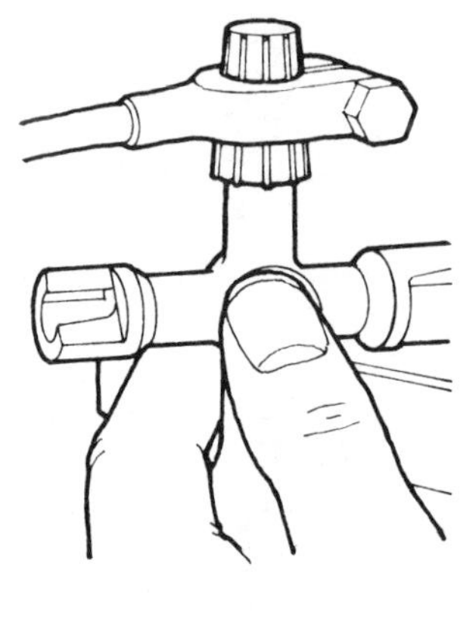

Battery terminals must be kept clean and free of corrosion. Check these connections every couple of months and clean as necessary. When reattached, coat with petroleum jelly as indicated in the sequence shown.

chance of corrosion of terminals and wires themselves. Now all electrical systems lose current through leaks and distant wire runs. However, boat systems are more prone to current loss than most others, and guarding against this is worth as much as 20 amp-hours of battery storage in one evening's use!

One of the best and simplest ways of avoiding this is to keep wiring out of the bilges. This should be self-evident, but a surprising number of builders who should know better persist in running major circuits through the dark, dank reaches beneath the floorboards. Any wires in the bilge should be rerouted as soon as possible.

Likewise, in the best of all possible worlds, all wiring should be run through plastic conduit with junction boxes located at easily accessed points throughout the ship. These must be openable with gasketed, watertight covers and also made of plastic. Thus, if a wire needs to be run or replaced, it's an easy matter to open boxes at both ends and draw the new wire through while making any connections in the box itself. If installing conduit for the first time, insert a running line to aid in drawing the wires through, especially in long runs. Likewise, make all bends or directional changes in runs at a box, not midway along a wire.

Choosing wire is something to consider with care. The longer the run, the greater the current loss and you shall have to employ heavier-gauge wire in the installation. Use multistrand, wire with which there is much less chance of a complete loss of current and less brittleness than in single-strand wire. Insulation should be neoprene or a similar rubber compound which is waterproof and of very low conductivity.

All ends should be twisted and attached using crimped connectors. However, each connection should be soldered as well as crimped to lessen the chance of breaking the circuit and to add to a more positive current path. Once the connectors are in place and male and female terminals are joined, cover the parts with a thin film of petroleum jelly. Do not use electrical

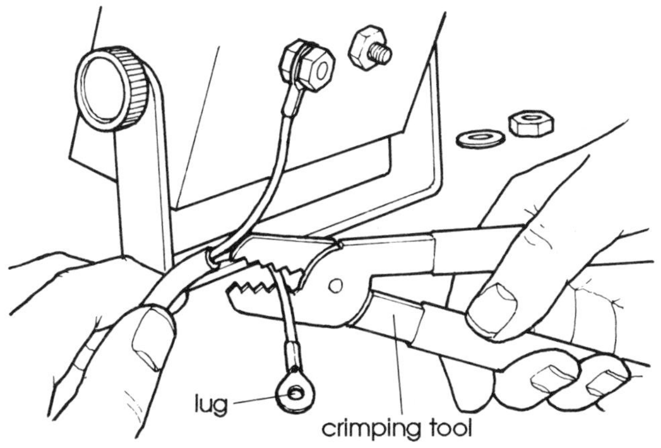

When connecting wires to terminals, use lug connectors crimped to the wire. This will assure better contact as well as less chance of individual strands breaking and causing a current loss. After making the final connection, coat the terminal lightly with petroleum jelly to keep it waterproof.

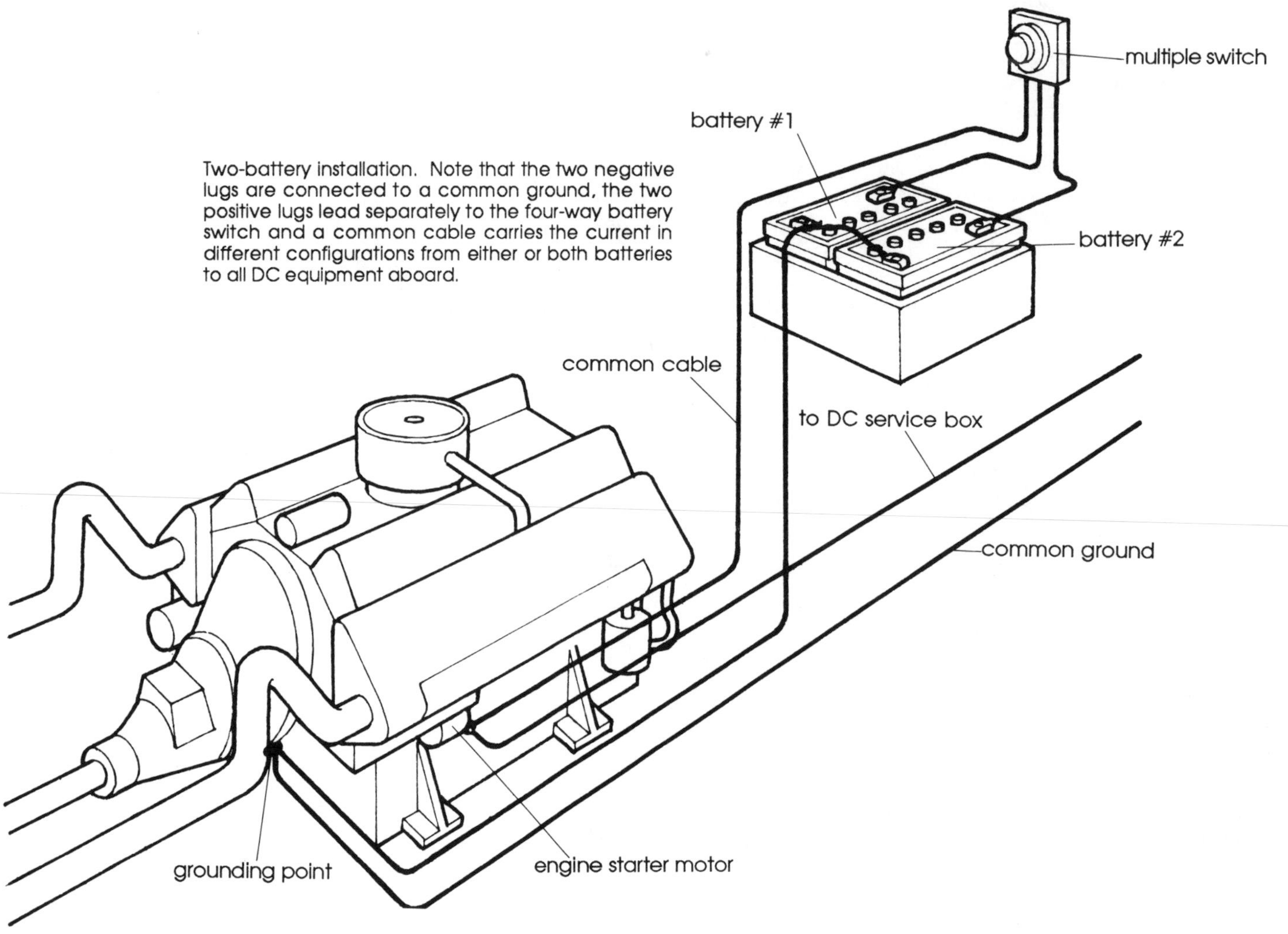

Two-battery installation. Note that the two negative lugs are connected to a common ground, the two positive lugs lead separately to the four-way battery switch and a common cable carries the current in different configurations from either or both batteries to all DC equipment aboard.

tape to cover these connections. It will invariably trap moisture and lead to corrosion and failure.

Leads from the batteries to the circuit-breaker board or the fuse board must be sized to the maximum possible load. To calculate this, add up the total wattage ratings of all lights and appliances and divide by the voltage of the system. For example:

Lights	6 @ 25 watts=150 watts
Navigation lights	4 @ 10 watts= 40 watts
Electronics	20 watts= 20 watts
Misc. equipment	72 watts= 72 watts
Total possible load	=282 watts

12-volt system: 282 divided by 12=23.5 amperes
24-volt system: 282 divided by 24=11.75 amperes

Thus the wiring should be heavy enough to carry this load should everything be turned on simultaneously, allowing for surges in heating and motorized equipment. Generally speaking, the leads from batteries to switchboard should be on a par with heavy-duty battery booster cables (8 gauge or lower in thickness). Despite formulas for working out resistance and length, a good rule-of-thumb is to choose cable sizes up by one gauge size for each yard of running length of any electrical cable.

GROUNDING

All electrical current leaks to some degree, and all circuits have both positive and negative pathways. The negative, as in an automobile, must be grounded to prevent surges and damage to the circuitry. The best way to do this depends on your hull. A steel or aluminum hull is totally a ground plate, a wood or GRP hull needs some piece of metal in contact with the water to take the ground. The best method, if you have an external keel, is to secure the ground wire to a keelbolt head.

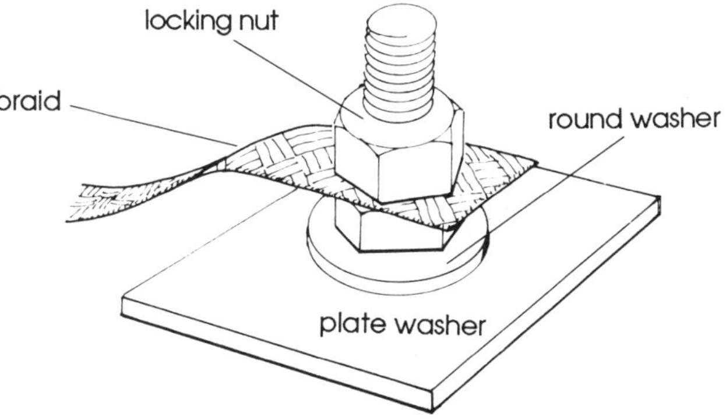

Where the boat is fitted with an external keel, bonding can be accomplished by leading a ground wire–better yet, braid–to one of the keel bolts as illustrated. All ground wires should be led to a common point first, then to the bolt.

Should the keel be encapsulated in GRP, an external plate made for the purpose can be installed on the hull near the centerline, possibly just before the turn of the bilge. This is important as any rolling in heavy weather, particularly thunderstorms, will otherwise expose the plate and leave the vessel ungrounded.

Grounding wire should be at least #8 braided copper or a copper tube of ca. 1/2 inch outside diameter, flattened at the ends, drilled and bolted to the grounding plate and the maststep. Needless to say, all stays and shrouds and any other large bulk of metal–the engine, prop shaft, electronics, etc.–should be attached to this plate by braided wire of #12 size for smaller items, #8 or 10 for larger.

Since a lightning strike is always possible, this system will help negate some of the possible damage. However, lightning is very unpredictable and cases are on record where even fully "protected" vessels have been burned and holed. Nevertheless, if you sail in areas where lightning storms are prevalent, grounding is an absolute must. If you are cruising into such an area for the first time, some measure of protection is possible by keeping a length of chain aboard to be shackled to a shroud. Make sure it is long enough to keep well below the waterline when the boat might be heeled. If your boat is fitted with inboard shrouds, trail the chain from the backstay. If it is a power vessel, your best bet is to rig a lightning rod from the mast to the engine grounding plate or the propeller shaft.

ELECTRONICS

Depth sounders, radars, loran, radios and other electronic devices, mostly for navigation and communication, but some–autopilots, navigation interfaces, etc.–used for active piloting, have become extremely sophisticated pieces of equipment. What used to be mechanical and highly power consumptive has become, through the use of integrated circuitry and computer chips, far more reliable and accurate and less of a power drain. However, the days when an amateur could fiddle about with a screwdriver and soldering iron are likewise gone for good.

With a few exceptions, most electronic equipment should be installed and serviced by professionals. The sophistication is beyond most of us and the cost of repairing DIY mistakes may be as much as a replacement. Some modern equipment is designed to use plug-in circuit boards, so that when something goes wrong, replacement doesn't involve more than snap out/snap in. However, very few sailors have access to the electronic diagnostic gear necessary to decide *which* of several boards has malfunctioned.

In choosing electronics for your yacht you obviously considered whether to power the devices from the ship's system or by self-contained battery power. For certain instruments such as depth sounders and radio direction finders, self-contained batteries have much to recommend them. Should the main power supply go by the board, at least you will have the basics of navigation at hand. Logs, as well, might be battery-powered or backed up with a trailing log of mechanical pattern.

However, larger electronics or those which demand especially high power–transmitters, radar–must be connected to the main battery system of the boat. On smaller auxiliaries or power boats, the norm is now to install two batteries, one for engine starting, one for ship's systems, the two segregated by means of a battery selector switch which can isolate either battery, connect them in series or charge both or one. For any yacht equipped with a serious navigation compartment–RDF, echo sounder, log, wind instruments, loran, radar, VHF, SSB, course computers, etc.–a *third* battery specifically for electronics is highly recommended. Motor activated navigational items like autopilots and radar scanners should be isolated to the ship's systems battery, as the draw and current surges can adversely effect some electronic systems.

All electronics should be installed in a relatively dry area with protection from driven spray or rain coming from any quarter. Cables should be routed to keep them out of the bilge and all should terminate in a junction box devoted specifically to electronics, preferably near the navigation area. Certain electronic devices–satellite navigation systems, loran, radar–need grounding and this should be done by a trained electronics engineer, since interference can drastically limit the range and utility of these devices.

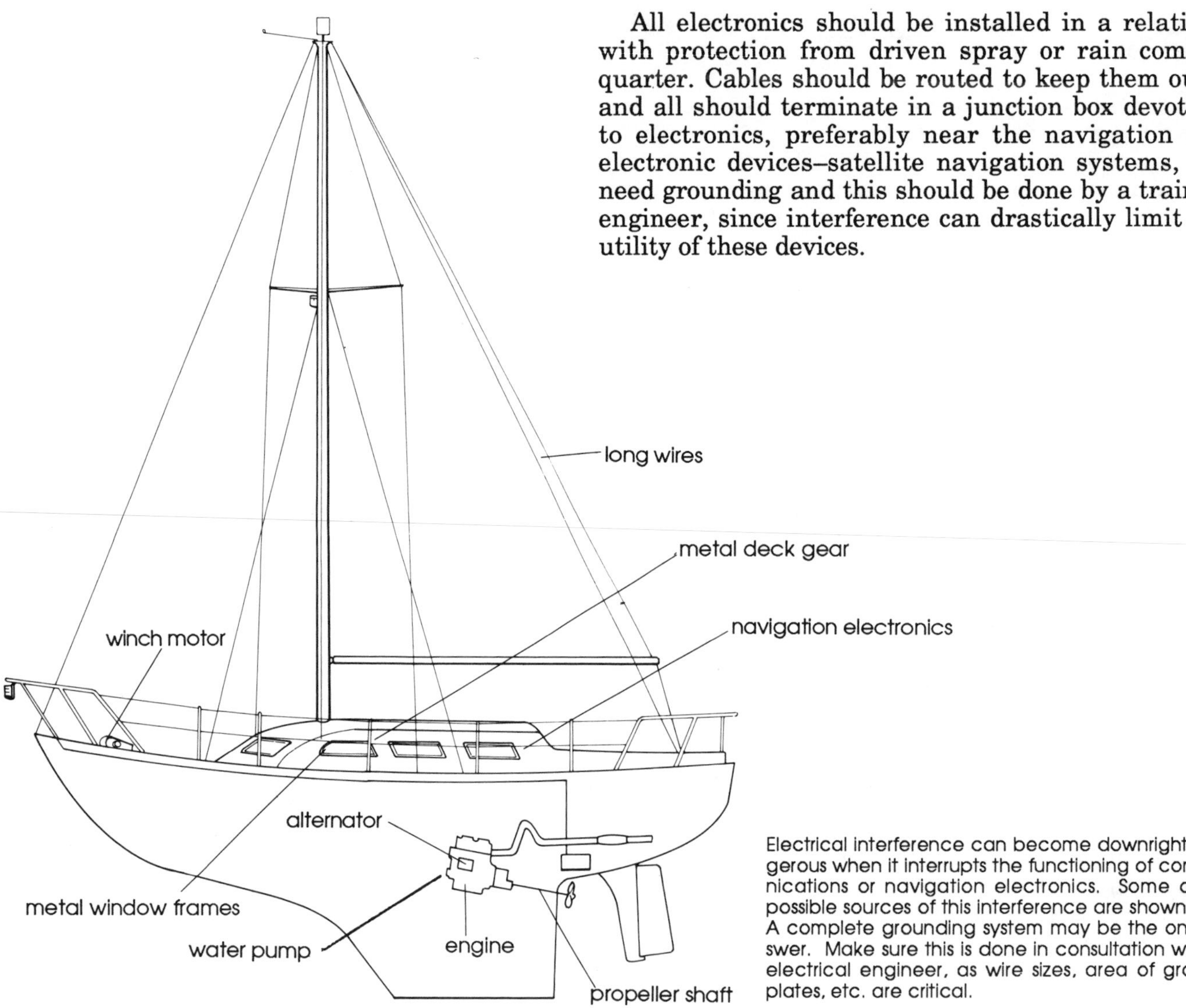

Electrical interference can become downright dangerous when it interrupts the functioning of communications or navigation electronics. Some of the possible sources of this interference are shown here. A complete grounding system may be the only answer. Make sure this is done in consultation with an electrical engineer, as wire sizes, area of ground plates, etc. are critical.

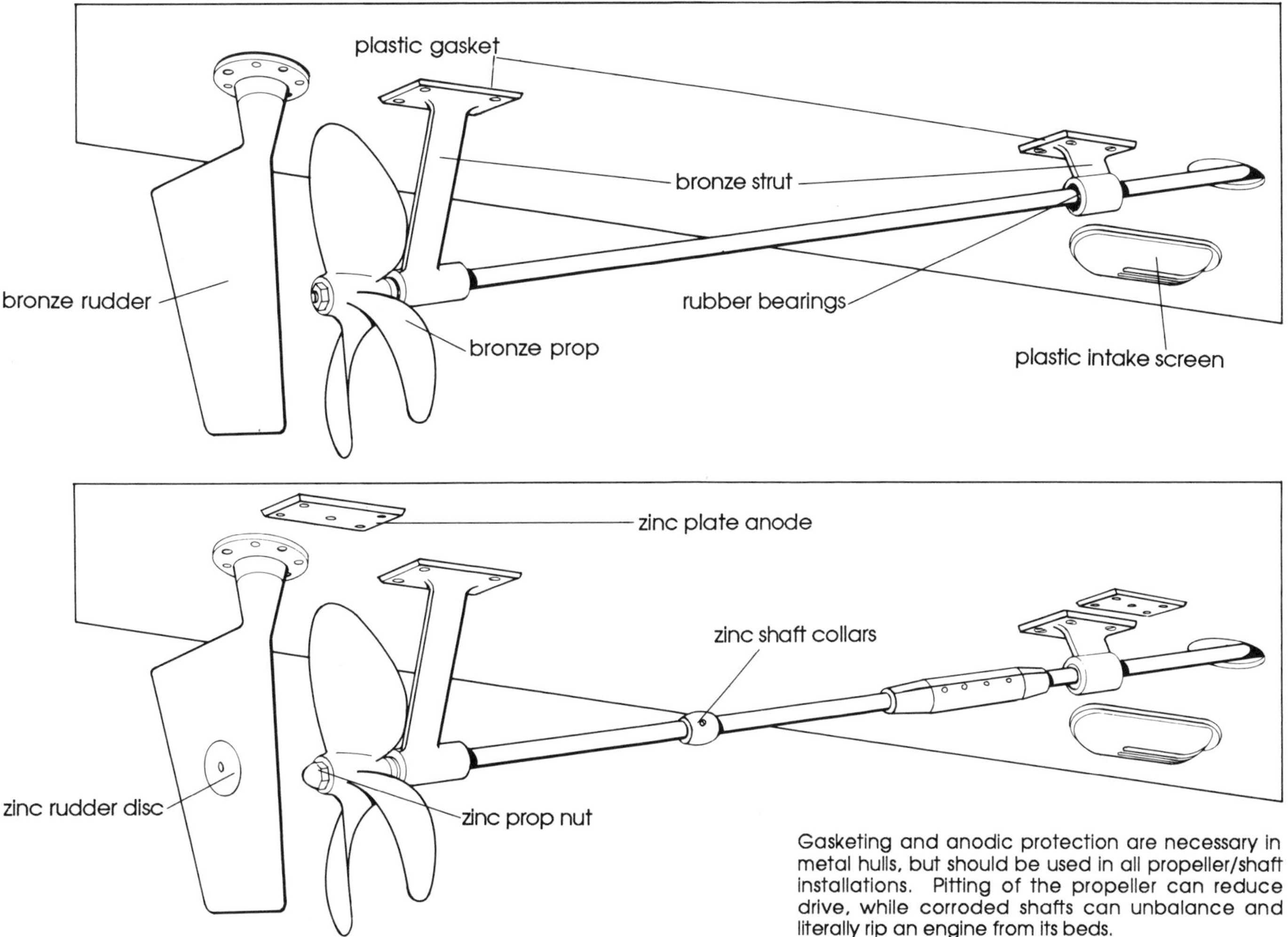

Gasketing and anodic protection are necessary in metal hulls, but should be used in all propeller/shaft installations. Pitting of the propeller can reduce drive, while corroded shafts can unbalance and literally rip an engine from its beds.

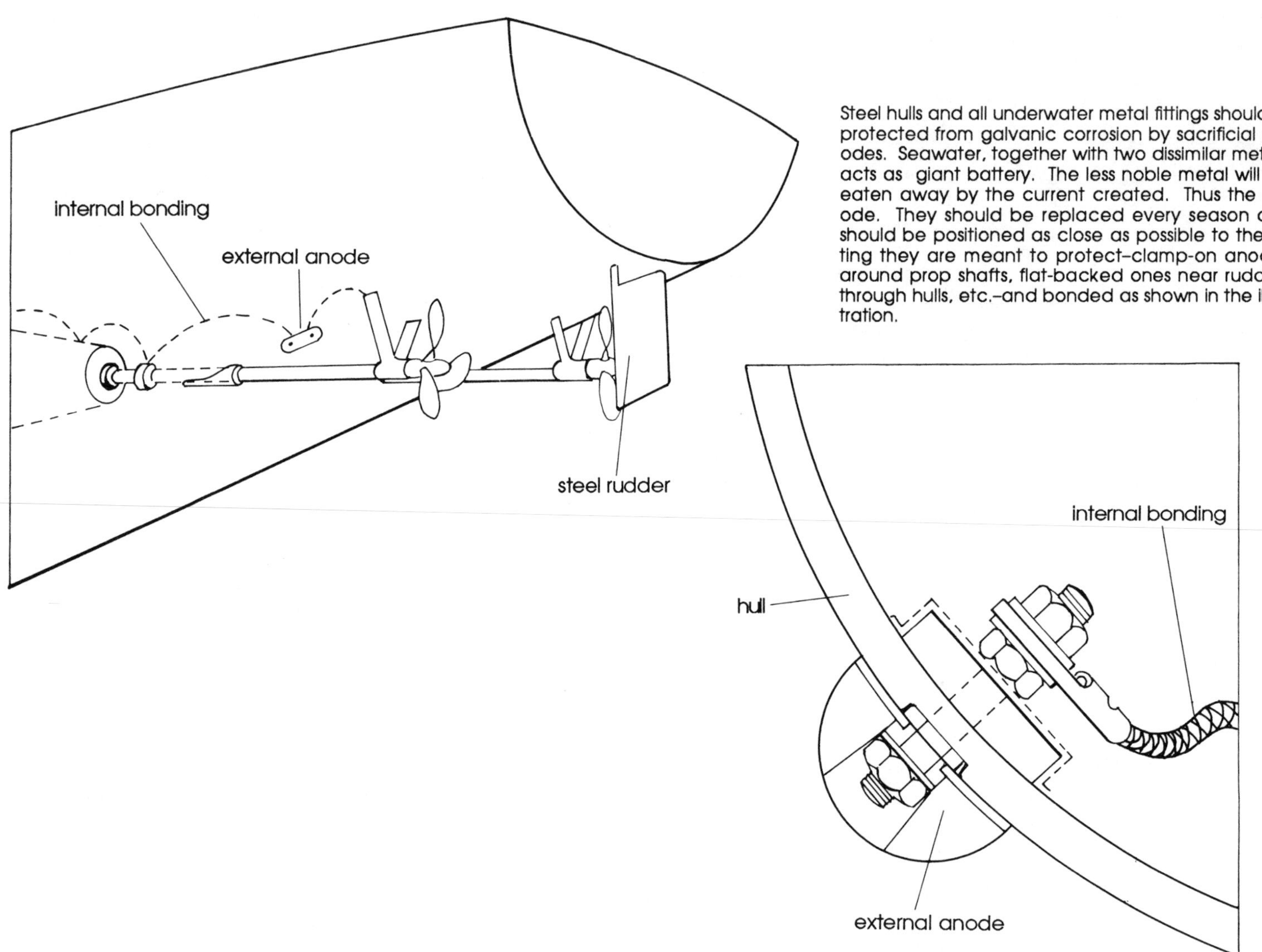

Steel hulls and all underwater metal fittings should be protected from galvanic corrosion by sacrificial anodes. Seawater, together with two dissimilar metals, acts as giant battery. The less noble metal will be eaten away by the current created. Thus the anode. They should be replaced every season and should be positioned as close as possible to the fitting they are meant to protect–clamp-on anodes around prop shafts, flat-backed ones near rudders, through hulls, etc.–and bonded as shown in the illustration.

9
FINISHING AND PAINTING

The one aspect of yachting that occupies the greatest percentage of maintenance time is keeping the surface finishes in top condition. In fact, I suspect that more time is spent on cosmetics than actually on the water going somewhere! Nevertheless, a yacht is judged by her finish, and a gleaming hull, Bristol varnishwork and polished metal all add to your pride of ownership as well as to the value of the ship.

The task of keeping any vessel looking her best is facilitated by preventive maintenance, and this can be succinctly described in three words: keep it clean! Grime, in the form of oils, grit, airborne pollutants, acid rain, sulphurous fumes, mud and hundreds of other carried aboard dirt-makers, will quickly deteriorate any surface–wood, GRP, metal or ferrocement.

The best and most readily available method of cleaning is water, endless water. The secret is to get rid of the grime before it is ground into or penetrates the surface of hull and deck, mast or rigging or sails. Ideally, fresh water should be used, but not all of us can partake of the luxury of a slip with plumbing. Bucketsful of salt water, provided it's not covered with fish scales, oil and other muck, will work almost as well. Yes, the salt will crust as it dries. Yes, it is not good for brightwork. But it is better than nothing. Besides, most salt can be prevented from drying if it is sponged or chamoised off after dousing.

When yachting was a gentleman's sport and a paid hand was carried aboard, the first thing he did every morning was to swab down the decks–to keep the sun from drying out seams–and wipe off the brightwork. Obviously, few of us can sanction paid help anymore, and frankly we get aboard only on weekends. Preventive maintenance becomes even more important.

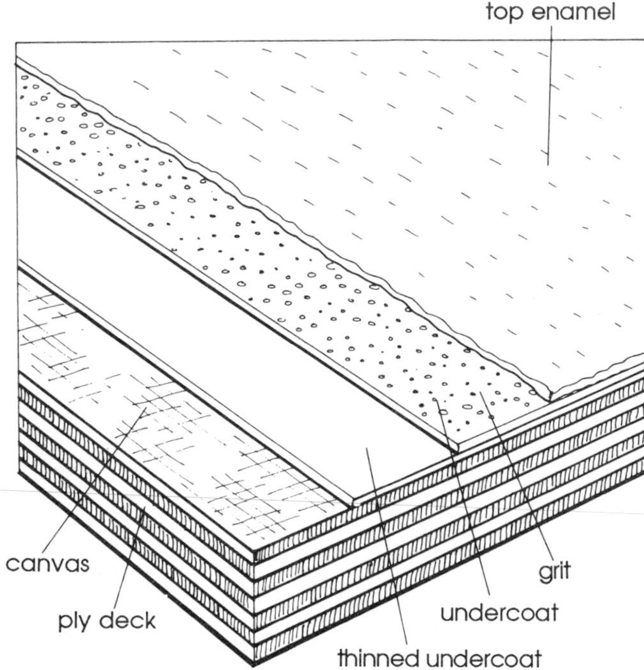

Composition of a canvas covered deck. Note that both undercoats as well as finish coat should be applied as evenly and lightly as possible to avoid paint buildup and cracking.

If you keep your yacht in a predominantly warm and sunny climate, you will have to expend greater effort to keep things looking shipshape. Sunlight, despite the pleasures it gives, has horrendous effects on decks and fittings, sails and ropes. Ultraviolet rays will cause most all materials to break down to some extent, especially synthetics. Surface protection, in the form of covers, paints and waxes, becomes very important indeed.

CLEANING

Water will rid surfaces of superficial grit, but the number of materials that will almost instantaneously penetrate wood or gelcoat is astonishing. Let's run down a list and see what can be done to eradicate various types of cosmetic gloom:

1. Bird droppings: scrubbing with a stiff brush and a mild abrasive cleanser will usually get rid of most dried guano. However, acids in the droppings can cause discoloration and fading in gelcoat. Auto or GRP buffing compound can be used to lessen these.

2. Grease: depending on the type of grease, first try a commercial spray cleanser. If the grease is ground into the gelcoat, use mineral spirits rubbed lightly with a constantly turned cloth or paper towels. Do *not* use acetone; it will soften the gelcoat. On wood decks, use paper towels soaked in mineral spirits in layers. Press down with a heavy weight. After the grease has been lifted by the towels, use a mild bleach-to-water solution (1:4) to rid the spot of any residual discoloration.

3. Acids: If you can act immediately after the spill, wash off the area with bucketsful of water. If time has passed the acid, depending on its strength, will have eaten away at the surface. With wood, this will mean a discoloration more than anything else. Gelcoat can be dissolved and the underlying GRP softened. Metal can be badly corroded. Wash and allow to dry thoroughly. GRP may need extensive repairs and, if in doubt, a qualified professional should be called in. A large enough spill

may damage part of the vessel structurally, requiring cutting out glass and relaminating the area. Most acids will not eat directly through steel or aluminum. However, the damage will be unsightly. An epoxy filler, applied strictly according to directions and allowed to cure thoroughly before painting, is the best answer.

4. Dirt: everything else can be classed as one form or another of dirt–grit ground into the deck, tar, airborne pollution, etc. A thorough washing with a good detergent, followed by oiling (wood decks), waxing (GRP) or painting (any painted surface) is the best answer. For small areas of GRP, where the gelcoat has been removed, patch kits can be purchased at most chandleries. For large hull and deck areas, it is best to have a pro undertake the job under controlled conditions or else to resort to a proper two-part linear polypropylene paint job.

PREPARATION: EXTERIOR/ BOTTOM

Once a yacht is clean, and only then, you can decide what needs painting, varnishing or waxing. With the yacht in a cradle you are first confronted with the bottom, the least visible and probably most critical area of the boat. The condition of the immersed hull is vital for speed, fuel economy, watertight integrity and structural soundness. This last has to do with possible osmosis (see the Hulls chapter for details).

If you are starting with a new hull, which has never been painted, wipe off the entire below-waterlines surface with a clean rag saturated in solvent, refreshing it constantly. This will get rid of residual mould wax in GRP construction. New wood hulls will need sanding with progressively fine wet-and-dry papers down to #600 grit if you are a perfectionist. For most, #200 grit will suffice. The key is to get the hull as fair as possible. Use a flexible batten to best visualize low and high points. Fairing a steel hull is a job for professionals unless you feel secure with a grinder; aluminum hulls are best faired with filler compounds, either epoxy or microballoons in a compatible resin mixture.

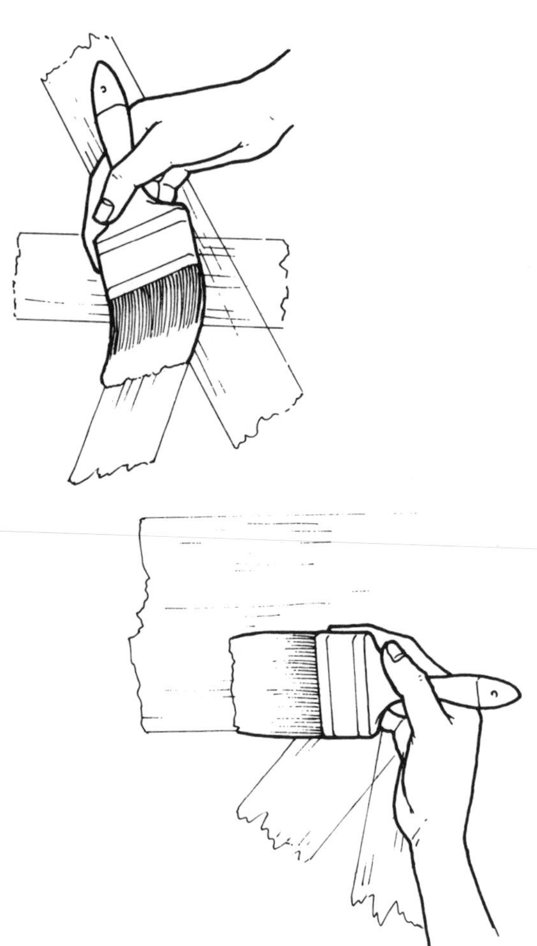

Initial paint strokes should be brushed on in an X-pattern, then smoothed out with back-and-forth strokes running parallel to the work.

Once a hull has been faired, it must be primed. No matter what anyone says, a specially formulated primer designed to work with a specific bottom paint cannot be too highly recommended. I have experienced the grief of midseason repainting as the initial coats quietly flaked off to sink to the bottom of the seabed. I didn't prime. And this was after totally stripping several layers of old paint. Spend the extra money and be sure of positive adhesion. It is well worth the time and effort. More to the point, that primer coat will act as a partial sealer as well, making osmosis perhaps a more distant prospect.

Preparation of a wood hull bottom demands that the caulking and seam compounds be in absolutely sound condition. If you have recaulked and refilled the seams, the boat should be launched and allowed to soak up for at least a week–with the pumps going–to permit the wood to stabilize and to allow excess seam compound to be squeezed out. Unfortunately a number of compounds will fall out completely. If it reacts as it should, the excess can be scraped down flush with the planking and the whole sanded before applying bottom paint. Oddly enough, one of the most effective seam compounds is ordinary roofing tar: that filled with GRP fibers is usually best and can be purchased at hardware and building supply dealers at a fraction of the cost of marine compounds.

Steel and aluminum hulls must have a barrier coat or two between the hull and the bottom paint to prevent any possibility of galvanic action. Tri-butyl-tin bottom paints are preferred for metal hulls, but the barrier coats should still be there. There are some problems with these, however, in that various government authorities are questioning their use as they have been proven harmful to spawning shellfish. They may not be available much longer. While going about prepping a metal hull, thought should be given to replacement of any metal through-hull fittings with plastic substitutes. New formulations are as tough as metal and far less liable to cause any hull deterioration.

SANDING

The key to effective hull sanding is evenness of touch. This is easily achieved–so to speak–by hand-sanding. However, on anything larger than a dinghy, the labor involved will be long, dirty and tiring. Power sanding is the logical alternative. Unless you are a pro, practice on a plywood panel first, especially if you plan to use either a belt or disc sander. Neither should be used on glass hulls, but are likely candidates for any plank-on-frame yacht. Modern, laminated (cold-moulded) wooden hulls should be sanded by hand or with an orbital power sander, as the laminates are usually one-eighth-inch thick and can easily be gone through with anything more powerful. Not a pleasant thought!

Sanding should always proceed from top down and from bow to stern. This is not arbitrary, but you will have the best "feel" for the look and finish of the job following this sequence. Follow each plank fore-and-aft and then downward, keeping the sander just in touch with the work so that the paint comes off in discernible layers. Since this can be a tiring job, especially above your head level, use staging when working heights exceed your chest level. Another good idea is to suspend the machinery with a block-and-tackle arrangement from the toerail or gunnel. The weight gets supported and you are free to concentrate on the finish.

The papers to use depend on the materials to be finished. Generally, for removing heavy coatings from all materials, #80 grit will suffice. Anything coarser will pose a threat to the surface. With belt and circular sanders, a finer grit, say #100 or #120, will be a more prudent choice, just because you have less control over the speed of the operation.

Be especially careful in working on GRP, as you can easily eliminate layers of glass and create an unholy mess. Long, even strokes–either by hand or with machine–are best to insure no sudden surface dips or gouges.

OTHER METHODS

Though sanding is the most efficient method of removing old finishes, it may not be the most appropriate for a particular job. Traditionally, wood boats were stripped or *wooded* using a scraper and blowtorch. Very few yards will permit an owner to engage in this hot pursuit today. The danger to your yacht and surrounding vessels, whether of GRP or wood, is just too great. Furthermore, it takes enormous experience to wield an open flame without damaging the hull planking. In any case, very few insurance carriers will allow it and the yard cannot be expected to cope with the potential liabilities. Heat guns, on the other hand, are pretty much fail-safe, but slow and not to be used except on wood. Heat and GRP do *not* mix.

Paint removers and strippers can be used. The paste type is better as you are working on a series of vertical surfaces and it will run less. They are all highly irritating and should be used with proper precautions, especially rubber gloves, an apron and long-sleeved garments. Additionally, they can be toxic and flammable. They will work very well on multilayered paint on wood surfaces. Also, special types are made for removing bottom paint from GRP hulls. Do not use them interchangeably! You will be very, very sorry when your plastic hull changes shape. No matter what method you use, finish work will involve sanding, so why not start that way and save yourself the potential for damage.

SAFETY

Working on the bottom of a hull means, by definition, you will be in contact with toxic chemicals and compounds. Not only can the surface coatings come in direct contact with your skin and any cuts or abrasions, but the dust released by sanding will most certainly invade your eyes, ears and respiratory system. Wear a respirator and goggles. Not one of those fiddly little dust masks which have only marginal effectiveness. Use a proper respirator mask with changeable filters and an industrial rating for toxicity. Copper, lead, tin and other metals have all been shown to cause a wide variety of diseases and cancers over a period of time. Sure, you are only doing this once a year, but the effects of heavy metals are cumulative. Your body does not get rid of them, and effects can appear twenty years later. Take care!

BOTTOM PAINTS

For years, bottom paints consisted of a combination of linseed oil, white lead and copper or bronze dust. They were soft paints, intended to work by being scrubbed occasionally so as to expose a fresh and toxic surface. And until the 1960's, most antifouling used greater or lesser amounts of copper to achieve its effectiveness. In the sixties, various polymer plastic bases were developed to make a stronger, harder and smoother binder for the antifoulants. These were and are particularly successful for improvement of speed, but they must be made strong initially since they will not wear as the season progresses.

Finally, in the 1970s we saw the development of TBT (tri-butyl-tin) paints. These are highly effective, smooth-based and reasonably hard-surfaced paints. They work exceedingly well. Too well, in fact, as they are about to be considered as environmental pollutants in more than one country and may be extinct in the near future.

Choosing a paint is dependent on the average water temperature, time the boat spends in motion, speed of the vessel and the salinity of your home waters. Additionally, the existent toxicity of your mooring area affects how well the boat's bottom will remain unfouled. Usually it is best to ask in local yards or of local yachtsmen what has worked best over a period of time. If you plan to fish or putter around or use the boat for commercial purposes, a traditional soft copper paint will suffice, wearing off with each successive scrub during the season and leaving you with minimal cleaning at the end of the year. Racers will demand a hard paint, usually a vinyl-based paint which

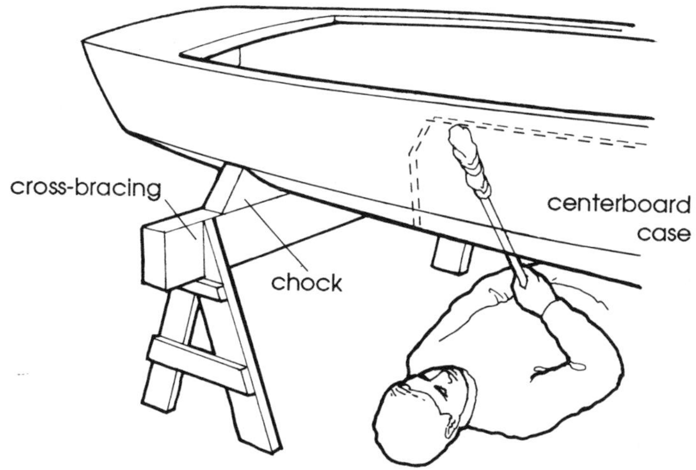

Perhaps the most effective way to paint the interior of a centerboard case with antifouling is to wrap a piece of toweling around a long stick (1"x2" cross section). Attach the toweling with staples for the most secure hold.

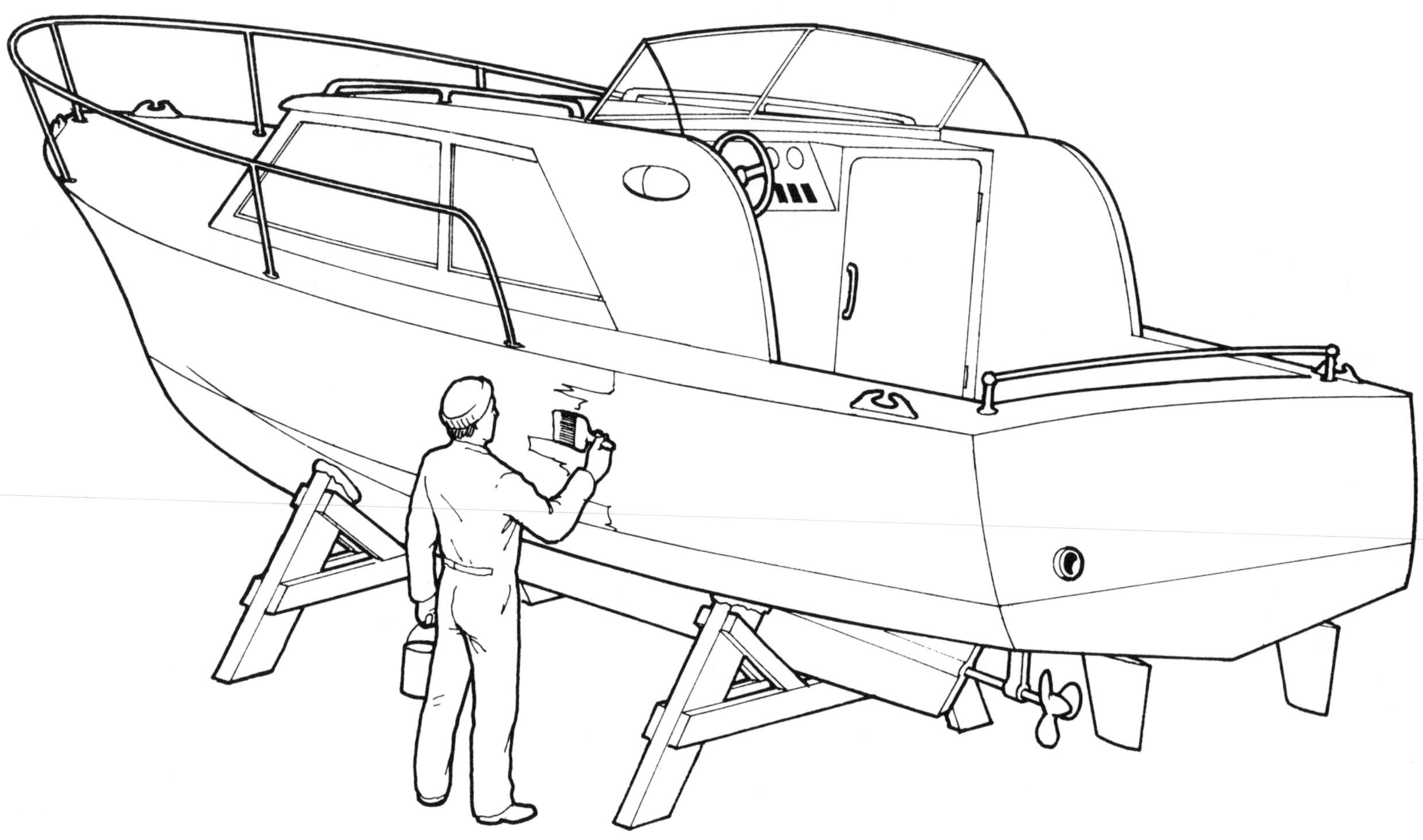

Painting a hull, one should start at the bows and work aft, first one side, then the other. Try to work at the time of day when each side is in the shade. Thus, if the port side is shaded in the morning, paint that first. Wait until the starboard side has cooled in the afternoon shade before painting.

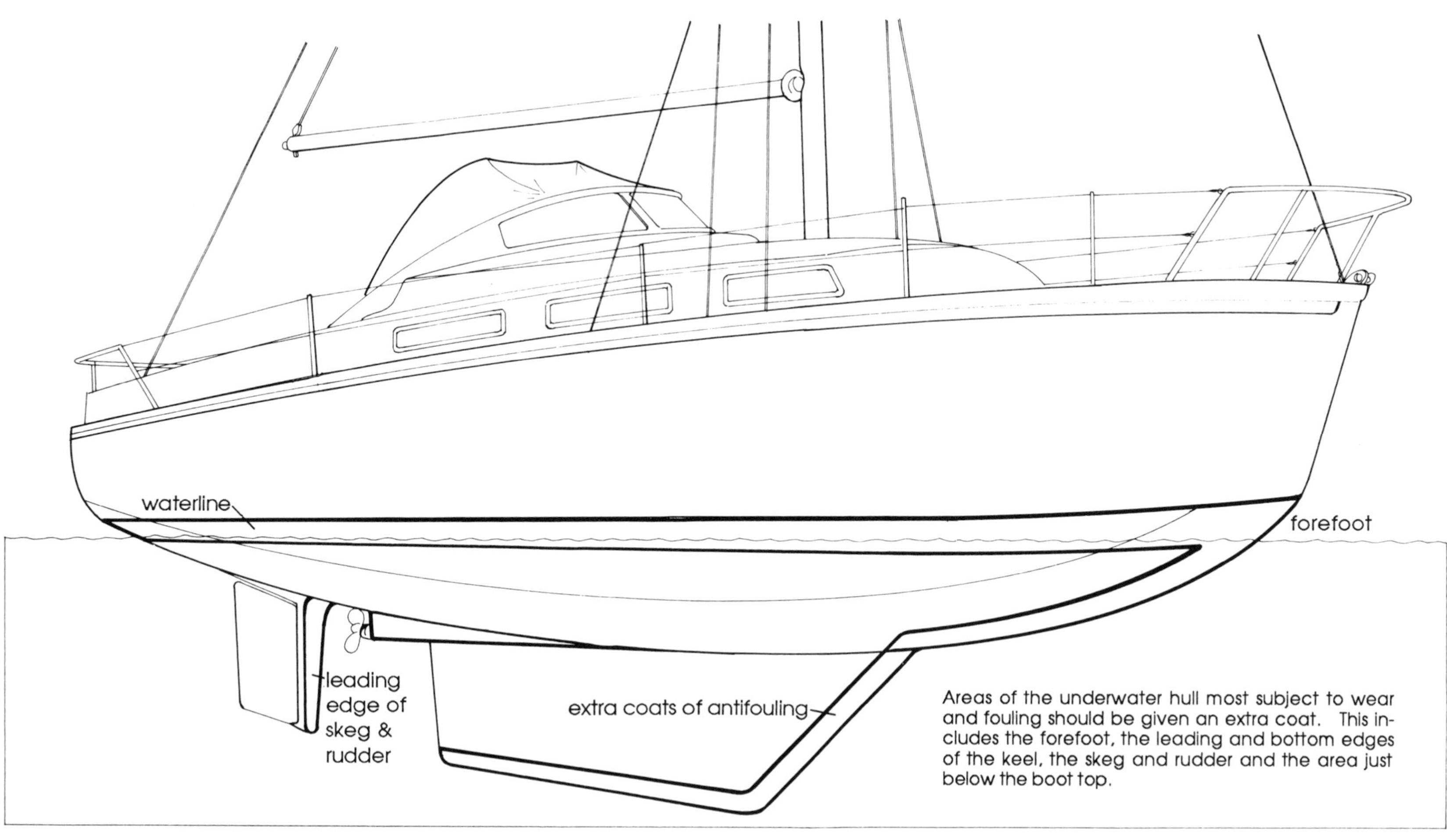

Areas of the underwater hull most subject to wear and fouling should be given an extra coat. This includes the forefoot, the leading and bottom edges of the keel, the skeg and rudder and the area just below the boot top.

can be burnished to a gloss finish. If the average water temperature is above 60 degrees F, go for the highest-toxicity paint you can afford. If you keep the boat in fresh water, paints are formulated for those conditions. Another possibility is to sheath the entire bottom in copper foil. Several proprietary systems have been developed but must be professionally applied and are quite costly. However, claims are made of seven to ten years without replacement, and if you are taking delivery of a new vessel, this is something to look into.

Application, once the surface is properly prepared, is a simple matter. You may use a brush, roller or spray, though the latter is only recommended for still days, great distances from other boats and skilled hands. All bottom paints–all paints, in fact–contain solids suspended in a binder. Constant stirring is a must to keep the toxic solids in an even suspension. Of late, roller painting has become very popular, but there is no way one can apply a coat as evenly or smoothly as with a brush. It need not be a badger-hair beauty. Any natural bristle brush, not much more than three inches in width, is a good choice. Buy cheap ones used for GRP layup. They have solid bristle anchoring. Trying to clean bottom paint out of any brush is not worth the effort.

Plan on two coats of any paint, following manufacturer's instructions to the letter. Deviations are at your own risk and, considering the cost of antifoulings, hauling, and your time–*read the label!* Start from the bows and work aft, out of the sun if possible. Complete one side, then return to the bows and work aft on the other. Small areas blocked by poppets or cradles, and the bottom of the keel, can be reached when the yacht is in slings, just prior to launching.

VARNISHING

The bane of all cosmetic care is brightwork. No matter how hard you try, this is not a once-a-season chore. Again, preparation is all. You want a surface like silk before you apply a single stroke of varnish. Despite all that has been written and ritually chanted about the difficulty of getting a pristine varnished surface, the procedure is really quite simple. It does take time, care and patience for optimum results, however.

As with bottom preparation, but even more so, all wood to be varnished needs to be clean and smooth. This means that virgin timber must be sanded with progressively finer papers until it resembles the proverbial baby's bottom. Wood that has been previously finished must be brought back to a *totally* unfinished surface. Paints and previous coats of varnish can be sanded down. Oil finishes–certainly common enough on contemporary brightwork–must be cleaned and bleached using a two-part cleaner specially formulated for the task. The best are highly caustic and rubber gloves must be worn as well as long sleeves and goggles. Wood so treated will need only sanding to make it ready for varnishing.

Laying down a smooth coat demands moderate temperatures, no wind and a dust-free environment. After sanding, wipe down the work with a clean tack cloth and hose down the wood and surrounding decks. Let it dry, bone dry. Any grain raised by this wetting will have to be further sanded with #220 grit paper and carefully wiped clean. The key to good varnish adhesion is priming or sealing. Use either a compatible primer recommended by the varnish manufacturer or varnish thinned by half with thinner or mineral spirits. Several coats of this will soak into the wood fibers and make for a far more compatible surface for the unthinned final coats.

The choice of brush is yours, and a number of people swear by disposable foam. However, experience has shown that for a truly even coat a badger brush of two-inch width with a tapered edge will give better results than anything else. Don't use this for any other painting, and keep it moist with thinner between coats. Otherwise, you will have granules of dried varnish marring your work.

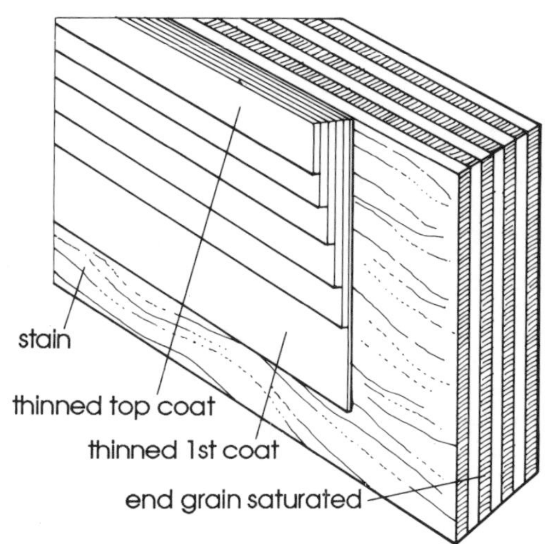

Varnishing is often considered the trickiest part of finishing. For a gleaming finish, a number of coats–usually 5 or more–of varnish need be applied. The trick is to prepare the surface carefully and to give each successive coat a light sanding to assure adhesion between coats. Otherwise you will find the surface peeling and cracking in a very short period.

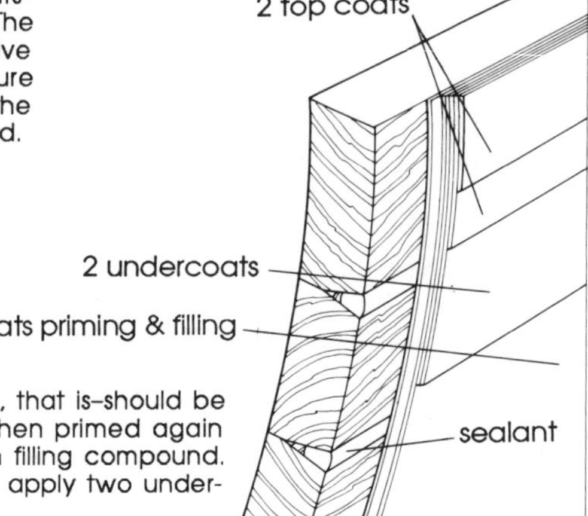

Conventional wood hulls–carvel, that is–should be primed, then sealant applied, then primed again and any rough spots faired with filling compound. After that has cured, sand and apply two undercoats and two top coats.

Thorough preparation is needed for any finish, but especially so in a steel hull. Primer must be applied as soon as shot blasting is completed. Otherwise, the chance of scale forming is significant. At least two coats of primer should be followed by filler or fairing compound. Final coating must be two undercoats, followed by two or more topcoats.

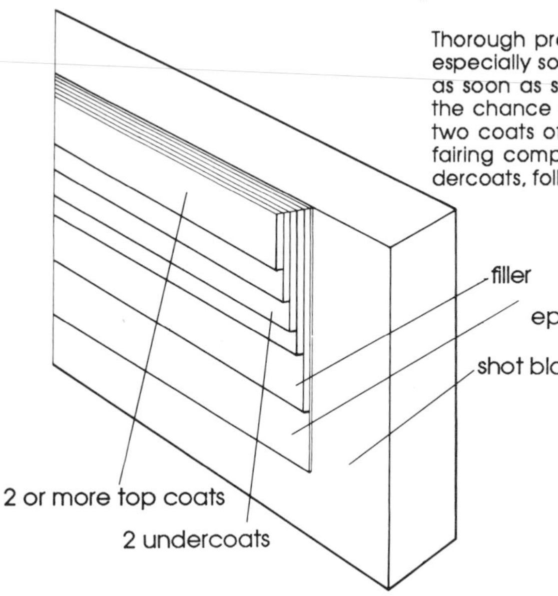

Painting GRP, ABS or ply hulls demands a schedule of primer–without it the finish will surely fail–followed by two top coats. Be sure the hull is thoroughly cleaned before priming. When using 2-part polyurethanes, resign yourself to the fact that it's a two-person job–one to apply, one to smooth out.

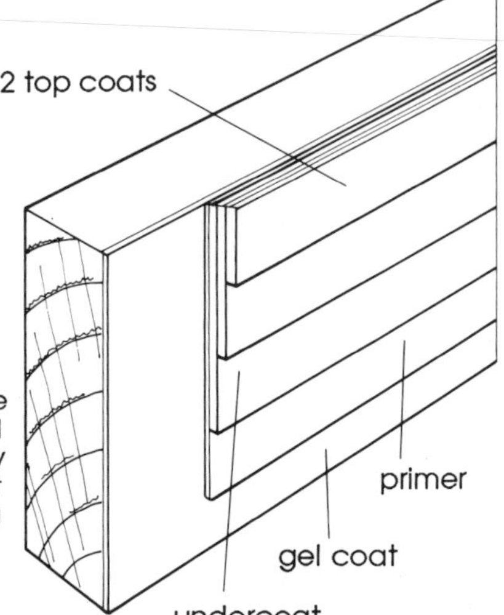

REPAINTING

Sooner or later, all yachts will need repainting, and GRP hulls will need painting for the first time. No matter what you are told, no paint, gelcoat or finish lasts forever. All will fade, lose gloss and luster and cease to protect the structural components of the boat. For any new finish to adhere, look and function as it should, the surface must be brought to a condition suitable to both the underlying material and the coating.

In wood hulls, this means stripping the wood down to its virgin state. Sanding, chemical strippers and scraping can do this with a lot of work and not too much chance of harm to the wood surfaces. However, remember that–especially in older boats–these processes do remove wood and must be accomplished with a light hand. Otherwise, the planking will lose both thickness and strength. Remember, after the original paint is taken off, the hull will have to be sanded smooth and faired. This will remove a fraction more wood. Be careful if you value your investment.

GRP hulls are a bit more of a problem. The gelcoat–which has probably dulled and is nicked–is measured in thousandths of an inch. Nevertheless, the gloss must be totally removed, all gouges filled and the whole smoothed and faired before you even think of what color it should be. Probably the best way to accomplish this is to use a reciprocating pad sander with a fine grade of paper, say #180 grit. Your arms will get tired, and you will have to develop just the right pressure to cut through the gelcoat without gouging the first layer of glass.

Only after the gelcoat is uniformly dull should you think of repairing any deep or shallow gouges. Since the hull is to be painted, a good two-part epoxy patch compound is recommended. Follow directions, but remember to wash down both the area to be repaired as well as the entire hull with an appropriate solvent prior to painting. You must be sure that all traces of wax, grease or other foreign matter are removed. Otherwise, no patch or paint will adhere for long.

Coating a surface with alkyd or oil-based paints is comparatively simple. Use a tapered, 3-inch brush (anything larger will be unwieldy, anything smaller inefficient) and rinse it out first in mineral spirits to rid it of any foreign matter, loose bristles and dust. Wipe down the surface of wooden hulls first with a tack rag, a cotton cloth soaked in a mixture of one part linseed oil mixed with three parts mineral spirits. GRP hulls should have a final wipe down with the compatible solvent recommended by the paint manufacturer.

Always start your painting at the gunnel and work down, but work from bow to stern in strakes of no more than eight inches. Smooth out each application as it goes on, working aft. If the help can be found, it's better to have one person apply the paint, while the second smooths it out. Make sure the paint is stirred regularly in the can and that it is thinned if necessary. Any contact with air will thicken paint, especially on a hot day.

10
SAILS

Gone are the days of flax and canvas, hemp and cotton, when half one's time was spent with sizing, stretching, drying and other interesting but tedious occupations. Modern sails are strong, stable and, with moderate care, will last a long time. However, the word "modern" has to be defined, especially in the recent past. No longer do we mean simply dacron/terylene or nylon. The adoption of new fibers by sailmakers and their use in composite sails has radically changed the way we look at fabric propulsion.

DACRON

The majority of sails are built from Dacron/Terylene fabric, either filled or virgin. Dacron itself is a manmade fiber that can be drawn into threads of varying density and diameter and woven, much like any cloth. It is a very stable, stretch-resistant material with a hard surface and light weight for its strength. It is not overly resistant to ultraviolet light and, in its virgin state, rather soft.

Most sails utilize a resin-filled Dacron cloth that gives the sail a degree of stiffness and shape retention. However, since few sails are handled with jeweler's care, this resin soon starts to break down, especially in the way of recurrent creases. Likewise, prolonged exposure to sun will cause a chemical breakdown in the cloth, as will chafe and oils. However, much as some gung-ho sailmakers would like to dispute the fact, Dacron cloth is still the best *all-around* fabric for sailmaking. Better, though not as stiff, and thus not as appealing to racing sailors, is unfilled cloth. This Dacron has been very tightly woven and is both easier to handle and less liable to be damaged by creasing and folds.

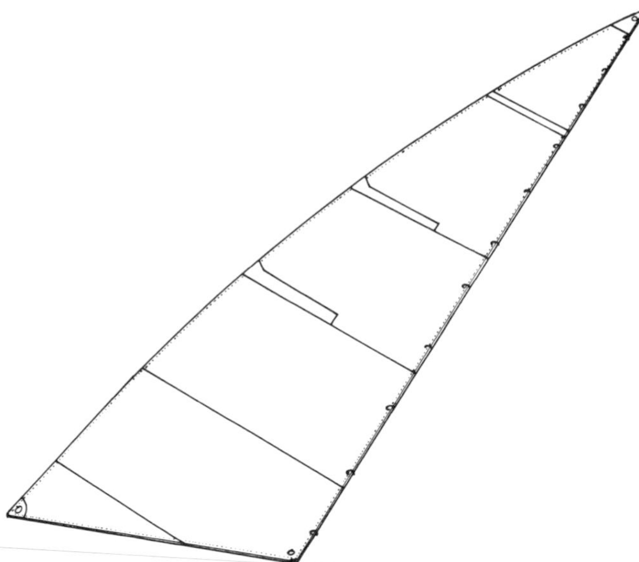

To fold a triangular sail, lay it flat–or considering deck space, as flat as possible–flake it down, then roll it up leech to luff.

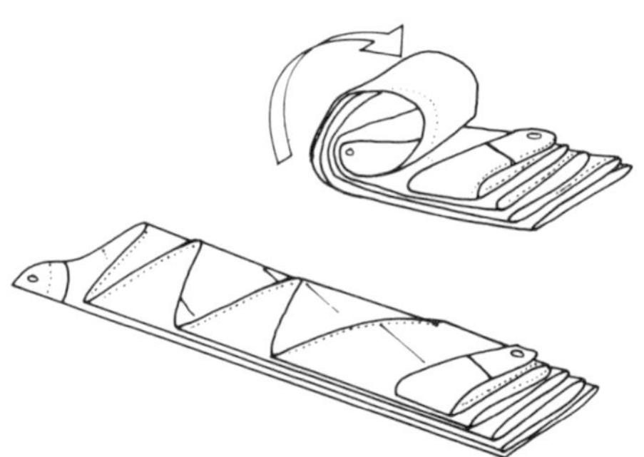

NYLON

Nylon is much stretchier stuff than Dacron. Used almost exclusively for spinnakers and asymmetrical cruising chutes, nylon is lightweight, perfect for downwind sails, where shape retention is not as critical as on other points. It is even more subject to ultraviolet deterioration than Dacron. Its inherent shape retention after stretching makes it a perfect shock absorber, thus its downwind role.

Nylon can be treated slightly more cavalierly than Dacron. It can be haphazardly folded with less chance of permanent creases developing. Like all sails, however, it should be washed, dried and stored carefully. Tears can be repaired with ripstop tape or by stitching, though the latter is best done by a sailmaker as the cloth has neither the weight nor the ability to lie flat as Dacron does.

MYLAR AND KEVLAR

These are the latest synthetics to invade the sail loft. Both are extremely strong and very stable. Mylar, in particular, is not woven, but rather extruded or pressed into a continuous sheet of varying widths. Since it is an impervious membrane, the wind will flow much more smoothly across its surface, making for a more efficient sail. However, it is very thin and fragile and creasing will destroy its airfoil properties. Thus, it is often laminated with special glues to a comparatively thin Dacron backing or sandwiched with Dacron to make a stronger sail. Kevlar is a thread of truly remarkable strength, roughly five times stronger than high-tensile steel. Currently it is used for reenforcing clews, heads and the lower portions of mainsails, though continuing development will bring about increased use in headsails. It does give a sail an odd beige color and purists will have to get used to that.

CARE

Sail care is actually one of the easiest bits of maintenance to undertake. First, and most important, is to keep the sails as crease-free as possible. After a headsail change, don't stuff the old sail into the bag. Push it down the forehatch and fold it below. f course, this will not be too simple with large genoas, but at least attempt to keep the sail as smooth as possible until conditions permit a proper fold. Mains should be flaked down over the boom and tied firmly but lightly. Don't try to garotte the sail with ties. You merely wish to keep it from falling into the cockpit.

Likewise, each sail should have its own sailbag, identifying the sail. Sails kept bent on–mains, club staysails–should have fitted covers to protect them from atmospheric grit and sunlight. The best material for covers is without question acrilan, a synthetic canvas which will withstand just about any abuse. Colors are to be preferred as white will eventually get dirty beyond cleaning.

At the end of the season, all sails should be cleaned. This can be done with any mild detergent–*not* soap–and warm water. Grease and other stains that will not come out by this method can be attacked with a household cleaner or with a mild solvent. In all cases, the sail must be rinsed with copious amounts of clean water and left to dry spread out on a lawn or deck or other clean surface. Do not fold and store wet or damp sails for the winter. They will mildew (yes, even synthetics can support microorganism growth) and crease even more. After they are totally dry, fold them loosely and bag them. Store sails in a dry, room temperature space with as much air circulation as possible. Above all, don't leave them on board.

The alternative is to deliver them to your sailmaker for vetting and winter storage. You pays your money and takes your choice. Actually, this service is usually fairly cheap and repairs, if any, will be made professionally.

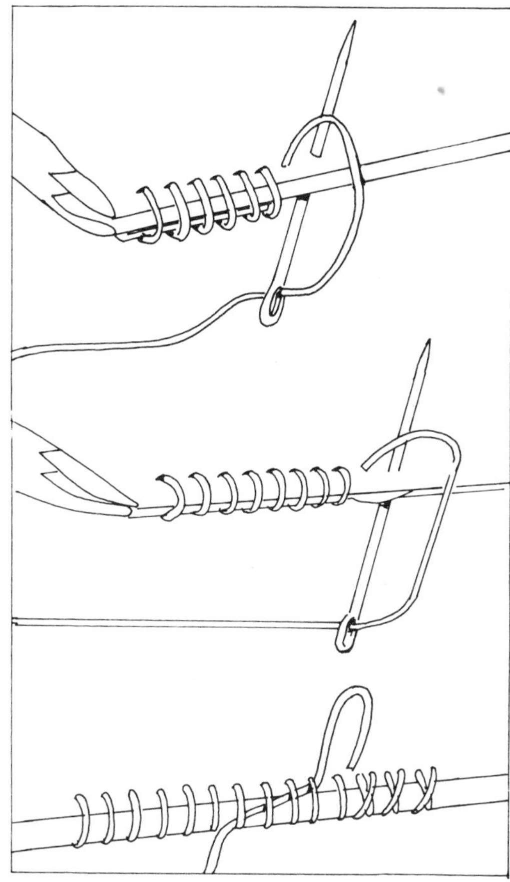

Stitching up a seam with an overhand stitch, then locking the stitches in place by reversing the procedure and backstitching up the seam.

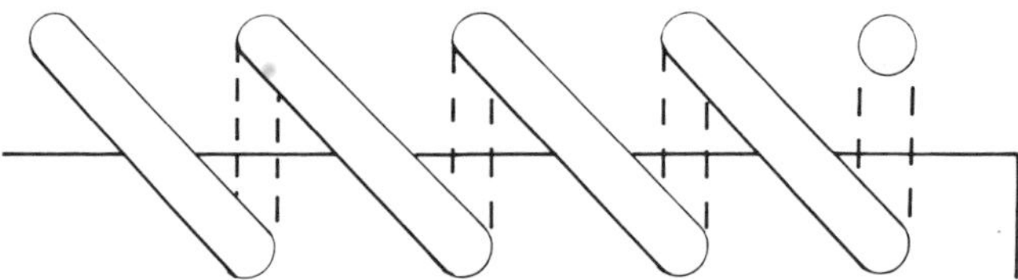

A. The overhand stitch, used for securing patches. Six stiches per inch is optimum.

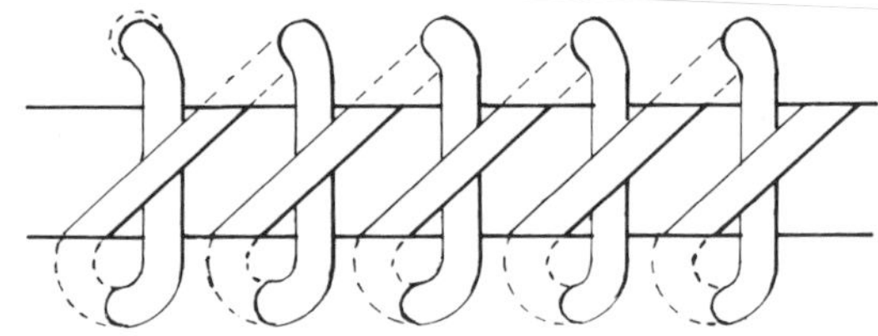

B. The sailmaker's darn, used for closing up tears. Six stiches per inch is optimum.

REPAIR

Sail damage breaks down into three major areas: tears in the cloth, broken stitching, and damage to sail fittings. Each repair can be undertaken without fear of major disaster, providing you learn some basic techniques and take your time. Sewing is one of the essentials for all sailors. Even if you can't sew a button on a shirt, you should be able to execute those stitches necessary to keep your sails in good order. Despite claims to the contrary, sail needles, except in the smallest sizes, will actually damage Dacron and nylon cloth. These are not comparable to canvas or flax and the triangular point will chafe and tear modern materials.

Instead, a round shaft needle of about 3-inch length will simply penetrate between the threads of the sail cloth. All needles will rust, no matter how heavily plated, and they are best kept in a plastic vial, wrapped in a scrap of oiled cloth and well sealed. Except in heavy cloth, a palm is not really necessary. Finding a good one is not easy! It should be adjustable, with a buckle or Velcro-fastening strap, and fit snugly. Leather is the only acceptable material and be sure to get one made for your configuration–right- or left-handed.

Thread for stitching should be of Dacron. Do not be tempted to use a spool from the home sewing basket. This is either cotton or polyester and will break instantly. Dacron thread made specifically for sails is extraordinarily strong and has been treated with an ultraviolet inhibitor. In fact, you will not be able to break the thread with your hands, so keep scissors or knife handy when you work. If you are ordering new sails, one good idea is to have the stitching done with contrasting thread, as any chafe or breaks in the stitching will be easier to spot.

Since modern sail cloths are "hard," the thread that holds the panels together lies on top of the cloth, not bedded into it as was the case on old natural fiber sails. Thus, the most common area of damage is to the thread where it catches or chafes against rigging, lines or fittings. The best way to lessen this is to rig various preventive devices to eliminate or lessen possible chafe points. Baggywrinkle, the old standby, really has no place aboard a modern vessel. It is clumsy, unsightly, adds windage and will soil sails. Far better is the polyvinyl split tubing sold for snapping around shrouds and stays. It should roll freely. This will make handholds a bit less secure, but will keep the sails well-protected.

Likewise, spreader ends must be smooth and unobstructed. Molded boots are available, but a better solution is to fit spreaders with captive ends of a semispherical shape. The less aloft, the fewer chances for hang-ups and less windage. Also, most spreader fitments are taped on. The tape unravels during the season, trailing like a sticky serpent and allowing the boot to fly off.

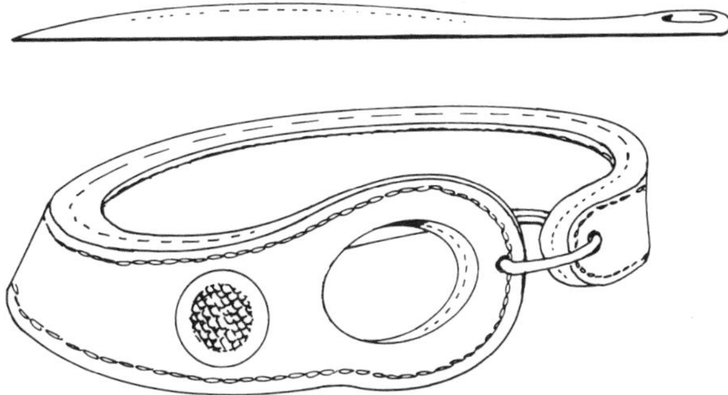

A palm and properly sized sail needles are musts for quick and effective sail and canvas repairs. Palms should be adjustable and fitted for either right or left hand work. Needles should be large enough to part the threads in the cloth, but not so large as to tear them.

FURLING AND REEFING SAILS

Roller-furling and roller-reefing sails have become extremely popular in the past decade and are certainly a godsend when shorthanded or while cruising. Simply due to the fact that they must wrap around a foil or stay, they need to be cut differently than hanked-on sails, flatter and with different reinforcements. Additionally, they are stressed along the cloth parallel to the luff much more than hanked-on sails. Due to the roll, each area of cloth exposed at the new "luff" is liable to distortion, as well as stitch chafing. Care must also be taken to protect the furled sail from ultraviolet deterioration. Many sailmakers will attach sacrificial strips of cloth along the foot and leech of the sail; otherwise a sleeve, fitted with a downhaul, is a good idea.

Roller-reefing mainsails are particularly valuable for shorthanded sailing. These must be battenless, but the tradeoff is enormous strain in the outhaul. Insist on triple stitching at all reinforcements.

mitered corners

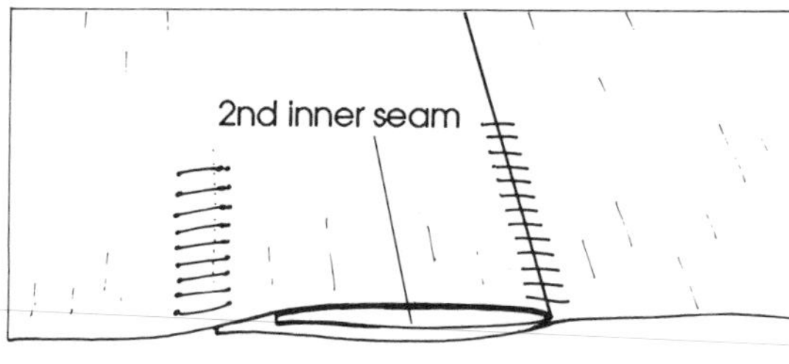

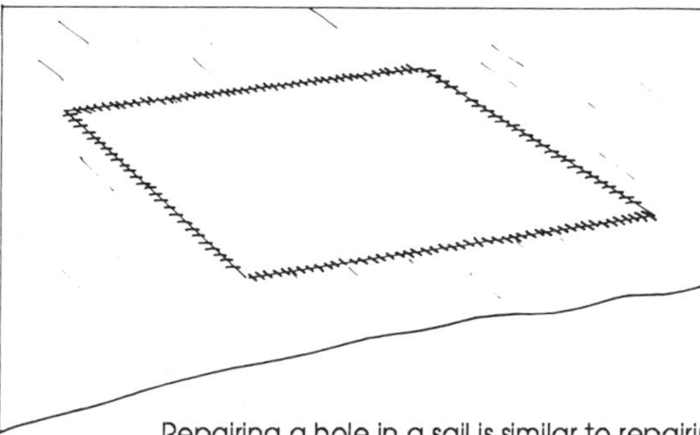

Repairing a hole in a sail is similar to repairing a tear in a canvas deck, except that stitching is used instead of tacks to hold the old fabric and new together. The mitered corners of the old material are turned under and a double seam is formed with the new piece of fabric overlapping, making for a doubly secure patch.

REPLACEMENT

Sooner or later, all sails will lose shape, get torn beyond repair or just plain wear out. Before ordering new sails, always consider in some detail just what type of sailing you intend to do. Sailmakers, as a rule, are race oriented. After all, this is how they make their living, advertising their wins. However, many racing sail design and construction features are actually a hindrance to the cruising sailor: Mylar, infinite sail adjustments, monster headsails.

For racing, you will need to go to the limit of what your class or rule requires. This can be an expensive proposition and should be discussed in detail with the sailmaker. For cruising, much depends upon rig and goals, but a few thoughts on the subject:

1. There is never enough crew while cruising. Therefore, sails should be of soft cloth (unresinated), woven of ultraviolet-treated material and of a size easily handled by a small crew.
2. Battens are a way around certain racing rules. Though the loss of sail area can be up to 15 percent in a roped-leech sail, the advantages, particularly for long-distance cruising, may well outweigh the loss of area.
3. Headsails for cruising should be fitted with foot pennants to allow clearance from the deck and the pulpit. Once again a small loss of drive, but at the saving of sail, especially in green water conditions.
4. If fitting roller-reefing sails, make sure that they are cut for the job: fairly flat and with triple stitching at all stress points.
5. Avoid D-rings at the clew; better would be O-ring grommets set into the sail with appropriate stitching to strengthen the sail. D-rings can cause serious injury to anyone on the foredeck while the sail is flogging.

Much of what you get in a sail depends upon the tastes and inclination of your sailmaker. The more you can tell him what you need, the better the chance of getting the sail *you* want. Many sailmakers will try to get you to go along with all the latest technological developments. Whether you need these is a matter for you to decide. Kevlar and Mylar laminates have little place in the average cruising or daysailing wardrobe, and even for racing, your competitive spirit and pocketbook will dictate how many refinements will be incorporated.

Triple-stitching is for ocean crossing and is of little value to the weekend sailor. Likewise too many sail shape control lines. An outhaul and cunningham for the main and leech lines for the jibs are the most most people need. A great deal of variation is available through the use of halyards, travelers and downhauls, and these should be taken into account when ordering a new sail.

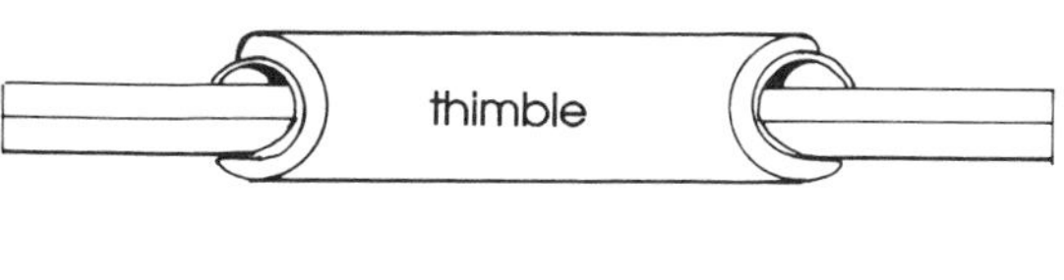

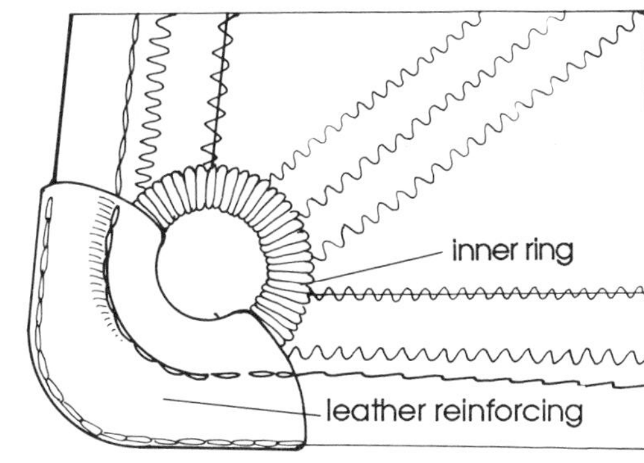

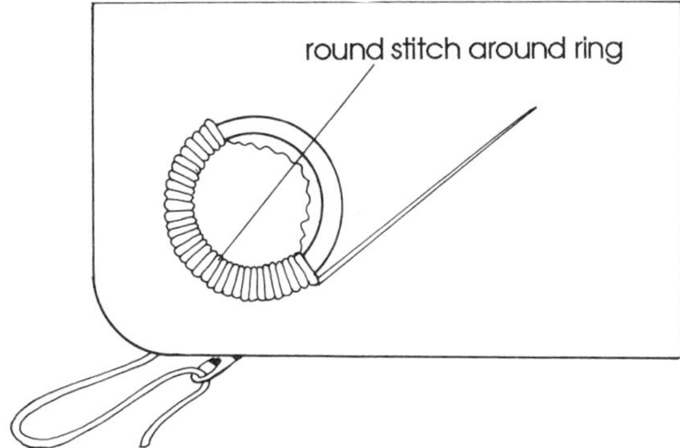

A clew thimble is pressed in place with a hydraulic press. Leather patches can be used to reinforce the assembly and stitching all around will prevent against chafe and aid in anchoring the thimble in place.

STORAGE

During the season, sails should be folded and bagged after use, with the exception of boomed sails which may be flaked over the boom and protected with a fitted sail cover. Though cockpit lockers are the usual location for storing sails, they are far from ideal. Since these lockers are usually filled with other items, ofttimes hard and unwieldy, the sails will be crushed, battered and subject to possible tears. Additionally, these lockers are usually wet with bilge water or condensation, upping the chance of mildew.

Far better would be to store bagged sails in the forepeak, either in vented bins or stacked against the forepeak bulkhead. Assuming no one will actually sleep there, this a fine solution. If the forepeak berths are to be used for human habitation then the sails might be stacked in the hanging locker. The idea is to keep them as dry and ventilated as possible.

11
WINTERIZING AND COMMISSIONING

The two most regular sets of chores for any boat owner are spring commissioning and winter layup. During the spring, the pent-up energies and frustrations of a winter without one's beloved boat burst forth, resulting in devilish activity, lists, new projects and endless polishing, scrubbing and painting. During the autumn, the regret at putting her up for the season allows one to be less than thorough in preparing one's beloved for the harsh abandonment of winter. I realize that this may be a bit poetic for some, but the fact is that rarely are the two ends of the boating season treated equally, and they should be. For the continuing prime condition of the vessel, both layup and commissioning should be treated with diligence and thoroughness.

WINTERIZING

Come the end of the season and the yacht is hauled out, usually without your presence. Nevertheless, you must be there in spirit; more importantly, if you are not present, make sure the yard has an underwater profile of your boat, to scale, so they can rig slings for the travel hoist or a cradle for a railway without damaging any appendage–rudder, skeg, keel, etc. Once ashore, if the boat does not have a permanent cradle, make sure that supports and poppets are correctly positioned and the boat is shored up to distribute weight as evenly as possible.

The minute a boat comes out of the water, the bottom should be scrubbed down, either by hand or with a pressure washer. Even a day's delay can make bottom weed, slime and stains that much harder to remove. In addition, the area around the waterline, usually covered with weed and stained with oil and

God-knows-what-else, will probably need cleaning with a stiff brush and possibly solvent or a patent cleaner. Household cleansers should be given a try first as they are cheaper and highly effective on grime and grease. Do not use abrasives, with the possible exception of rubbing compound formulated for GRP. Most powder cleansers are far too harsh and will quickly grind away gelcoat.

EQUIPMENT REMOVAL

Once the boat is firmly propped up on dry land, the removal process begins. By and large, if something can be removed, remove it. This of course assumes some place to store it all. A yard or club locker is never large enough, and if you are an apartment dweller, forget it. Ideally, a garage helps, providing of course that you have no intention of keeping your car in it.

If it's a sailing yacht, the mast should come down. The yard should unstep it before they haul. It should be washed down, any masthead instruments removed, spreaders removed, the stays and shrouds tied together with twine every two to three feet and then tied around the mast, and turnbuckles removed and stored separately. It must be stored on a rack off the ground and supported every few feet. Tapered and flexible masts need greater support than straight ones. The purpose of the exercise is to keep the spar in column.

Booms should be stored with the mast, and halyards from both should be tied securely with the stays or else removed, washed and stored in loose coils. This is a good time to check over all fittings, splices, terminals and shackles. Be particular about clevis pins and, as a matter of course, replace all cotter pins. The turnbuckles can be cleaned, greased and wrapped in oiled cloth or an old towel. Do not keep them in plastic bags.

Masthead instruments are extremely delicate and must be removed the minute the mast comes down. They should be carefully wrapped in some sort of padding after cleaning and oiling and stored indoors for the winter. The same is true of radar scanners, satellite antennas, VHF aerials and the like. Mast-mounted winches should be taken apart, cleaned and re-greased. Do not cover them with plastics of any sort as this will only promote condensation and corrosion. On powerboats, all electronics mounted above deck should be removed as well as any mast-mounted sensors and antennas.

Water tanks should be emptied prior to hauling, so as to minimize balance problems in the slings; likewise, make sure bilges are pumped dry. Next, all tanks must be thoroughly drained: water, fuel, and holding. Care must be taken to make sure that all liquid is removed so as to lessen any condensation problems or freezing with its concurrent expansion and possible damage to the tanks or piping. An alternative with the fuel tanks is to top them up with fresh fuel and add appropriate additives made specifically for winterizing. However, the possibilities of fuel contamination and separation, not to mention sedimentation, are ever-present, and draining the tanks is preferred.

In conjunction with tank draining, all plumbing should be be drained and cleared, especially any piping which leads to the engine, fuel supply or head. Any remaining water can freeze, expand and cause leaks or ruptures. Any fuel can vaporize and lead to a potentially explosive condition. While you're at it, make sure all through hulls are properly fastened and bedded and that seacocks and other valves are positive in action. Seacocks should be taken apart, once the boat is hauled, and cleaned and greased. Also, make sure all hoses are tightly clamped and should any be only held in place by a single clamp, add another.

All movable equipment should ideally be removed from the boat: fenders, cushions, food, outboard motors, rafts, instruments, books, charts, galley ware, spare parts: anything that can either deteriorate or tempt a would-be thief. Since condensation is a particular problem, especially with single-skin GRP hulls, anything that can be damaged by the damp should come off. This includes all electronics below deck, all

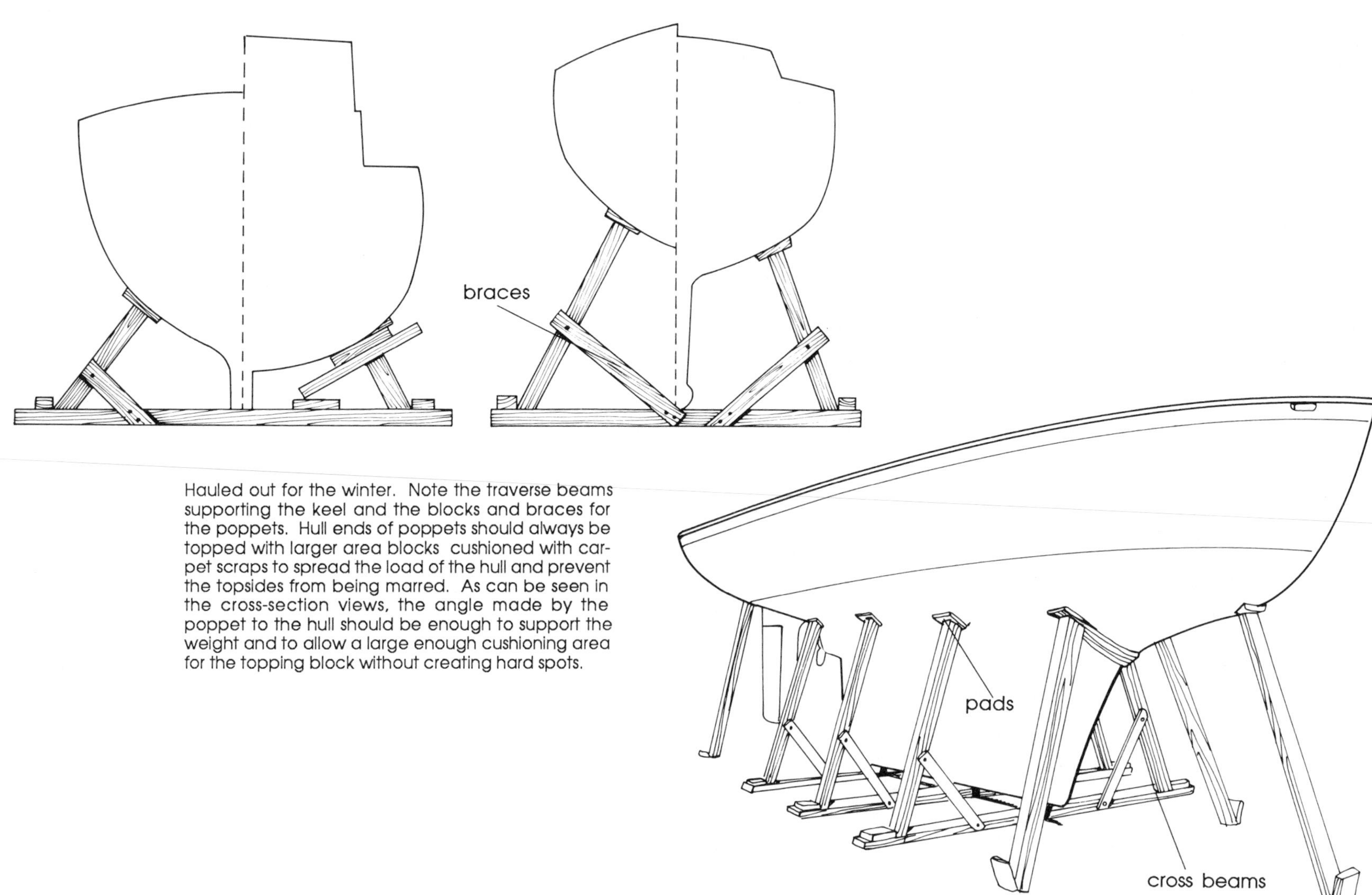

Hauled out for the winter. Note the traverse beams supporting the keel and the blocks and braces for the poppets. Hull ends of poppets should always be topped with larger area blocks cushioned with carpet scraps to spread the load of the hull and prevent the topsides from being marred. As can be seen in the cross-section views, the angle made by the poppet to the hull should be enough to support the weight and to allow a large enough cushioning area for the topping block without creating hard spots.

instruments, cushions, etc. All lockers should be left partially open and the same goes for bilge traps. In conjunction with this, it's a good idea to remove the drain plug in the bilge–if there is one–to allow any collecting *interior* water to depart. Be sure to replace it in the spring!

Since electrical circuits are especially subject to damp, remove the batteries, charge them fully and store in a dry and warm place. Cold storage can permanently affect a battery's ability to retain a charge. If you take them home, connecting them to an automatic charger is not a bad idea. The amount of electricity paid for over the course of a winter is but a fraction of the cost of a new marine battery. This a good time to inspect the wiring, fuses or circuit breakers and terminals and connectors. Any signs of corrosion, fraying or loose connections should be taken care of now or added to the spring checklist.

ENGINES

Winterizing an engine should follow manufacturer's recommendations. However, a few points can be mentioned as standard to all. First, make sure all collection points for fuel are thoroughly drained: carburetors, fuel filters, fuel lines. Second, make sure the crankcase is drained, and new oil as per specifications is added. Turn over the engine a few moments to spread this clean oil throughout the system, insuring against engine corrosion. Third, clean the exterior of the engine and touch up any spots with the appropriate engine heat-resistant paint. Be sure to prime all surfaces to be painted after removing any rust and grease.

For outboards and gasoline inboards, spark plugs can be replaced with special vapor-releasing plugs which will lessen combustion chamber corrosion. Spray a good penetrating oil into the carburetor air intake while the engine runs its last. Flush out all cooling systems with fresh water and then pour in a mixture of half water/half antifreeze, making sure the mixture is fully distributed throughout the cooling system (when it exits the exhaust). Otherwise, let the engine run at full throttle until dry to assure empty combustion chambers and a high enough temperature to help reduce built-up carbon deposits. Each cylinder should have a small amount of lubricating oil sprayed into it after the engine is stopped for good.

Diesels should have the injectors cleaned, the valve clearances adjusted and the fuel system thoroughly bled. Failure to bleed the system can lead to condensation and bacterial growth in the off season and the result will be a major overhaul, to say the least.

CLEANUP

Once all has been removed, it is imperative that all surfaces likely to harbor mildew and mould should be washed down with a 1:4 solution of bleach and water or a good liquid cleanser. Make sure everything is thoroughly dried before closing up the boat. Also make sure that all food stuffs or any cans containing soda or liquids are removed as all are subject to freezing and possible explosion. Clean the bilges with patent bilge cleaner and drain thoroughly. Anything which might cause an odor or allow mildew or vermin to prosper has to be cleaned and aired.

On deck, all metalwork should be cleaned with detergent and lots of fresh water, then coated with a thin layer of petroleum jelly or wax. Do not buff the wax. It can easily be removed in the spring and buffing will just diminish its protective powers. Teak will need cleaning and oiling, varnish work should be touched up and lifelines should be slackened. A minor but not unimportant point is to remove stanchions from bases, clean the ends and coat the ends with a light grease. Stanchion bases are a prime area for corrosion and if this procedure is not followed yearly, the upright and base can fuse,

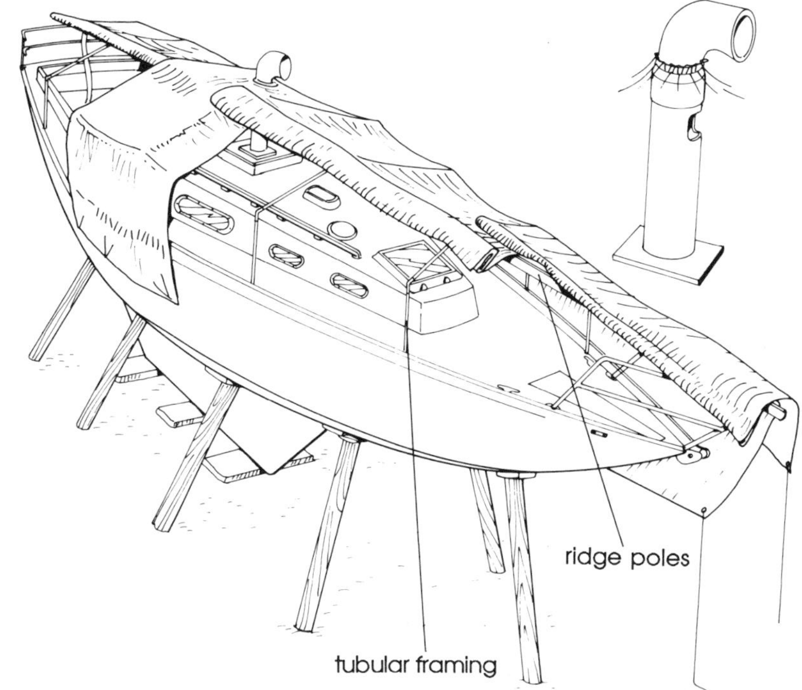

Winter covers can be framed out in different ways. The sailboat on the left has a frame made up of interlocking sections of pipe fitted into the stanchion bases. The ridge pole is then lashed across the tops of these pipes at right angles making for a rigid and secure structure. The powerboat on the right, with a solid rail surrounding the deck, has a frame made up of cross members lashed to the rail at the stanchions and a ridge pole arrangement carried out in the same way as on the sailboat. Winter covers should be held down by ropes running individually from each grommet around the perimeter of the tarp, tied to parts of the supporting frame or cradle. Lacing, or tying ropes to ropes, is not good practice, as it will allow the cover to shift in high winds and tear.

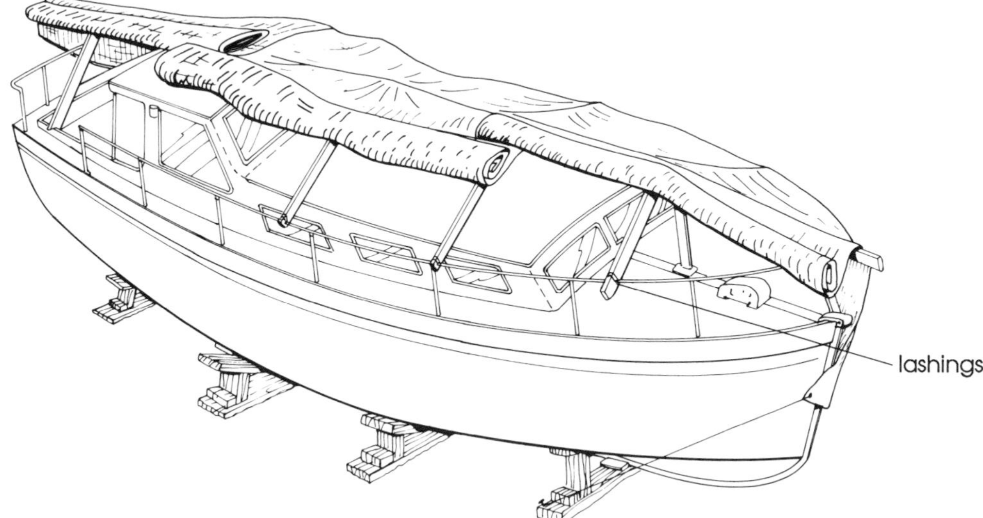

weakening each considerably. Replace the cotter pins holding the two together.

While on deck, make sure all cockpit lockers are cleaned out and the contents removed. Also, wash all ropes, decide which will need replacement, dry thoroughly in loose coils and stow in the cabin. Blocks should be removed, washed, lubricated and taken off the boat. Anchors can be left in place, but should be scrubbed and this is as good a time as any to paint or spray with galvanizing paint. Anchor lockers, by the way, are sure to be the mustiest and dirtiest places aboard and ought to be cleaned out now. Make sure tank filler caps are tightly secured.

Below the waterline, clean out all through hulls, which are perfect dens for barnacles. Sand them smooth now so you won't have to chisel out the creatures come spring. Make sure transducers and paddle wheels are intact and undamaged. Check the propeller for nicks and dents. If any cannot be removed by minor filing, pull the prop and send it off now for repairs. Make sure shaft alignments are alright and that any struts or supports are securely attached to the hull. Check rudder bearings and alignment. Replace sacrificial anodes in the fall–one less thing to worry about in the spring. If the keel is bolted on externally, check the condition of keel bolts and any gaskets or flanges at the hull-to-keel join. This is a very critical area and is subject to flexing and heavy strain. It's a prime source of leaks and hull weakening and must be absolutely without weakness. Trim tabs must be thoroughly inspected and lubricated. The same goes for any I/O units. Make sure any hydraulic linkages are leak-free and responsive. All these points will require a haul-out for repair, so better to correct any deficiencies now, rather than wait until next season.

COMMISSIONING

Springtime is when every yachtsman's thoughts turn to getting the beloved into the water. You have spent the winter hoarding new equipment, making wood bits-and-pieces and planning the season's cruises and outings. Most likely, the boat has been diligently neglected since the flurry of work at haul-out. When you get to the yard, you will find the winter cover torn and tatty, the hull and deck encrusted with grime and dead leaves, the cabin coated with dust and reeking of damp, fused charts and two essential pieces of hardware missing!

It needn't have been that way, of course, if you had followed the preceding advice. But you have to tackle it anyway, so let's begin. Take off the cover. If it's in good shape, spread it out on the hard and carefully fold and secure it for next winter. Disassemble the frame. If it is a carefully crafted, bolted together ensemble, tie all the pieces together and store them in an area of the yard where they will not be mistaken for staging lumber or firewood. Start cleaning!

Since the deck will get dirtier, there is little to be gained by cleaning it now. However, the hull should be washed down, any repairs made and the whole, from gunnel to waterlines, waxed if GRP, painted if wood (that is, if it needs it; most wood hulls need at least a light topcoat yearly to maintain their pristine looks). Prior to this, however, any wood toerails or rub rails should be refinished, as bleaches, cleaners, solvents and the like will only force you to refinish the hull. If these are varnished, and it's very early in the season, you shall have to wait, of course, but at least protect the hull with a skirt of plastic sheeting when you do get around to the actual varnishing.

Now is the time to attack the bottom. With the newer self-cleansing bottom paints, all you need do is a light sanding and recoating with two coats. Other bottom paints will need a heavier sanding and, should the bottom have to be stripped down to bare glass or wood, a coating of primer before recoating. All through hulls should be checked for free passage; all instrument transducers and paddlewheels need to be totally clean and working prior to launch. Make sure the rudder and keel are secure and that all bearings, struts and stuffing boxes are aligned and adjusted to function properly.

On deck, make sure that any repairs you noted at haul-out are attended to. Also, make sure that the yard has done everything it was supposed to do, especially in the way of engine and hull repairs. Now is not the time to tackle major jobs. If you did everything you were supposed to do in the fall, other than cleaning, painting and waxing, there should be little to bother you. Restow all you removed from the boat in the fall. Make sure rigging is in good condition. Flush out and lubricate the engine, make sure seacocks are operating smoothly, strap down the *fully-charged* batteries.

Check out all deck hardware, lubricating where necessary. Since all was cleaned before winter, all should need little looking after. Be sure to replace all cotter pins with new stainless steel ones. Tighten up all steering linkages if there is any slack in the cables, and lubricate all sheaves and gears.

AFTER LAUNCHING

Once the boat is in the water, there are still many chores to be done. Deck gear must be installed and adjusted, masts must be stepped and rigging tensioned, seacocks opened where appropriate, gear loaded aboard, tanks filled, instruments calibrated and compass swung, and the entire boat cleaned. This is a set of tasks which can usually be accomplished over a weekend, but the larger the yacht, the more complicated the systems, the longer it will take. Try to get it all done before you get under way for the first time. The care taken up front will repay you with hours, days of enjoyment and fewer last-minute emergencies.

12
SAFETY GEAR

Safety and emergency equipment is good if it works. Though this may seem self-evident, it's suprising, not to say frightening, how much gear kept aboard for emergencies doesn't function properly or at all when it is truly needed. And since we have become so dependent on the *idea* of its necessity, and we have gone to the expense–considerable in most cases–of actually purchasing and installing it, we really must take the trouble to make sure it is in working order.

LIFE RAFTS

In dire emergencies, when one is forced to abandon ship, the life raft is probably the single most vital piece of equipment. Unfortunately, it is also the one piece of equipment aboard that no one has ever tried out. Now, admittedly, it is an expensive process to test a life raft as the CO_2 cannister must be recharged, the raft refolded and the whole repacked. Considering the purpose of the equipment, though, it really ought to be checked out by a certified raft servicing facility once a year, at the beginning of the season. Too often, this is done in the autumn and the whole kit is left in some damp place over the winter and God knows what can happen! In fact, the most usual failure point in a raft is the inflation valve(s). Since any metal valve can corrode or oxidize enough to limit free movement, this must be carefully checked and coated with the recommended lubricant. Do not use just anything at hand! Viscosity for valve lubricants of this sort must be low enough to allow for no possible thickening in cold or wet.

Where a life raft is stowed has a major impact on its proper functioning. The ideal is a ventilated, waterproof locker. Since this is a virtual impossibility aboard most vessels, the best solution is in a cockpit locker which may be opened instantly, no

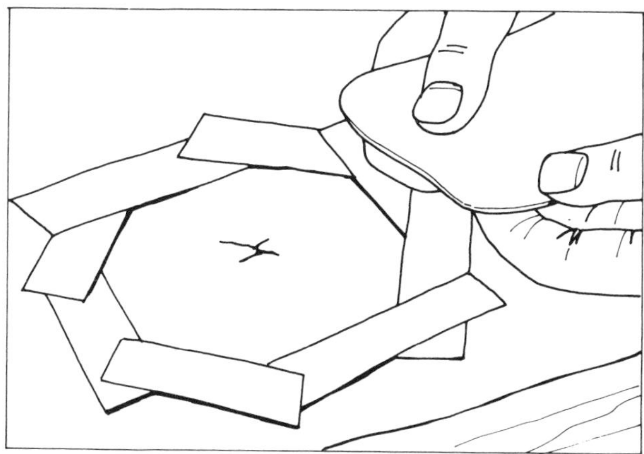

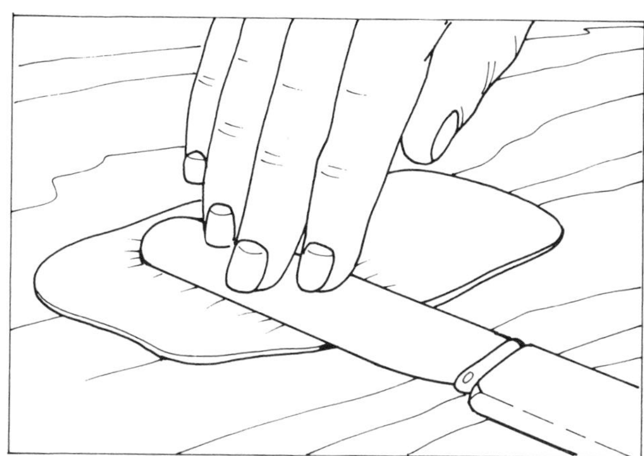

To repair punctures or leaks in inflatables, first allow the boat to dry out, then select an appropriate size patch. Trace the area of the patch on the surface of the boat around the puncture. Mark off the area with masking tape, then lightly abrade with #200 grit paper. Finally apply adhesive to both the patch and the damaged area and allow to dry.

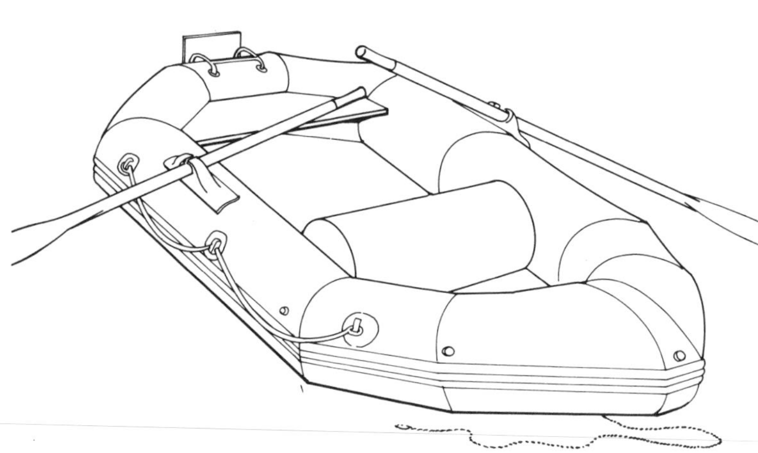

Inflatables are not to be thought of as life rafts. However, as safety appliances, they can be of utmost value. Check them at the beginning of each season for leaks and make any repairs necessary. Make sure all fittings are secure and oarlocks and oars are operational.

matter what situation the yacht is in. Mounting the raft on the forward end of the coach roof or the foredeck is to court malfunction. And no matter what, a moulded cannister is the only reliable containment for a raft. Soft valises can allow breakage, corrosion and actual material tears and rips.

Remember also that many of the contents of a survival pack are liable to deterioration over the course of a season. Emergency food and water supplies are particularly susceptible. Anything even slightly suspect should be discarded, as to survive only to come down with food poisoning is not exactly a fair trade-off. Likewise, knives and fish hooks that have corroded, lines that have frayed or plastic evaporation stills that have cracked or ruptured will do no one good. Rarely can these items be repaired. They should, at the time of repacking the raft, all be coated with rust preventative or a light oil–providing the coating will not have a detrimental effect on the raft materials!

All fastenings that hold the raft to the deck or raft cradle need yearly inspection also. Often a raft is held in place with lashings. These must be inspected for chafe and for proper knotting. Any knot must be of a sort that is releasable instantly. Patent latches should be checked for corrosion and kept lubricated and free-moving.

HARNESSES

Personal safety harnesses should be considered a must for small children, night sailing and any passage offshore in heavy weather. Basic requirements include strength-tested specifications, positive and tested hooks and a secure means of adjustment. Yearly inspections should include checking the carbine hooks for hairline cracks, the stitching in the body webbing and that which hold the rings in place, and making sure no chafe or fraying has damaged the tether. Stitching can be easily renewed, but make sure to use Dacron/Terylene thread, doubled.

Any damage to the hardware indicates the immediate need

for replacement. A distorted hook or D-ring can only lead to fracture or failure under stress. Since most of these hooks are made of stainless steel, and this alloy is subject to fatigue, every effort must be made at constant inspection. If in doubt, the fitting can be saturated with special dyes made to locate hairline cracks.

Tethers take the most abuse–whether nylon rope or webbing–and splices in rope are apt to chafe against deck gear, shrouds and lifelines. The same precautions apply to all lines.

Harnesses that are integral with foul-weather jackets are more protected, needless to say, but also hidden. If the harness cannot be removed from the garment for inspection, don't buy the jacket! Otherwise, check out all the parts as above.

MAN OVERBOARD LIGHTS

If crew goes overboard at night, no light–either personal or attached to a dan buoy–will be of any assistance to recovery if it doesn't work. Of course, all members of the crew should have flashlights/torches when on night watch. In addition, it's a good idea to equip each crew member with a personal safety light to clip on to his or her foul-weather gear. This is in addition to the self-activating light which must be permanently and securely attached to the life ring or horseshoe.

Any and all of the above must function without fail when needed. This is not as simple as it sounds, as very few so-called waterproof lights are truly shielded against the ingress of moisture. Taping battery compartments closed is not a good idea and often ineffective. Better, purchase a good light to start with, make sure the seals are tight and replaceable and that any openings can be clamped or screwed closed. Snap-apart fixtures have no place on a boat. Batteries should be replaced at the beginning of each season and discarded at the end of the season whether or not you have actually used the lights. Batteries left in place over the winter can swell, deteriorate, explode or leak. Likewise, bulbs should be changed at the start of

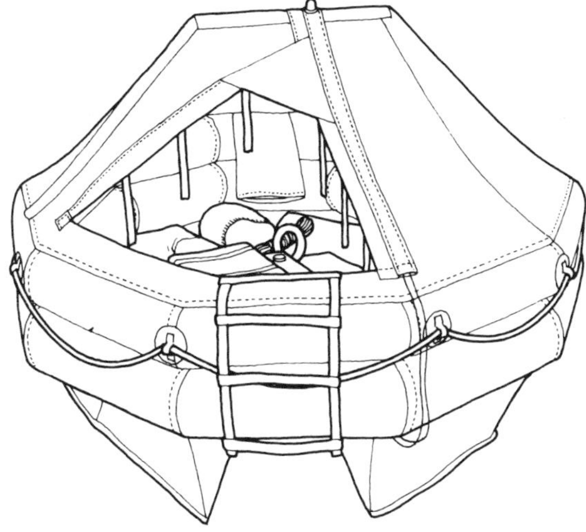

For venturing offshore, all boats should carry a liferaft and emergency equipment. The raft should be certified, with a double floor, canopy, etc. Rafts should be inspected yearly by an approved service center. In addition they should be equipped with an emergency pack and, on long voyages, with extra water and supplies.

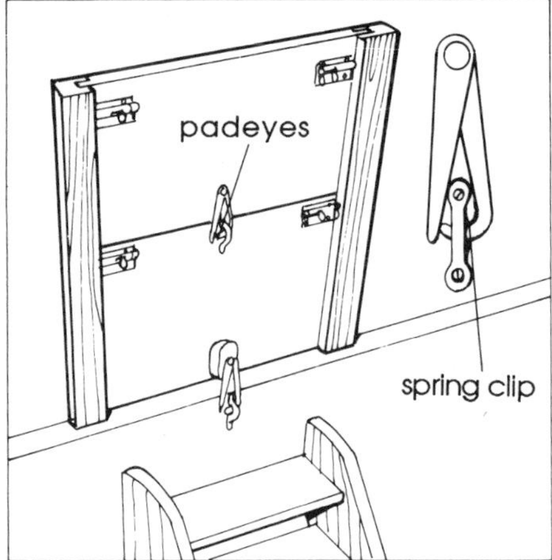

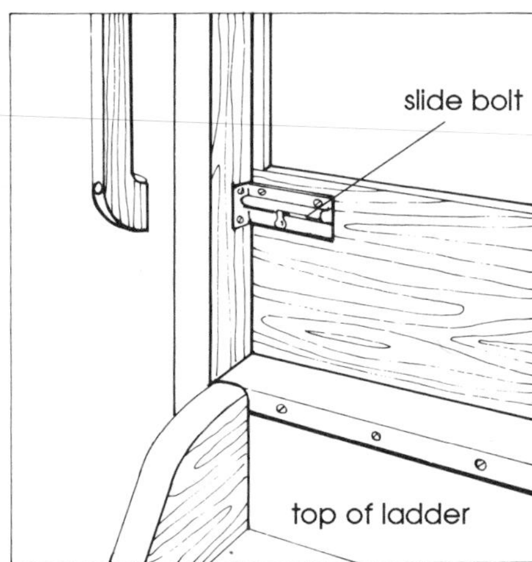

Washboards, to close in the companionway, should be numbered sequentially and provision should be made for the bottom board to be secured in place. Additionally, in really heavy weather, some system must exist for securing the boards in case of a knockdown. One possibility, using spring clips, is shown here.

the new season. If one should suddenly burn out when needed, a life can be lost.

DECKS

In any sort of seaway, in fact in any weather, the antiskid properties of a deck are your most immediate aid in preventing injury or going overboard. Sadly, very few stock boats have proper antislip decking. Most are moulded-in patterns of varying effectiveness. All have some sort of gelcoat in places. And gelcoat is the enemy of sure footing. It looks good, and will continue to do so for a few years, but once the gelcoat has worn you will have grubby-looking decks and still not much protection from spills. Better you should attack the problem at its source, and go about making your decks truly safe.

Probably the best antiskid decking is teak. However, in today's light-displacement boats, the weight of teak is a real safety hazard, not to mention the expense and care needed. A more practicable solution is to install Treadmaster or similar material. This is sold by the sheet, weighs little and is impervious to most anything. Compounded of cork and rubber, Treadmaster is put down with a special two-part epoxy adhesive and, providing the deck is properly prepared, will last for years.

If that is not cheap enough–and for a large deck area it most certainly is not cheap–the best method of saving your neck and other parts of the anatomy is to paint the decks and sprinkle sand, microballoons or ground walnut shells over the still-tacky paint, letting it dry, then vacuuming up the excess. This will need replacement every few years, but the cost is minimal and the labor can be done in one weekend. Although it's fashionable to demarcate different areas of the deck with bands of gelcoated GRP, better to cover the entire deck with nonskid; then there should be no question of slipping on a hatch surround on a dark and wet night.

Besides the deck, cockpit seats should be sheathed in teak–

especially if you value your posterior. Coamings, which get trod upon constantly, should likewise be sheathed or have self-adhesive nonskid strips affixed to them. Cockpit floors are much helped by teak gratings and, though expensive, they will repay the cost in resale value and comfort, especially keeping your feet out of collected water.

LIFELINES AND GUARDRAILS

Provided you have a secure deck under you, there is still a need for some means of restraining yourself from going over the edge. Lifelines and guardrails–in theory–serve that purpose. Nothing, however, will do any good if the uppermost line is too low. And in many production boats this is all too true. Twenty-four inches will catch most people just above the knees, acting as a perfect fulcrum to tip them over the deck edge. The bare minimum should be 30 inches and, on larger yachts, even higher.

To make any rail effective, it must be anchored so firmly to the deck that a large person thrown against it will not make it give way. In practical terms this means that all stanchions must be of thick wall or solid tubing and through-bolted even on a wood deck. No screw, no matter how long, will hold under the wrenching stress of 200 pounds going at high velocity. In turn, the bolts used should be sized to the mounting holes in the stanchion bases and long enough to extend through the deck and backing plates and still allow length enough for a washer, nut and locknut beneath that. Since stanchions get jerked around a lot, they will need rebedding every few years. Don't try to squeeze silicone in cracks. The entire base must be removed, cleaned with solvent (as well as the deck area it rests upon), and reattached with a generous spread of sealant under the entire base area. This is a two-person job, unless your stanchion bases are drilled for stove bolts, in which case everything can be put in place and the job can then be finished off below.

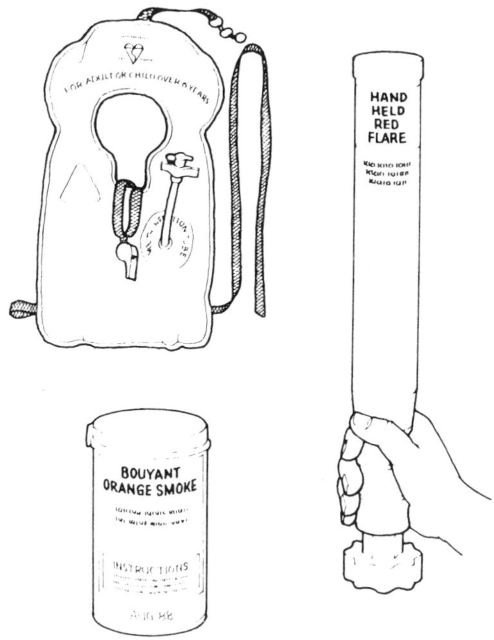

All boats, no matter what type or size, should carry life vests for each crew member and both day and night signals of an approved type. Crew should be familiarized with their operation under all conditions. Make sure all straps and fastenings are secure and operating correctly.

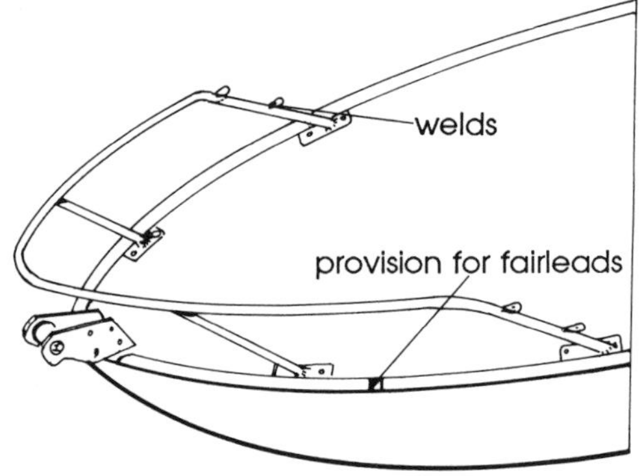

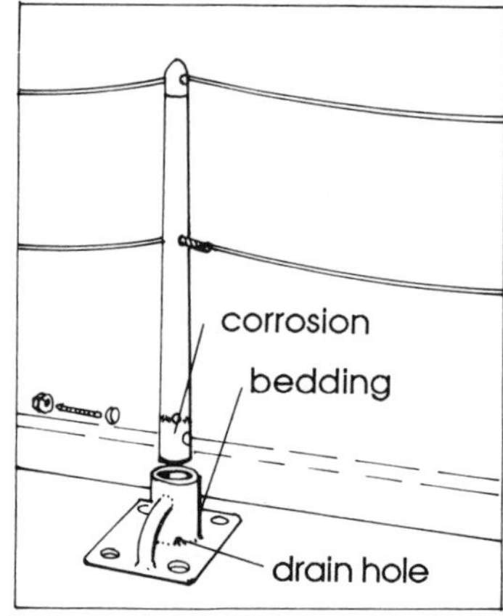

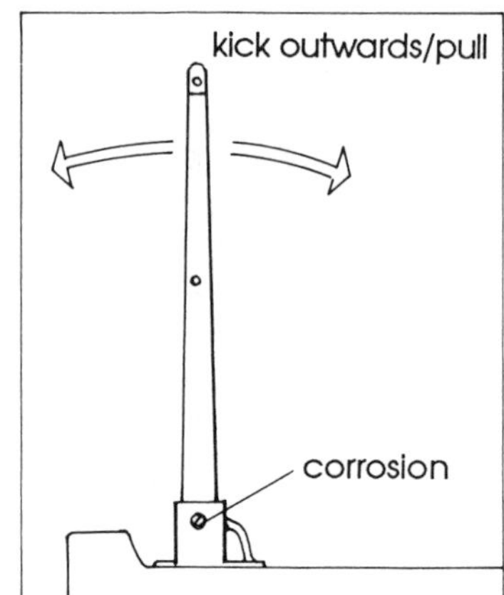

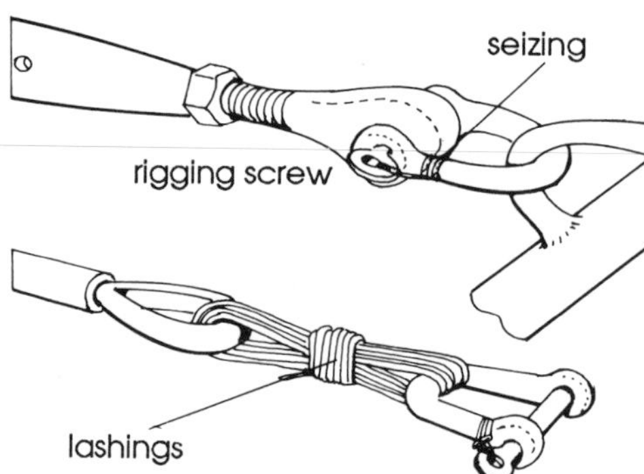

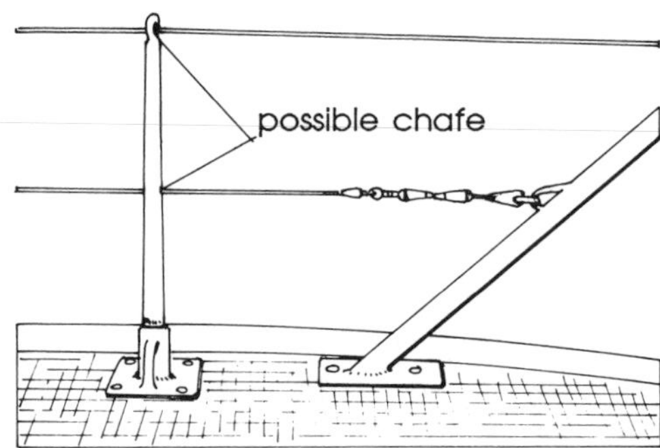

Stanchions and lifelines can mean the difference between life and death. Make sure all are corrosion-free, there are no signs of metal fatigue, all are properly bedded and through-bolted, and that drain holes are free. Lifelines can be secured using turnbuckles, pelican hooks or lashings. Lashings have the advantage of being slashable when it is necessary to bring someone aboard from the water. They will also act as a natural interference break in radio transmission. Make sure pelican hooks are the fail-safe type with double closures.

Check stanchion bases for corrosion. Quite often a stainless steel base will be used with an aluminum stanchion. Invariably, the two will fuse after a couple of seasons. This may not affect strength, but it will make it impossible to replace one or the other. Once a year, remove the stanchion from the base, clean it and coat the end of the stanchion with silicone spray or light grease. Make sure drain holes are kept clear and replace as necessary

Wire lifelines, especially those covered in plastic, are subject to chafe and corrosion. Especially inspect the end fittings, usually swaged. If there are cracks visible, replace with Sta-Lock or Norseman terminals. Make sure the stanchion holes through which the lines pass are burnished and that lower lifeline guides are fitted with bushings. While you're at it, check over all line anchoring points on stern rails and pulpits. Usually welded, these welds are subject to twisting strains and if any sign of a break or fatigue appears, have the yard reweld the eye or loop in the rail.

ROPES

Though it may seem odd to include ropes and lines in a discussion of safety, they are vital to the well-being of the ship. For docking, anchoring, sail control, kedging and warping, if a rope breaks both you and your yacht can be put into a position of grave danger.

All lines should be checked every season. Since virtually all rope used today is synthetic, mildew and rot are no longer problems, but ultraviolet deterioration is, especially in nylon. Any rope which passes over a sheave ought to be reversed end-for-end once a year. Anchor lines, especially, must be inspected carefully where they pass over rollers or through chocks and also at the thimble end shackled to chain. If any chafing appears around the thimble, cut it out and splice a new one in. Any other chafe must also be cut out. If any fraying shows up

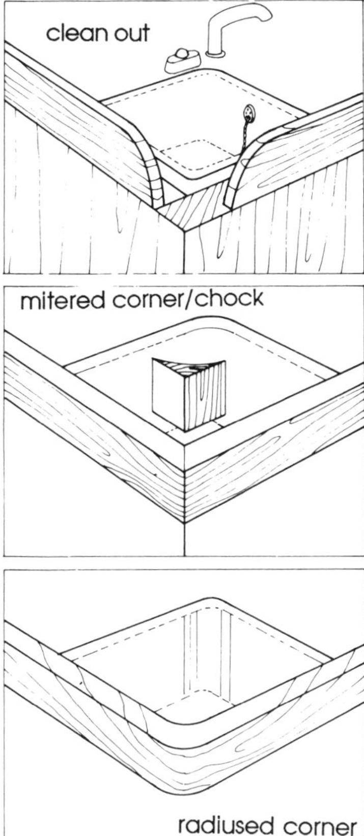

Safety at sea demands a place for everything and everything in its place. This is especially true in the cabin. All flat surfaces–tables, counters, etc.–should be fitted with stout and high (2-inch minimum) fiddle rails. Fiddles around galley counters should have provision for clean-out. They can be made removable as well. No matter what, all rails must have a plumb inside surface, otherwise objects will slide over them. For offshore work, rails can easily be 3-4 inches high.

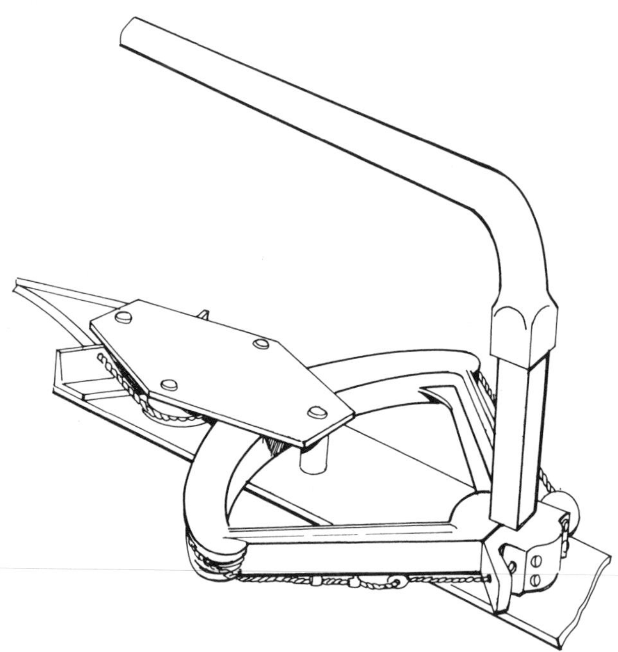

All vessels equipped with wheel steering should have some provision for fitting an emergency tiller. This must be arranged to allow a view forward for the helmsman, and must be both very strong and long enough to provide leverage. Also, make sure there is clear access and swinging room when fitting one. Ideally it should key into the rudder head fitting.

in the middle of the rode, cut it up for docklines and get a new one.

Too often docklines are tattered and in very lowly condition. They are oddments demoted from other tasks. Demote, for sure, but please use sound rope. Docklines are in constant motion and need to be especially strong and free from defects to cope with the stresses put upon them from wakes, tidal surge and sharp edges. Though it's usual to have large eye splices in docklines, an unspliced length is both stronger and more useful. A loop can always be tied in with a bowline. Best use rope of a larger diameter than usual for any lines used to hold the boat for longer than usual–wintering, for example–or in anticipation of a storm. By larger than usual I mean up one or two sizes, i.e., 3/8 inch to 1/2 inch (8mm to 10mm) increase.

Fire Extinguishers

Not often thought of as safety equipment, the various appliances in engine compartments designed to extinguish fires or prevent them are as important as anything in keeping vessel and life together. Since most engine compartments–except in outboard-powered boats and workboats–are enclosed to a greater or lesser extent, their ability to contain a fire is directly related to the ability to cut off oxygen from the engine intakes, as well as the speed at which any extinguishing system works and the amount of fireproof materials surrounding the engine room. A steel boat is best able to contain a fire; a GRP boat least able, due to the extreme flammability of GRP as a substance.

The first thing to check out is the fire extinguishing system installed in the engine compartment. Is it functioning? Do the valves work freely? Was the powder or foam recently recharged. All charging should be clearly dated and renewed according to manufacturer's recommendations. Placement of the outlets for the system are very important. Make sure that they do not spray indiscriminately over the block, but are directed to the air inlet, so as to cut out combustion as soon as possible.

The two most common types of permanently installed fire extinguishing equipment are foam or dry pressurized cannisters and halon gas systems. Both will work under ideal conditions, but certain precautions should be taken. Halon, especially in the earlier installations, would often be exhausted through the engine before it could work. Current systems have a solenoid-valve activating device to close the exhaust on the engine just prior to activation. Halon works by robbing the oxygen needed for combustion from the engine proper and is highly effective. Dry powder and foam systems may be better for electrical fires.

Ideally, both systems should be installed as well as a number of hand-held extinguishers of an approved type at key locations around the boat. There must be a minimum of one in every separate compartment of the vessel, including for good measure the cockpit lockers (especially handy if the companionway is blocked by flames and smoke). All hand-held units should be recharged at least every three years or according to manufacturer's specifications.

Not only a fire extinguisher but a fire blanket should be located near the galley stove. Alcohol and kerosene (paraffin) stoves do flare up now and then and the danger is that some part of the overhead will catch fire. Have no curtains in the galley, and be sure that the overhead is insulated with fireproofing material covered with a stainless or aluminum sheet, allowing at least 1/2 inch of air space between the overhead and the fireproofing. Ceramic spacers made for home woodstove installation are particularly good for this purpose.

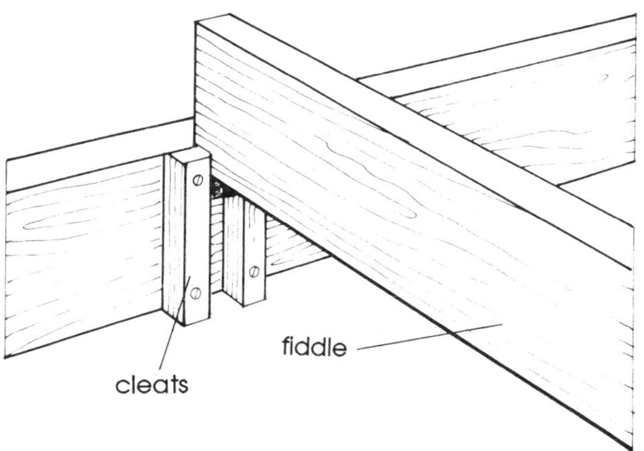

One method of constructing a removable fiddle. Make sure cleats are both glued and screwed in place. Beveling the cleat or fiddle end edges will make for easier installation and removal.

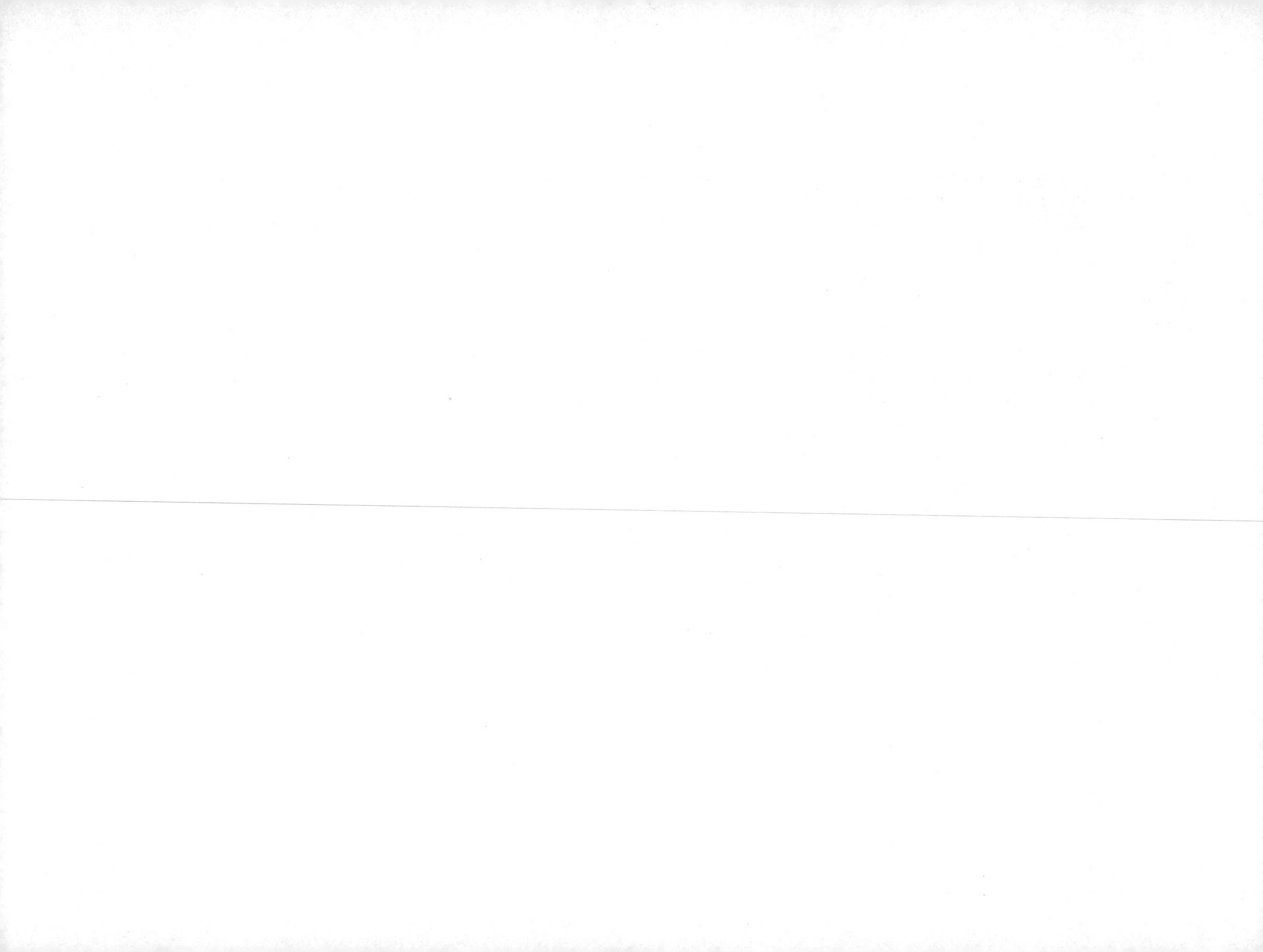

13
THE BOSUN'S LOCKER

Everything for repairs, painting, spares and emergencies collectively can be called the bosun's locker. One should plan this equipment with reference to the size of the boat, stowage space aboard, type of voyaging expected and cost. Obviously, if you are planning a voyage to the South Seas of three years' duration, what you must plan for and carry with you is likely to be vastly more and different than if you take a two-week coastal cruise every summer. Unfortunately, many seamen stock up on everything–at great cost and with little forethought–without taking into account what it's all for!

The need for specific items depends on your boat's construction, size, engine, rig and type. A large powerboat will not need spare shrouds for a long passage, obviously, but it will pay to take a spare propeller and shaft, especially in out-of-the-way spots. Also, one would need tools or means to pull the prop with the boat careened or beached at low water. Likewise, 4 gallons of bottom paint make sense carried along on a year's cruise. There's no need for any paint aboard the weekend boat. Following are several lists of spares and tools to be kept aboard different-size yachts. None are to be taken as gospel, as each of us has different needs and aims.

FOR BOATS UNDER 30 FEET (9 METERS)

Tools

8" (20 cm) adjustable wrench
medium-size pliers
medium-blade screwdriver
10" (25 cm) vise grips

pocket rigging knife with spike
waterproof pouch to carry tools

Sail repair kit
scissors
sailmaker's wax
palm
seam ripper
hot knife
3 spools waxed polyester thread
assorted needles
1 roll ripstop tape
3'x3' (1x1 meter) piece of adhesive, sticky-backed Dacron/Terylene
light thread for spinnaker repair
telltale yarn
waterproof ditty bag

Spare parts
assorted stainless steel nuts, bolts, washers, sheet metal screws
bulbs for compass and running lights
winch pawls and springs
cam cleat springs
assorted cotter pins and split rings
clear, compartmented box to hold all

Miscellaneous
1 roll duct tape
tube of clear silicone seal
1 spray can penetrating oil
small can general-purpose lubricating oil
can of Teflon spray lubricant
indelible marking pen

FOR BOATS FROM 30-45 FEET (9-14 METERS)

Tools

Allen wrenches
chisels (1 cold chisel)
hand drill plus set of bits
files (8" or 20 cm mill bastard, 1 medium rattail, 1 triangular)
medium ballpeen hammer
50' (15 meters) measuring tape
nail set
oil stone
pliers (10" or 25 cm channel lock, needle nose, regular)
hacksaw with extra high-speed blades
6 assorted-size regular screwdrivers
2 Phillips screwdrivers
1 set jeweler's screwdrivers
vise grips (7" and 10" or 18 and 25 cm)
wire brush
wire cutters
work gloves
wrenches (8" and 10" or 20 and 25 cm adjustable, set of combination–open end and box)
toolbox

Electrical parts

spare bulbs for each light aboard
3 each spare fuses for each type aboard
assorted wire crimps
wire strippers/crimpers
flashlight (torch) batteries and bulbs
continuity tester
black electrician's tape

Engine and mechanical spares

3 cans oil for hydraulics

hydraulic hose and assorted end fittings
transmission fluid
set of engine filters
assorted grits wet/dry sandpaper
complete set of engine belts
one complete oil change
new voltage regulator for each alternator
6'x6' (2x2 meters) canvas drop cloth with grommets
length of 2x4 lumber
section of marine grade sheet plywood
assorted stainless steel hose clamps
drift punch
spare water pump impeller

Spares
assorted nuts, bolts and washers
assorted cotter pins
assorted clevis pins
assorted D-shackles
assorted snap shackles
1 spare turnbuckle with toggle
1 genoa car
winch pawls
winch pawl springs
winch roller bearings
spare winch handle

Sail repair kit
scissors
sailmaker's wax
2 palms
2 seam rippers
hot knife
light thread for spinnaker repairs
6 spools waxed polyester thread

assorted needles
ripstop tape
3'x6' (1x2 meters) piece of sticky-backed Dacron/Terylene
yarn for telltales
25' (8 meters) stainless-steel or monel seizing wire
3 D-rings
sailmaker's pliers
ditty bag

Sealants and lubricants
2-part epoxy
2 tubes clear silicone sealant
2 cans spray penetrating oil
1 can general-purpose lubricating oil
1 can Teflon spray lubricant
2 rolls duct tape
silicone or lanolin grease
indelible ink markers
1 spray can seize preventative

FOR YACHTS 45 FEET (14 METERS) AND LARGER

Tools
Allen wrenches (long and short)
awls (small and large)
block plane
chisels (1 cold, 2 wood)
hand drill with set bits
variable-speed rechargeable electric drill with set bits
files (8", 10", 12" or 20, 25, 30 cm mill bastards, 3 wood files, 2 rattails, 1 triangular)
hammers (16-oz. or 500-gram ballpeen, baby sledge, claw, rubber mallet)

measures (100' or 30 meters tape, fold-up rule, calipers)
mirror (1 retrieving)
nail sets (5 assorted)
oil stone
pipe cutter
pipe, 18" or 1/2 meter (as battering ram and as Spanish windlass)
pliers (2 channel lock, 2 needle nose, 4 regular in assorted sizes)
2 putty knives (1" or 2.5 cm)
saws (crosscut, hacksaw and 40 blades, jigsaw and 12 blades)
screwdrivers (17 assorted regular, 6 assorted Phillips, 2 offset, 1 jeweler's set)
tap and die set (sized to your needs)
tin snips
propane torch with varying tips
vise
vise grips in assorted sizes
wire brushes (steel and brass)
wire cutters
work gloves (leather palms)
wrenches (6", 8", 10" or 15, 20, 25 cm adjustables, 14" or 36 cm pipe wrench, strap wrench, complete 3/8" or 1 cm drive socket wrench set, set combination wrenches, set open-ended wrenches)
X-Acto knife and 6 blades
tool box

Electrical parts
compass-light assembly
running-light bulbs
spare bulbs for each lamp aboard
3 of each type of fuse aboard
assorted wire crimps
wire strippers-crimpers

flashlight (torch) batteries and bulbs
assorted lengths and gauges electrical wire
black electrician's tape
silicone grease
multimeter
solder
soldering gun or iron (12-volt or flame heating)
spare anemometer cups
spare wind vane
spare knotmeter transducer
storage box

Sealants and lubricants
2-part epoxy
2 tubes clear silicone sealant
2 cans spray penetrating oil
2 cans spray silicone lubricant
2 cans multipurpose lubricating oil
2 rolls duct tape
2 indelible ink markers
silicone or lanolin grease
2 cans antiseizing spray

Sail repair kit
scissors
sailmaker's wax
2 palms
2 seam rippers
hot knife with spare tip
light thread for spinnaker repairs
8 spools waxed polyester thread
assorted needles
2 rolls ripstop tape
2 pieces 3'x6' (1x2 meters) sticky-backed Dacron/Terylene
yarn for telltales

2 weights seizing wire (25' or 8 meters each)
3 D-rings
3 O-rings
50' (15 meters) tubular webbing
sailmaker's pliers
assorted weight sailcloth
roll 5 oz. Dacron tape, 6" (15 cm) wide
spool of light stuff for flag halyards, etc.
6 awls
grommet set (stainless steel or brass)
ditty bag

Rigging parts
Nicopress (Talurit) tool (sized to halyards and shrouds, 2 preferably)
12 Nicopress (Talurit) sleeves for each size wire aboard
assorted stainless steel thimbles
assorted snap shackles
assorted D shackles
assorted stainless steel wire in 36" (1 meter) lengths
spare turnbuckles and toggles
assorted clevis pins
assorted track cars
link plate set
spare main halyard
spare jib halyard
one length stainless steel wire 2' longer than longest stay or shroud

Engine and mechanical spares
1 gallon (2.5 liters) oil for hydraulics
10' (3 meters) length hydraulic hose with fittings
2 cans transmission fluid
oil for engine oil change
set engine filters, gaskets

complete set engine belts
voltage regulator for each alternator
6'x6' (2x2 meters) canvas drop cloth with grommets
assorted stainless steel hose clamps
section of marine grade sheet plywood
2-3' (1 meter) lengths 2x4s
drift punch
set of injectors
grease gun with lithium grease
2 cans starting spray
keel-bolt wrench
rudder-packing wrench
spare impellers for engine pumps (4)
spare set steering cables
master links (12) for steering chain

Spares
assorted cotter pins
assorted nuts, bolts, washers
head repair kit: pump parts, diaphragms, etc.
hand pump for oil changes
high volume bilge pump mounted on board
electric drill pump with hoses
bronze wool
assorted wet/dry sandpaper
assorted crocus cloth and emery paper
spare packing for propeller and rudder glands
winch spares: pawls, pawl springs, assorted roller bearings, split rings, toothbrush, tweezers, dental pick, extra handles

Optional
banding tool, bands, clips
spare propeller and shaft
300' (100 meters) nylon line equal to heaviest line aboard
assorted softwood plugs sized to all through hulls

Needless to say, putting everything on a small boat would quickly lead to foundering. Nevertheless, you should have on board all the basics needed to make those repairs which are vital to the voyage you are undertaking.

OTHER BOSUNRY

In addition to the tools and spares above you should have other spare supplies on hand, logged in and replaced when necessary.

Paints

For the average yachtsman, this is a once-per-season job and paint need not be carried aboard. However, if you are planning any long voyage, the bare minimum would be enough bottom paint for a complete recoating. If you have a wood boat, paint for the hull and deck, along with sandpaper, brushes, solvents, scrapers, etc.

Adhesives

A tube of silicone sealant, a package of 2-part underwater epoxy, a small can of 2-part patching compound, a tube of all-purpose cement.

Rope

At least 100 feet (30 meters) of the heaviest line used aboard, spare halyard, extra dock lines, extra anchor rode (nylon), assorted small stuff for sail ties, lashings, etc.

Miscellaneous

Rigging knife, extra flashlights, spare batteries for every piece of equipment aboard, anchor light, stove fuel, spare engine oil, emergency flares, etc.

14
FASTENINGS AND ADHESIVES

Every piece of hardware, every repair to wood, metal or GRP, every last change or modification to any vessel is going to use various glues, resins, screws, nails, bolts, staples and other methods, chemical and mechanical, to keep two objects or surfaces together, secure and watertight. The sheer variety and number of fastenings and glues available for household and marine use is formidable. What we'll attempt in this section is to give you some ideas on what to choose for whatever purpose and why.

MECHANICAL FASTENERS

Under this category comes every sort of device to hold two or more pieces of whatever together *without* chemical bonding. The most common are screws, nails, bolts, rivets and staples, but there are countless variants on all and certain ones are better than others for different applications. Screws are probably most useful on wood boats and for interior work. Generally available are screws fabricated from stainless steel, brass, bronze, steel (galvanized or not), or anodized or plain aluminum. For marine applications except in the cabin, only bronze or stainless steel are appropriate. The others are just too subject to deterioration from galvanic or electrolytic action or wood sickness.

For hull refastening, bronze screws 2 1/2 times the planking thickness are the usual recommendation. Flat head screws should be used. Unlike many, I personally think Phillips-head screws are better than slot-head screws for all applications (if you can find them). There's less slippage, thus less chance to damage surrounding surfaces. However, in certain applications, Anchorfast nails–that is, ringed nails with the rings an-

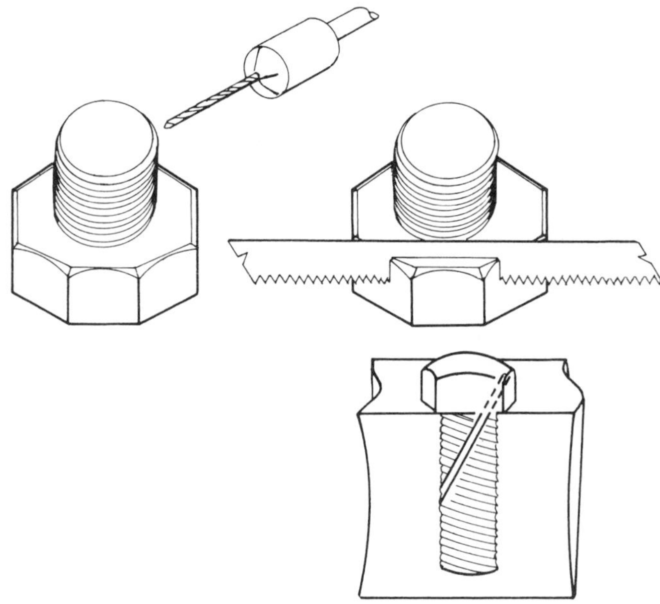

Some cures for frozen nuts and bolts: A. drill the nut at an angle and force in penetrating oil. B. hacksaw the bolt off. C. drill the bolt at an angle, squirt in oil and remove.

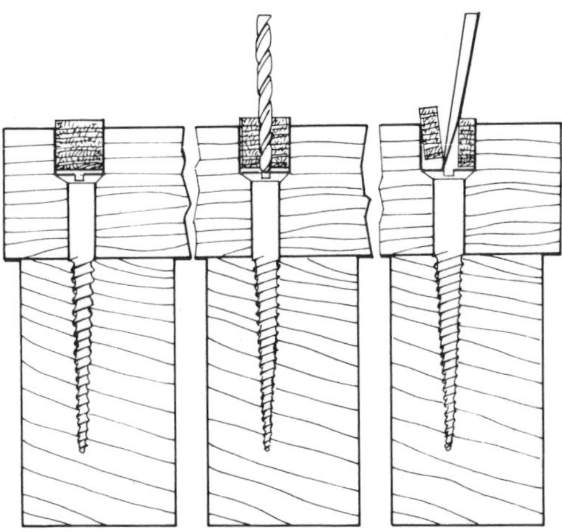

A. To remove a bung to inspect the screw underneath (when the bung has popped, the screw may be corroded), first drill a hole on the centerline of the bung, then use a scratch awl to pry out the halves.

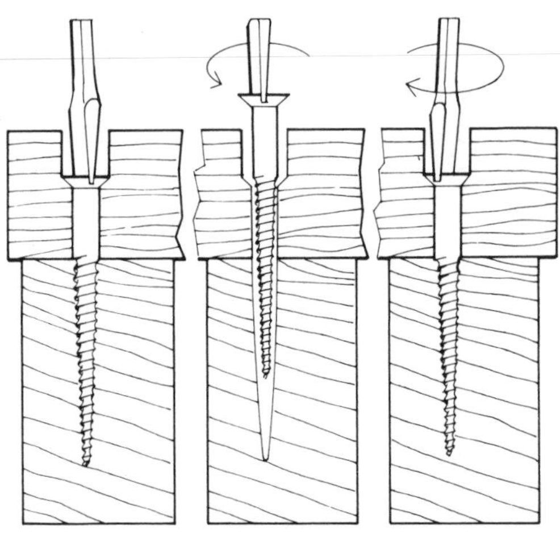

B. Using a screwdriver, tap the handle with a hammer to loosen the screw. If a new screw is needed, use a slightly larger diameter and length and coat it with soap or paraffin before driving it home.

gled to prevent pull-out–in either bronze or monel may be easier and faster to use. All planking fastenings must have pilot holes drilled first, and the use of a compound bit to allow hole, countersink and bung hole to be drilled in one operation is highly recommended.

In the past, a number of boats were fastened with galvanized boat nails. If you can find a source for honestly hot-dipped, galvanized nails, fine. Don't try it with hardware store roofing-type nails. They won't hold and they won't last! Proper galvanized fastenings can last 20 years. With flash-coated nails, your boat may fall apart in five years.

Stainless steel is a wonderful material, but is actually a number of different alloys, and you can't always be sure what you are getting. For interior use, no problem arises, but for underwater applications, hull fastenings or, in the case of metal boats, hull material can make a drastic difference in the overall performance and durability of the fasteners. In some areas, stainless will deteriorate as fast as brass. Underwater fittings, in all but metal vessels, are best fastened with bronze alloy fasteners. In steel vessels, welds are preferable to any screws or bolts. In aluminum hulls, careful–very careful–isolation of fitting and hull and fasteners is required to keep any of the metal components from deteriorating. Plastics are probably the best way to go with an aluminum hull, fastened in place with epoxy resins.

All underwater metal fittings–prop, shaft, P-brackets, rudders–should be fitted with sacrificial anodes of zinc. These should be renewed each season. They are made in various forms, from clamp-on bullet-shaped anodes for the prop shaft to buttons which are bolted through the rudder blade. It is vital that any anode installation makes complete contact with the area of its installation, and some filing or grinding may be necessary to achieve this. Always follow manufacturer's instructions and try to make the anodes as streamlined as possible. Do not coat them with antifouling paint, and make sure all bolt heads are countersunk. Any projections or unfairness will have an effect on boat speed and possible fouling with lines and debris.

New types of fasteners are always coming on the market, but remember that except for the USA, everyone else in the world produces them in metric sizes. Actually, most US-made products are metrically sized also, if only to allow for export sales. Most tools can be had in both metric and traditional sizing, but this should be a consideration when looking for new fastenings.

Screws, nails and bolts must always, as mentioned above, be sized to the job. Do not err in excess and choose sizes too large. An overly large screw or nail can split materials, distort them and otherwise create leaks and other havoc.

ADHESIVES

The purpose of all adhesives is to bond two objects together chemically. Subsidiary effects include waterproofing and sealing. But like nuts and bolts, there are hundreds of different adhesives, some more effective in given situations than others. Two, however, dominate the boat arena: epoxy and Resorcinol types. These are primarily building adhesives. That is, they are used in gluing together various structural members of masts, hulls, interiors and decks. They are not, except for major repairs, the sort of glues one uses on an everyday basis.

I qualify this in the case of epoxies. There are many different varieties of epoxy-type glues on the market. Here we are not speaking of construction epoxies such as West System or System-3, which are intended for major construction. Rather, our concern should be with those used for repairs that can be bought off the shelf in hardware stores and chandleries. Glue will hold but mechanical fasteners will hold better unless the structure is designed for gluing. In other words, for a quick and permanent repair, use mechanical fasteners; for a more complex and perhaps more cosmetically acceptable repair, use epoxy.

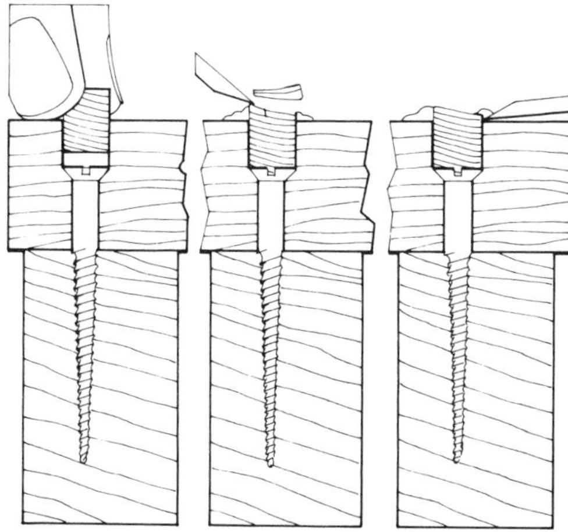

C. New bungs should be coated with glue or white lead before inserting. After the coating dries, chisel off the bung with the grain, almost flush with the plank. Then sand and paint. Always insert a bung with its grain parallel to the planking grain to avoid splitting.

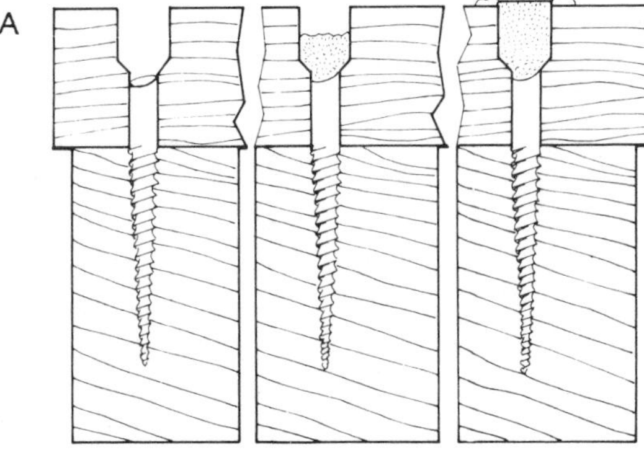

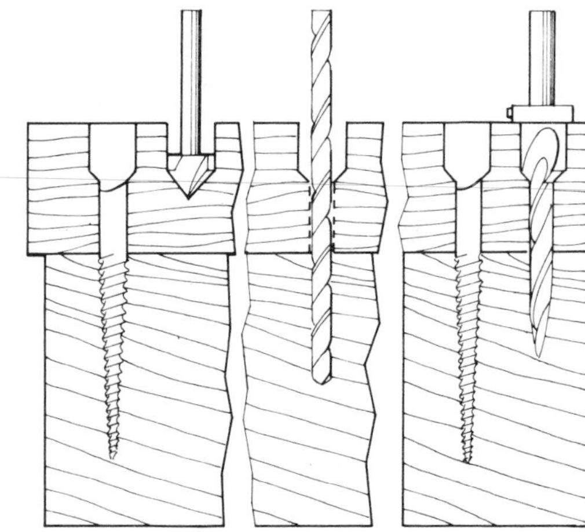

Should a screw head break off or corrode away, either A. seal the bung hole with epoxy as illustrated or B. drill a sister hole as close as possible in new wood to the old screw, countersink and install a new screw and bung. You may also use a combination bit for drilling both screw hole, countersink and bung hole in one operation.

Epoxy has many advantages for repairs that have to be sealed, waterproofed and are between dissimilar materials. Very few adhesives will bond wood *and* metal. Epoxies can! Certain types can even be used underwater and will gradually cure to a sound bond, very useful to stem some leaks. All epoxies are two-part adhesives: base and catalyst. They are mixed in fairly precise proportions just prior to using and have a fairly short pot life. Take this into account when using them, as all are expensive. Mix only what you expect to need.

Many modern adhesives are highly toxic. When working with epoxies, always wear plastic or rubber gloves, and if for anything longer than a minor patch, always use a respirator mask. Contact with the skin can cause irritations and inhaling the fumes can lead to nausea, dizziness and possible long-term complications. Even in hot weather, wear long-sleeved shirts and long trousers. Wear socks. Ankles are subject to splatters and despite the fact that boat shoes are usually worn barefooted, this is only a sensible precaution. Do not smoke around any glues or resins; they are highly volatile and fire or explosion is always a possibility.

Glossary

Adze A shipbuilder's axe, used for shaping timbers.
Afloat On the water.
Afore Forward of.
Aft Toward the stern of the boat.
Aground State in which boat is resting on bottom; not afloat.
Alternator Dynamo belted to engine supplying alternating current for ship's services.
Anchor Metal device for holding the boat tethered in position in the water.
Anemometer Instrument for measuring wind speed.
Antifouling Paint containing toxic substances applied to boat's bottom to keep it free of weed and animal life.
Apron Timber fitted on the afterside of the stem to receive the plank ends.
Astern Behind the boat.
Athwartships From side to side of the boat.
Auxiliary Engine used as secondary means of propulsion.

Back To maneuver the boat astern.
Backbone The assembly made up of keel, stem and sternpost; the main structural member of a wooden boat.
Backstay Standing rigging supporting the mast from the truck to the stern of the boat.
Baggywrinkle Bunches of yarns or unlayed rope used as protection against chafe in the rigging.
Balance The total sum of characteristics that allow a boat to sail with a near neutral helm under a variety of conditions.
Ballast Weight, usually in the form of iron or lead, carried in the lowest part of the vessel or under the keel to increase stability.
Bare poles A sailing vessel with no sails set.
Barnacles Shellfish that adhere to boat's bottom, thereby reducing speed. Kept at bay by use of proper antifouling paint.
Barometer Instrument that measures changes in atmospheric pressure and indicates coming weather changes.

Battens Narrow strips of wood or plastic used to keep the leech of a sail in shape.
Beam The width of a boat at the widest part.
Becket A loop or eye at the end of a rope or a strap on a block to receive a secondary line.
Before The forward side.
Belay To make fast around a cleat.
Below In the cabin.
Bend Any easily cast off knot, used to fasten two ropes together, or a rope to a spar.
Berth Resting place for the boat afloat; also, any sleeping place aboard.
Bight Bend or loop in a rope.
Bilge(s) The lowest internal part of the hull.
Binnacle The housing for the compass.
Bitt Vertical member for securing mooring rope.
Block Pulley used to gain mechanical advantage.
Bobstay Stay between cutwater and end of bowsprit to counter the strains of the forestay.
Bollard Post used to secure ship's ropes.
Boltrope Rope sewn to edges of sail to prevent tearing and chafe.
Boom Any spar used to support or extend the foot of a sail.
Boot top The markings indicating the light and loaded waterlines of a boat, usually painted.
Bow The stem or forward end of a boat.
Bowline Knot used to tie a loop in a rope. One of the most useful knots.
Breast hook A piece of wood shaped as a knee and used to hold the gunwales and apron to the stem.
Bridle Rope secured at both ends and controlled in the center.
Bulkhead Athwartships partition used to maintain rigidity and separate the vessel into compartments.
Bulwarks Raised planks at the deck's edge that act as railings and prevent objects from falling off the deck.
Burgee A swallow-tailed flag.
Butt The ends of plank; or two planks secured end-to-end.
Buttocks Lines representing fore-and-aft vertical sections in plans.

Camber The degree of slope in a deck athwartships.

Canvas Fabric, traditionally made of flax, used to cover decks and for covers and awnings. Other than deck covering, most canvas used today is woven from man-made fibers.
Capstan A revolving vertical windlass for hauling lines, etc.
Carlins Fore-and-aft timbers between beams.
Carvel Planking laid edge to edge against a rigid frame.
Casting Metal form made by pouring molten metal into mold.
Caulking Any material used to seal and make watertight seams, either in planking or under hardware, ports, etc.
Cavitation Excessive vibration caused by incorrect positioning or size of boat's propeller.
Centerboard A pivoted board–of wood, GRP, etc.–in the bottom of a sailing boat, used to prevent leeway and allow the vessel to point higher.
Chafing gear Any material fastened in place to prevent chafe against sails, rope, rails, etc.
Chain plates Metal plates or bars bolted to the outboard sides of sailing boats as attachment points for shrouds.
Cheeks Sides of a block.
Chine Intersection of sides and bottom of a hull, usually seen in metal and plywood vessels.
Chock Fairlead, usually for mooring lines.
Clamp Plank fitted to inside of frame that acts as a bearer for beams.
Clew After lower corner of a sail.
Clinch To rivet two overlapping planks with rivets and roves.
Clinker Lapstrake-built hull.
Coach roof The raised part of the cabin top.
Coaming Raised rail or partition around cockpits or hatches that prevents water from entering.
Cockpit The well from which the boat is steered.
Compass Instrument used to indicate relative magnetic North. Used for steering.
Counter Projecting stern from waterline aft.
Cradle Frame used to support a boat when out of water.
Cringles Thimbles or loops fitted to sails at the corners.
Crosstrees Spreaders.
Cuddy Small cabin in bows used mainly for storage.

Cutter Sailing vessel with mainsail, staysail and foresail.

Dagger board Removable drop keel, usually found in smaller boats.
Davits Supports from which tenders are held, usually from the stern of the boat.
Deadeye Wood block through which lanyards are rove, usually for shrouds.
Deadrise Angle of rise of boat's bottom above the base line.
Deadwood Wedge of wood angling the horn timber to the keel of a hull.
Deck Horizontal surfaces or platforms acting as both floor above and roof for the spaces below. Large yachts may have several decks.
Deck light Glass prism fitted flush in deck to give light below.
Diagonal planking Set at a 45-degree angle to the frames; usually covered with a second layer of planking set at right angles to the first.
Dinghy Small open boat used as ship's tender or for recreational sailing.
Ditty bag Small cloth bag, usually used to hold repair materials and tools.
Dodger Cloth screen attached to a frame, used to protect the occupants of the cockpit.
Double ender Any hull with both pointed stem and stern.
Doubling Turned edge of a sail to which the boltrope is sewed.
Downhaul A rope fitted to pull anything down from aloft, usually a sail.

End for end Reversing the ends of a rope to counteract chafe.
Epoxy Resin, glue or coating; very strong man-made adhesive impervious to water and used in many aspects of boat building.
Eye Loop of a splice.
Eye splice Rope end looped back and tucked into the standing part of the lay to make a loop.
Eyebrow molding Light wood molding around cabin top.

Fairlead Any nonmoving fitting through which a rope passes so as to lead it in the direction required.
False keel Secondary keel fitted for protection underneath keel.
Fashion piece Athwartships timber aft of the transom.
Fast, to make To secure a line.
Feather-edge Any plank with one edge thinner than another.

Fender Buffer of rubber, coir, wood, etc. that keeps the boat from hitting a dock, another boat, piling, etc.
Fiber glass Cloth or mat made up of woven or compressed extruded glass fibers.
Fid A conical wood or steel tool used to open the strands of rope–wire or fiber– when splicing.
Fiddles Vertical rails around countertops and tables that keep things in place in a seaway.
Fiddle block Double block with one sheave over the other.
Flake To coil a rope on deck so it will run freely.
Floorboards The walking surface over the floors proper.
Fluke Pointed end of the arm of an anchor.
Foot Lower edge of a sail.
Fore and aft In a line from bow to stern.
Foredeck Deck ahead of the mast.
Forepeak The small hold in the bows of a boat.
Forestay Wire rope running from the masthead to the stemhead.
Forward Near the bows.
Foul bottom Covered with marine growth.
Framing The supporting structure of the boat: frames, ribs, stringers, etc.
Freeboard Height from waterline to gunwale.
Furl To roll up, gather or fold a sail or other canvas work.
Futtocks Built-up pieces forming timbers.

Gaff Spar to which head of mainsail is bent.
Gallows Frame to support a boom.
Garboard Planking directly above and next to the keel.
Genoa Large jib.
Gimbal Suspension device that allows leveling of equipment when the boat is heeled and/or pitching. Used on compasses, stoves and lights.
Gooseneck Jointed fitting attaching the boom to the mast.
Grommet Metal or rope eyelet used as tying off point in a sail or awning.
Guard Rails Safety rails fitted around decks, etc. Refers to both solid rails and wire-and-stanchion lifelines.
Gudgeon Eyebolt fitted to stern of boat to receive pintle attached to rudder, usually outboard.

Gunter Rig much like gaff, but with the gaff hoisted almost vertical, giving the appearance and much of the efficiency of a Bermudan rig.
Gunwale Topmost strengthening timber around the uppermost part of the hull.
Guy Steadying line used to keep a boom, spinnaker pole, etc. from riding up or jibing.
Gypsy Winch drum, especially one keyed to accept chain links on a windlass.

Halyard Rope used to hoist sails, flags, etc.
Hatch Deck opening, usually with hinged cover.
Head Marine toilet; also, the compartment in which it is located.
Heel The base of a mast; also, point where keel and sternpost meet.
Helm Wheel or tiller controlling steering mechanism.
Hemp Cordage made from hemp plant.
Holidays Bare patches overlooked when fairing or painting.
Horn timber Wood joining transom to keel.
Horse Simple traveler for mainsheet consisting of metal bar with stops at the ends.
Hounds Shoulders supporting crosstrees or spreaders.
Hull Frame and planking of a boat.

Inboard Toward the centerline of the boat.
Inwales Inboard fore-and-aft hull members imparting strength.

Jackyard Small boom fitted to upper part of topsail.
Jacob's ladder Rope ladder with wood steps.
Jaws Horns of a gaff that hold it to the mast.
Jib Foremost triangular sail.
Jury rig Any makeshift repair that allows the vessel to continue under way.

Kedge Auxiliary anchor for warping without power.
Keel The basic timber of a ship; also, less correctly, the ballasted fin of a sailing vessel.
Keelson Inner keel tying the floors to the keel.
Ketch Two-masted sailing boat with mizzen stepped afore the rudder.
Kicking strap Preventer to keep the boom from rising when sailing with the wind aft.

King plank Centerline plank of a deck.
Knees End supports to athwartships timbers, such as deck beams, thwarts, etc.; they may be of wood or metal.
Knot Correctly, a measure of distance; more commonly, 1 knot=1 nautical mph.
Knuckle Sharp change of contour, usually in the hull near the bows.

Lacing Line used to bend on sails, etc.
Landing strake The plank next to the topmost strake on either side of a hull.
Lanyard Small line used to attach anything to the rails, etc.
Lap jointed Lapstrake, clinker-built.
Lash down Secure by means of a rope.
Lay Twist of a rope.
Lay up Take a boat out of commission.
Lazarette Stern locker.
Lazyjacks Lines running from the mast to the boom on both sides of the mainsail to assist in furling or flaking the sail.
Lead line Rope with attached weight used for taking hand soundings.
Leeboards Boards pivoted on either side of a sailing boat that act in the same way as centerboards but without piercing the hull.
Leech The after edge of a sail.
Legs Upright spars lashed to beam ends of boat to keep it upright when drying out.
Limber holes Gutters between planking and timbers in the bilge that allow water to drain into the sump.
Loom Handle of an oar.
Loran Electronic position-finding receiving device.
Luff The leading edge of a sail.

Mae West Life vest.
Main sheet Tackle used for trimming the mainsail.
Mainmast Principal mast of a sailing vessel.
Mainsail Sail hoisted on the mainmast.
Make fast Secure.
Manila Rope made from Philippine banana plant fibers.
Marconi rig Triangular, jib-headed rig.
Mark Object useful for navigation.

Marline Generally, any small stuff; more precisely, loose-laid, two-stranded hemp.
Marline spike Metal spike for opening lay of rope for splicing.
Mast Vertical wood or timber pole from which sails are spread.
Mast coat Canvas boots around base of the mast at deck level that prevents water entry belowdecks.
Mast step Support, usually atop the keelson, upon which the heel of the mast rests.
Masthead Top of the mast.
Mizzen Sail hoised on the mizzen mast.
Molds Battens used to transfer lines from the loft floor to the vessel bulding.
Mooring pennant Rope, chain or wire running from a mooring buoy and taken aboard to make fast.
Mortise Chiseled-out area in wood, as when a mortise is made for a hinge or lock.

Navel pipe Through-deck fitting through which anchor chain passes to the chain locker.
Necklace Rope used to secure a hanging block, usually from the mast.
Nip of a splice Rope surrounding the thimble.

Oakum Tarred hemp used for caulking.
Oar Rowing device with loom at one end, blade at the other.
Oarlock U- or O-shaped metal bracket used as a fulcrum for the oar in rowing.
Onboard In or on any boat.
Outboard Toward the boat's side; also, an engine-shaft-propeller self-contained unit used for propulsion.
Outhaul Rope used to pull or stretch out; most often attached to clew of mainsail to tighten foot.
Overboard In the water.
Overhangs Parts of a boat extending beyond the waterlines at either end of the hull.

Paddle Small oar for propelling canoes, etc.
Painter Rope used for tying up a small boat or dinghy.
Palm Leather band with socket used in sewing and sailmaking.

Parcel To cover a rope tightly with canvas for protection.
Parrel Rope or fitting used to attach a yard or gaff jaws to the mast.
Pawl Bar used to keep a winch or capstan from running backward.
Pay To fill caulked seams with sealant.
Peak Upper corner of a sail.
Pelican hook Opening hook used to secure lifelines.
Pintle Metal pin used in conjunction with gudgeons to hang a rudder.
Pitch To plunge, bows-down, in a seaway.
Pitch (propeller) Distance one turn would advance the propeller.
Planing Action of bows rising out of the water; lessens the displacement and wetted surface, hence increases boat speed.
Planking Fore-and-aft covering of a hull.
Poop Breaking sea over the stern when running.
Port Left-hand side of the boat.
Pram Small dinghy with a cut-off bow.
Primer Undercoating to increase adhesion and prevent base material from showing through the top coats of paint.
Propeller Screw made up of curved rotating blades.
Pulpit Tubular metal guardrail at bow or stern; stern rail is sometimes called the pushpit.
Purchase Tackle used to obtain greater power.

Quadrant Rudder head fitting connecting the rudder assembly to the steering gear.
Quarter Side of ship between midships and stern.
Quarter knees Strengthening crooks between gunwale and transom.

Radar Electronic device for obtaining bearings and distances.
Rake Angle or slope of masts aft.
Ratlines Ropes or slats lashed to shrouds to allow climbing aloft.
Reef To reduce sail area by tying up part of the sail.
Reeve To pass a line through an opening.
Refit Repair or replace.
Ribs The athwartships frames of a boat.
Rig The layout and design of the masts, booms, sails, etc.

Rigging The wires and rope that support the masts and work the sails.
Rigging screw See *turnbuckle*.
Ring bolt Metal ring attached to a bolt or plate; used as an attachment point for a block or tackle.
Roach The curvature on the aft edge of a triangular sail.
Rocker Degree of curvature, fore-and-aft, of the keel.
Rubbing strake Protective strip of wood, plastic or metal attached fore-and-aft to the ship's side below the gunwale.
Rudder Device for steering the boat, attached near or to the stern.
Rudder head Top end of rudder shaft to which is attached the tiller or steering quadrant.
Run After underside of the hull where lines converge.
Runners Stays, usually removable, that support the mast when sailing downwind.

Safety harness Webbing harness with lanyards and safety hooks for attaching wearer securely to boat.
Sail plan Diagram showing measurements, in profile, of all the sails for a particular boat.
Sail track Metal track attached to mast and boom to guide and hold in place one edge of a sail. Attachment is by means of sliders or lugs.
Sampson post A hefty bit, much like a bollard, usually of wood and bolted into the backbone of the ship.
Scantlings Structural dimensions of timbers in wood boat construction. With other materials, layup, thickness, tensile strength, etc. of structural members.
Scope Length of anchor chain or rode payed out and its relation to the depth of water–e.g., 7:1 scope.
Scull To propel a boat with a single oar over the stern.
Scuppers Openings in bulwarks or rails that allow drainage of water from the deck.
Seacock Positive stop valve for controlling ingress/egress, attached to through-hull fittings, usually below the waterline.
Seam Space between planking.
Seizing Binding two parts of rope together.
Serving Tightly wound marline covering parceling.

Shackle Metal link, usually U-shaped, used to connect eyes, etc.
Shank The long middle arm of an anchor.
Sheave The wheel in a block.
Sheer Fore-and-aft curve of a boat's profile.
Sheer strake Uppermost planking of the hull.
Sheet Rope used to trim a sail, attached to the clew.
Shelf Fore-and-aft timber that takes the deck beams.
Shell Frame that holds the pin of a block.
Shoe Metal or wood heel fitting.
Shrouds Athwartship standing rigging supporting the mast.
Skeg Fin supporting the leading edge of a rudder.
Snatch block Block with hinged sheave opening used to change ropes without reeving the entire length.
Snotter Lower support for a sprit.
Soft eye Eye not fitted with a thimble.
Spar General term for any boom, yard or mast.
Spinnaker Balloon-shaped running sail, set flying afore the forestay.
Splice To join two ropes or two parts of one rope by unlaying strands and interweaving them.
Spring line Rope tied amidships when alongside to keep the boat from moving back and forth.
Sprit Boom set diagonally across sail.
Sprung Unsound or damaged spar.
Staff Small pole that carries an ensign.
Stanchion Upright metal pillar for supporting lifelines.
Standing rigging Permanent supporting rigging for mast.
Stays Standing rigging supporting the mast fore-and-aft.
Stem Foremost timber in the bows to which planking is fastened.
Stern After part of the boat.
Sternpost Aftermost vertical timber to which the rudder is attached.
Stock Crossbar of an anchor.
Stopper Fitting used to hold a rope or chain temporarily.
Stopwater Material used to plug a planking leak.
Strake Full length of one width of a boat's planking from stem to stern.
Stringers Fore-and-aft hull stiffeners.

Tabernacle Support frame housing the heel of the mast on deck that allows mast to be lowered.
Tabling Hem of sail in which bolt rope is sewed.
Tack The lower forecorner of a sail.
Tackle Purchase made up of multiple blocks and rope.
Taffrail Stern rail.
Tail Rope tied or spliced to a block so it can be used in different positions.
Thimble Grooved metal eye around which a rope or wire is spliced to make a hard eye.
Throat Upper forecorner of a sail.
Thwart Athwartship seat.
Tiller Wood bar attached to rudder head used to steer the boat.
Toggle U-shaped device used in conjunction with a turnbuckle to allow for movement both fore-and-aft and athwartships.
Topping lift Tackle used to support and raise the boom.
Topsides The boat's sides above the waterline.
Trail boards Decorative stern boards.
Transom The athwartships part of the stern of a boat.
Traveler Metal bar that controls the position of the mainsheet and thus the amount of twist in the sail.
Treenail Hardwood, tapered "nail" used to fasten planking.
Triatic stay Horizontal stay between masts.
Trunnion Hinge, allowing multiple movement.
Trysail Storm sail used in place of the mainsail, not attached to the boom.
Tumblehome The inboard curve of a boat's side.
Turnbuckle Rigging screw; a double screw and barrel device used to tighten standing rigging.

Vane Weathercock, mostly referring to a wind vane in a self-steering gear.
Vang Strop or tackle used to keep a boom down when running or reaching.

Warp Rope used for moving a boat.
Waterline The line the ship's side makes with the water when loaded to design displacement.
Waterways Side decks.

Well The foot space of a cockpit.
Whipping Binding the end of a rope to prevent the strands from unlaying.
Whisker pole Pole used to keep the jib standing out when running.
Winch Device used to haul in ropes on a drum. Gearing and drum size determine the mechanical advantage.
Windlass Mechanical, electric or hydraulic winch used for hauling in the anchor.

Yard Spar hoisted on the mast to extend sails, etc.
Yoke Device installed on rudder head to take steering ropes in a small boat.

Index

Numbers in *italic* indicate illustrations.